CHARLOTTE BRONTE

JANE EYRE

OUR BOOKS ON LITERATURE

Charlotte Bronte

JANE EYRE

[Edited with Background Studies, Character Analysis, Various Approaches to the Novel, Study Questions and Criticism]

Aditya Nandwani

B.A. English (Hons) , Delhi University;
M.A. (English), IGNOU; Print Journalism (English) YMCA

ANMOL PUBLICATIONS PVT. LTD.

NEW DELHI - 110 002 (INDIA)

ANMOL PUBLICATIONS PVT. LTD.

H.O.: 4374/4B, Ansari Road, Darya Ganj,
New Delhi-110 002 (India)
Ph.: 23278000, 23261597

B.O.: No. 1015, Ist Main Road, BSK IIIrd Stage
IIIrd Phase, IIIrd Block
Bangalore - 560 085 (India)
Visit us at: www.anmolpublications.com

Jane Eyre

First Published, 2009

PRINTED IN INDIA

Printed at Mehra Offset Press, Delhi.

Contents

Preface

Jane Eyre is one of the most popular British Novels penned by Charlotte Bronte(April 21, 1816 – March 31, 1855). Among the three popular Bronte Sisters, she was the eldest one. Charlotte Bronte was the third of six children to Mr. Patrick Bronte and Mrs. Maria Branwell. Her father was an Irish Anglican clergyman. Her mother died quite early, leaving five daughters and a son. She did her early education at Clergy Duaghters School. You could find the description of Lowood School in Jane Eyre.

Charlotte maintained bad health as well as physical and mental development throughout her lifetime. Her two elder sisters died of Tuberculosis in May 1826. On 31st March, 1855, Charlotte and her unborn child died because of tuberculosis.

The immense success of Jane Eyre lit a new movement to feminism in the world of English literature. The portrayal of Jane Eyre is quite parallel to Charlotte. Jane Eyre deals with the maturation of a child because of the circumstances and emotions. It features five major stages of development. They are childhood at Gateshead, education at Lowood School, Adele's governess at Thornfield, Rivers Family at Morton and at Marsh End, followed by the reunion and entering into marital bliss to Rochester at Ferdean. The whole novel narrates the circumstances that transform a girl called Jane to mature woman.

Author

Chapter 1

Introduction

Reader, if you have yet to discover the unique voice of Charlotte Brontë's Jane Eyre, you have a special delight awaiting you.

For this most acclaimed of novels—"English," "Gothic," "Romantic," "Female"—is always a surprise, in the very authority, resonance, and inimitable voice of its. As Jane Eyre states, "I resisted all the way", and this attitude, this declaration of a unique and iconoclastic female rebelliousness, strikes the perfect note for the entire novel. That a woman will "resist" the terms of her destiny (social or spiritual) is not perhaps entirely new in English literature up to the publication of Jane Eyre in 1847: we have after all the willful s of certain of Shakespeare's plays, and those of Jane Austen's elegant comedies of manners.

But Jane Eyre is a young woman wholly unprotected by social position, family, or independent wealth; she is without power; she is, as Charlotte judged herself, "small and plain and Quaker-like" — lacking the most superficial yet seemingly necessary qualities of femininity. "You are not pretty any more than I am handsome," Rochester says bluntly. Jane Eyre was a risk for her young creator as it was a fictitious character for the vocal consciousness of a long and intricately plotted novel of considerable ambition. Had not Henry Fielding gambled, and lost, on the virtuous but impoverished and less than ravishingly beautiful of his Amelia, of 1751, arousing the scorn of readers who had so applauded Joseph Andrews and Tom Jones? Jane Eyre, who seems to us, in retrospect, the very voice of highly educated but socially and economically disenfranchised gentility, as natural in her place in the literature of nineteenth-century England as Twain's Huckleberry Finn is in our literature, was unique for her time. She speaks with an apparent artlessness that strikes the ear as disturbingly forthright.

Compare the slow, clotted, indefatigably rhetorical prose of Mary Shelley's Frankenstein, of 1818; or the pious and ensanguine narrative of Esther Summerson of Charles Dickens's Bleak House, of 1853; and the melancholy, rather over determined self-consciousness of 's Lucy Snowe, the of Villette, of 1853: "If life be a war, it seemed my destiny to conduct it single handed. I pondered how to break up my winter-quarters—to leave an encampment where food and forage failed. Perhaps, to effect this change, another pitched battle must be fought with fortune; if so, I had a mind to the encounter: too poor to lose, God might destine me to gain. But what road was open?—what plan available?"

One of the reasons for Jane Eyre's authority over her own experience, and the confidence with which she assesses that experience, is that, as the romantically convoluted plot evolves, the reader learns that it is history rather than story. Jane Eyre, who is wife and mother in 1819, is recounting the events of 1799-1809 in a language that is unfailingly masterful precisely because it is after the fact. If the Romantic/Gothic novel be, in one sense, sheer wish, Jane's triumph represents a wish fulfillment of extraordinary dimensions. The material of legends and fairy tales, perhaps; yet also, sometimes, this time at least, of life. We were made to believe Jane Eyre's good fortune because we are led to believe her voice. It is, in its directness, its ruefulness and scarcely concealed rage, startlingly contemporary; and confirms the critical insight that all works of genius are contemporaneous both with their own times and with ours.

Jane Eyre was written under a pseudonym when Charlotte was thirty-one years old, a casualty, so to speak, of ten years of servitude as a governess. Though "Currer Bell" was an unknown author and of indeterminate sex, the novel was accepted almost immediately upon being offered to the publishing house of Smith, Elder; it was published within seven weeks and became an instant success. Like 's romantic hero Lord Byron, the new author "awoke one morning to find herself famous."

That Jane Eyre sold so well should force us to reassess our custom of casually dismissing the tastes and expectations of the large audience of "female" readers of the nineteenth century. For Jane Eyre, whatever its kinship to eighteenth-century Gothic and however melodramatic certain of its episodes (the one in which Rochester disguises himself as a gypsy is particularly strained), is nonetheless a work of stubbornly idiosyncratic intelligence; its strength lies as much in passages of introspective analysis as in conventionally dramatized scenes. Jane projects such rebellious undercurrents that some critics, including sympathetic readers, found the novel "coarse." Jane does not sentimentalize herself as an orphaned child any more than she sentimentalizes other children—in the scene in which she confronts Mrs. Reed her voice is "savage": "I am glad you are no relation of mine: I will never call you aunt again as long as I live.

I will never come to see you when I am grown up; and if any one asks me how I liked you, and how you treated me, I will say the very thought of you makes me sick." During Jane's stay at Lowood, when so many of her classmates sicken and die, Jane voices no false piety in noting that spring is "unclouded" nonetheless. Not coarseness but an unfashionable realism provokes the child's insight: "My mind made its first earnest effort to comprehend what had been infused into it concerning heaven and hell. For the first time it recoiled, baffled; and for the first time glancing behind, on each side, and before it saw all round an unfathomed gulf: it felt the one point where it stood—the present; all the rest was formless cloud and vacant depth: and it shuddered at the thought of tottering, and plunging amid that chaos." At a time when women were merely inhabited bodies meant to bear children, but being, in other respects, chastely bodiless, Jane rejects the proffered love of the martyrish St. John Rivers because it is merely spiritual. Surely, this suggests "coarseness" very much at odds with Victorian ideals?

Like Villette, Jane Eyre is a story of hunger; unlike that more complex and perhaps more aesthetically "pure" novel, it is a story of hunger satisfied. That young Jane Eyre supplants the formerly exotic Bertha (the Creole heiress whom Rochester recklessly married in his youth) is not, given the terms of the novel's logic, a matter of moral ambiguity. For in her deranged and diseased state Bertha is no longer a human woman but sheer appetite, and therefore beyond the range of Jane's (and presumably the reader's) sympathy. Her laughter is "demonic", her figure "hideous." Jane is necessarily repelled; for this is quite, truly other, lacking even the intelligence and sense of moral proportion so artfully voiced by Dr. Frankenstein's doomed monster. When Jane first sees Rochester's lawfully wedded wife the reader is as shocked as she is at that moment. In the deep shade, at the farther end of the room, a figure ran backwards and forwards.

What it was, whether beast or human being, one at first sight could not tell: it groveled, seemingly, on all fours; it snatched and growled like some strange wild animal: but it was covered with clothing; and a quantity of dark, grizzled hair, wild as a mane, hid its head and face. This secret wife lacks even a gender. She is it, and animal: "the clothed hyena rose up, and stood tall on its hind feet." Rochester mockingly addresses Jane as a "young girl, who stands so grave and quiet at the mouth of hell, looking collectedly at the gambols of a demon." (Rochester confesses to having married Bertha, the daughter of a West India planter, in a trance of youthful "prurience" and after it was too late he discovered, that their natures were antithetical.

Her "pygmy intellect" was "common, low, narrow, and singularly incapable of being led to anything higher"; she was sexually promiscuous—"her vices sprang up fast and rank"; and diseased—"her excesses had prematurely developed the germs of insanity.") That Bertha Mason suffers from atypical general paresis, the consequence of syphilitic infection, must be passed by in silence since, in realistic terms, Rochester too would be syphilitic; and would infect Jane Eyre if she married him.

Jane Eyre's hunger and that of Bertha Mason do not seem to overlap, one is qualified by intellectual scrupulosity and a fierce sense of integrity; the other is, and was, a sheer animal. Jane goes against the grain of her deepest wishes; she renounces emotional fulfillment in the service of an ideal that includes, as "Currer Bell" carefully notes in the preface to the novel's second edition, "the world-redeeming creed of Christ." Jane's self-banishment and the remarkably literal terms of her hunger—she comes close to starving after she flees Thornfield—identify her in fact as a kind of Christ: misunderstood, defiant, isolated, willing (almost) to die for her beliefs. The reiteration of "master" and "my master" in the narrative suggests Jane's ultimate if not immediate acknowledgement of her place in the hierarchy of a civilized cosmos.

In this, she strikes a chord of willful submission not unlike that of Emily Dickinson, whose insistence upon "Master" as a force in her emotional life carried with it an air of obsessive conviction. How seemingly passive, how subtly aggressive! Jane Eyre is the ideal as she is the ideal narrator of her romance.

It is interesting to note that the sisters— Charlotte, Emily, and Anne—began writing as children, creating a private mythology out of the exigencies of a motherless, isolated, and intensely private domestic life in Haworth Parsonage on the Yorkshire moor. In 1826, when Charlotte was ten, her father Patrick gave her brother, Branwell, a box of twelve wooden soldiers, which seemed to awaken a fervor of creativity in the children: they began making up stories in which the soldiers figured as characters. In time, they created plays, mimes, games, and serial stories transcribed in minute italic handwriting that mimics print; they were influenced by their father's storytelling and by their wide and promiscuous reading—among contemporaries, Scott, Byron, E. T. A. Hoffmann, and supernatural stories by James Hogg that appeared in serial form in Blackwood's Magazine. Out of the children's elabourate fantasizing grew two long-enduring partnerships between Emily and Anne (the "Gondal" sagas) and Charlotte and Branwell (the "Angrian" stories): Emily continued to live imaginatively in Gondal until she was at least twenty-seven years old, while Charlotte wrote her last Angrian story at the age of twenty-three.

Emily Brontë's Wuthering Heights is more clearly an adult's rendering of incestuous childhood obsession than are any of Charlotte 's novels, but the romantically dangerous Rochester is most likely a remnant of the children's sensational world, the poetic antithesis of all that was dull, dreary, routine, and circumscribed in the world of Haworth Parsonage. Here is Jane's first vision of the man she will adore: Something of daylight still lingered, and the moon was waxing bright; I could see him plainly. His figure enveloped in a riding cloak, fur collared and steel clasped; its details were not apparent, but I traced the general points of middle height, and considerable breadth of chest.

He had a dark face, with stern features and a heavy brow; his eyes and gathered eyebrows looked ireful and thwarted...; he was past youth, but had nor reached middle age. Like Emily's Heathcliff, that Byronic, doomed hero; yet unlike Heathcliff—who after all starves himself to death in his deranged attachment to the past—since, by the novel's end, after he goes blind, Rochester does become domesticated. The Gothic is tamed and redeemed by ordinary marital love. However, for 's time, or for ours, Jane Eyre ends upon a note of conjugal bliss: "I am my husband's life as fully as he is mine. No woman was ever nearer to her mate than I am, ever more absolutely bone of his bone and flesh of his flesh. I know no weariness of my Edward's society: he knows none of mine, any more than we each do of the pulsation of the heart that beats in our separate bosoms; consequently, we are ever together.... We talk, I believe, all day long: to talk to each other is but a more animated and an audible thinking". The orphan Jane is no longer "resisting all the way"; no longer, at this point, required to be Jane. The novel's passionate energies consume themselves as the apocalyptic fire at Thornfield consumes unregenerate Bertha.

Much of the power of Jane Eyre derives from a dialectic the author unobtrusively pursues on several structural levels. For instance, in the largest, most spacious sense the novel is about a character stimulated into growth—truly remarkable growth— by place. Jane Eyre, orphaned and presumably defenceless, and a mere girl, discovers the strength of her personality by way of the challenges of several contrasting environments. The Reed household, in which she is despised; Lowood School, where she discovers a model in Miss Temple and a spiritual sister in Helen Burns. Thornfield, where she cultivates, with agreeable naturalness, a measure of sexual power; Whitcross, where, at last, she acquires the semblance of a family; and Ferndean, Rochester's retreat, a manor house of "considerable antiquity... deep buried in a wood," where she is at last wed.

Just as these carefully rendered places differ greatly from one another, so Jane differs greatly in them, one has the sense of a soul in ceaseless evolution. As a child in the Reed household, rebuking Mrs. Reed, Jane feels a sense of precocious triumph: "Ere I had finished this reply, my soul began to expand, to exult, with the strangest sense of freedom, of triumph, I ever felt. It seemed as if an invisible bond had burst, and that I had struggled out into unhoped way for liberty." 's sense of human personality is that it is pliant, fluid, and living, in immediate (and often defiant) response to its surroundings; not that it is stable and determined, as if sculpted in marble. Jane Eyre is no portrait of a lady but the story of a young woman in a "heroic" mold, as susceptible as any man to restlessness and ennui when opposition fails to provide a cause against which to struggle. Grown bored at Thornfield, for instance, before the arrival of the master, Jane longs for a power of vision that might overpass the limits of her sequestered life, pastoral as it is. Very like the nameless governess of Henry James's The Turn of the Screw,1 Jane walks agitatedly about, alone, "safe in the silence and solitude," and eager for adventure: which is to say, romance.

Women are supposed to be calm, Jane says, but women feel precisely as men do, requiring exercise for their faculties and suffering from stagnation. On the third floor of Thornfield she paces about, not unlike the captive Bertha in her backward-and-forward movements, allowing "my mind's eye to dwell upon whatever bright visions rose before it. Certainly, they were many and glowing; to let my heart be heaved by the exultant movement, which, while it swelled it in trouble, expanded it with life. Best of all, to open my inward ear to a tale that was never ended—a tale my imagination created, and narrated continuously; quickened with all of incident, life, fire, feeling, that I desired and had not in my actual existence." Jane is Charlotte telling us of the mesmerizing psychological experience of the writing of Jane Eyre.

In recounting her story, Jane typically introduces a situation meant to provoke conventional associations on the part of the reader (to whom, as to a friend, Jane speaks candidly) and then, within a paragraph or two, deftly qualifies or refutes it. The narrative's dialectic constitutes a plot motion of its own, quite distinct from Jane's activities. A thesis of sorts was presented; but, should we respond to it, the narrator will set us right: for she is always in control of her narrative. We learn, with Jane that what seems to be rarely is; even when Rochester disguises himself as a fortune-telling gypsy, improbably fooling his guests, Jane is keen enough to suspect "something of a masquerade."

The novel begins with a blunt statement: "There was no possibility of taking a walk that day." The shrubbery is leafless; the winter sky overcast; the rain penetrating; Eliza, John, and Georgiana, and the despised orphan, Jane, were cooped up together in the house. But, should the reader be tempted to respond automatically to this privation, Jane immediately declares, "I was glad of it; I never liked long walks." Excluded from Christmas celebrations in the Reed household, Jane describes the festivities and exchanges of gifts she missed; then says, "To speak the truth, I had not the least wish to go into company." Given what is known of Charlotte's grief at the deaths of her two elder sisters at school, when she was a very small child, the dialectic of 9 is even more surprising. The typhus epidemic at Lowood Orphan Asylum is set against an unusually idyllic spring, and while disease, death, gloom, hospital smells, and the "effluvia of mortality" predominate, Jane, untouched by the disease, is frank about her enjoyment of the situation. Forty-five out of eighty girls are affected; some go home to die (as Charlotte's sisters did, from the Cowan Bridge School), and some die at school, like Helen Burns, and are buried "quietly and quickly".

But the ten-year-old Jane, clearly no kin to child s in works of George Eliot or Charles Dickens, responds instinctively to the bright May sunshine and the "majestic life" that is being restored to Nature. She delights in her freedom to ramble in the woods and to eat as much as she likes, for the first time in her life: with very little Victorian delicacy, but with a refreshing air of truthfulness, Jane notes that her breakfast basin is "better filled" because the sick lack appetite. Even the death of Helen Burns is sparely treated; and Jane's close questioning of Helen's religious convictions does not appear resolved: "Again I questioned; but this time only in thought. Where is [Heaven]? Does it exist?"

Jane Eyre is remarkable for its forthright declaration of its 's passions and appetites. Unlike Lucy Snowe, with whom she bears a family kinship, Jane hardly needs to work at cultivating a "healthy hunger": she is ravenous with appetite at Lowood, and, in fleeing Thornfield, in the brilliantly sustained nightmare of Chapter 28, she is in danger of literally starving to death. In the latter scene, Jane responds at first like any romantic, imagining a Wordsworthian solace in the moorland: "Not a tie holds me to human society at this moment—not a charm or hope calls me where my fellow-creatures are—none that saw me would have a kind thought or good wish for me.

I have no relative but the universal mother, Nature: I will seek her breast and ask repose." Outcast that she is from human society, Jane knows herself loved by Nature, to which she clings with an ingenuous "filial fondness": "Tonight, at least, I would be her guest, as I was her child: my mother would lodge me without money and without price. I had one more morsel of bread.... My hunger, sharp before, was, if not satisfied, appeased by this hermit's meal." As her reverie continues Jane speculates about God, a He set beside Nature's She: "We know that God is everywhere; but certainly we feel His presence most when His works are on the grandest scale spread out before us: and it is in the unclouded night sky, where His worlds wheel their silent course, that we read clearest His infinitude."

Jane's awakening next morning is to a bitter revelation: she begins to experience genuine hunger and to suffer the humiliation, mounting very nearly to physical terror, of near-starvation. Piety rapidly vanishes; romantic rhetoric is dropped. renders this painful interlude with such exactitude that one cannot doubt she wrote from first-hand experience, as her earliest biographer Mrs. Gaskell suggests, few scenes in English literature are so harrowing as those in which Jane overcomes her pride to beg for food and is given a crust of bread, or food meant for hogs, or rebuffed altogether. ("I blamed none of those who repulsed me.

I felt it was what was to be expected.") Hunger has become real to Jane in a way that the platitudes of "Nature" and "God" are not. (One is reminded of the "thin, haggard, and hollow-eyed" Lucy Snowe, who, confronted with a Renoir-like portrait of a voluptuous female, ostensibly Cleopatra, responds with startling violence. Indeed, Brontë herself is so incensed by this "enormous piece of claptrap" that, for some paragraphs, the fastidiously subdued prose of Villette is enlivened by a genuine passion: "I calculated that this lady... would infallibly turn from fourteen to sixteen stone. Indeed, she was well fed: very much butcher's meat—to say nothing of bread, vegetables, and liquids—must she have consumed to attain that breadth and height, that wealth of muscle, that affluence of flesh.... She had no business to lounge away the noon on a sofa. She ought likewise to have worn decent garments; a gown covering her properly." Lucy Snowe is an older and embittered Jane Eyre, recoiling from the very emblem of flesh.)

The plot of Jane Eyre is increasingly contrived and melodramatic—the novel is after all a late-Romantic, early Victorian form of the "manufactured fiction" of which Henry James spoke, in terms of Dickens, with some disdain—and, so far as "story" is concerned, the tensions of an interior dialectic sometimes lack subtlety. No aura of mystery or exoticism accrues to Rochester's visitor from the West Indies, Richard Mason: in Jane's sharp eyes he is sallow and unmanly, with something in his face that fails to please. "His features were regular, but too relaxed; his eye was large and well cut, but the life looking out of it was a tame, vacant life." Later, when Jane is brought in Bertha's presence and mockingly introduced to Rochester's wife, she is naturally revulsed—she feels no kinship with this creature.

Though Jane charges Rochester with cruelty in so despising and exhibiting his mad wife, claiming that Bertha cannot help her condition. Jane cannot really identify with the woman; and rather too readily forgives Rochester his curious (and ungentlemanly) behaviour.3 That Rochester had intended to dishonestly marry her, and, in the most fundamental sense, "deflower" her, matters less to Jane than the reader anticipates. But the legitimate Mrs. Rochester, along with Thornfield Hall itself and all it represents of a diseased past, will soon be destroyed in a refining fire.

Numerous readers have felt that the long Whitcross section, consisting as it does of nearly one hundred pages, is an awkward digression in Jane Eyre; and one is nudged to recall that the publishing firm of Smith, Elder had rejected Charlotte 's earlier novel, The Professor, as "undersized." (But if Currer Bell would write a full-scale, three-volume novel for them, they would be "most interested.") Still, the carefully transcribed section is required for symmetry's sake. 's authorial strategy is to balance one kind of temptation with its obverse (if Rochester is all romantic passion, urging her to succumb to emotional excess, St. John Rivers is all Christian ambition, urging her to attempt a spiritual asceticism of which she knows herself incapable). Jane Eyre is not an orchestrated novel of ideas, closer in temperament to the fiction of George Eliot than to that of Emily. The miraculously realised "family" of Diana, Mary, and Rivers himself strikes us as a benign adumbration of the novel's original household, in which Jane is despised by Eliza, Georgiana, and the spectacularly loathsome John Reed. Rochester, following the novel's design, must be altered too in some respect, but it is probably incorrect to read his blinding as a species of castration—as that perennial cliché of criticism would have it.

Not only is the blind and crippled Rochester no less masculine than before, but, more significantly, it was never the case that Jane Eyre, for all her inexperience, shrank from either her master's passion or her own: the issue was not Jane's sexual timidity but her shrewd understanding that, should she become his mistress, she would lose Rochester's respect. One might say, inevitably lose his respect. These were the hardly secret terms of Victorian mores, and Jane Eyre would have to have been a very naive young woman, as self-deluded as George Eliot's Hetty, to be believed otherwise. And Jane is anything but naive.

"Reader, I married him," Jane announces boldly in the novel's final chapter. The tacit message is that I married him—not that he married me. What greater triumph for the orphan, the governess, the small, plain, and "Quaker-like" virgin? The novel ends with a curious aside to St. John Rivers, away in India "labouring for his race" and anticipating, with a martyr's greed, his "incorruptible crown." It is St. John's grim and exultant language that rounds the story off, however ironically: "'Amen; even so, come, Lord Jesus!'" But those who have love have no need of this particular Lord Jesus.

Chapter 2

Charlotte Bronte : Biography and Works

Charlotte (April 21, 1816 – March 31, 1855) was a British novelist, the eldest of the three famous sisters whose novels have become standards of English literature. Charlotte is best known for Jane Eyre, one of the most famous of British novels.

Life

Charlotte was born in Thornton, Yorkshire, England, the third of six children, to Patrick (formerly "Patrick Brunty"), an Irish Anglican clergyman, and his wife, Maria Branwell. In April 1820 the family moved a few miles to Haworth, where Patrick had been appointed Perpetual Curate. Maria Branwell Brontë died of cancer on 15 September 1821, leaving five daughters and a son to the care of her sister Elizabeth Branwell. In August 1824, Charlotte was sent with three of her sisters; Emily, Maria, and Elizabeth, to the Clergy Daughters' School at Cowan Bridge in Lancashire (which she would describe as Lowood School in Jane Eyre). Its poor conditions, Charlotte maintained, permanently affected her health and physical development and hastened the deaths of her two elder sisters, Maria (born 1814) and Elizabeth (born 1815), who died of tuberculosis in 1825 soon after they were removed from the school.

At home in Haworth Parsonage, Charlotte and the other surviving children — Branwell, Emily, and Anne — began chronicling the lives and struggles of the inhabitants of their imaginary kingdoms. Charlotte and Branwell wrote stories about their country — Angria — and Emily and Anne wrote articles and poems about theirs — Gondal. The sagas were elabourate and convoluted (and still exist in part manuscripts) and provided them with an obsessive interest in childhood and early adolescence, which prepared them for their literary vocations in adulthood.

Charlotte continued her education at Roe Head, Mirfield, from 1831 to 1832, where she met her lifelong friends and correspondents, Ellen Nussey and Mary Taylor. During this period (1833), she wrote her novella The Green Dwarf under the name of Wellesley. Charlotte returned as a teacher from 1835 to 1838. In 1839 she took up the first of many positions as governess to various families in Yorkshire, a career she pursued until 1841. In 1842 she and Emily traveled to Brussels to enroll in a pensioned run by Constantin (1809 – 1896) and his wife Claire Zoé Parent (1804 – 1890). In return for board and tuition, Charlotte taught English and Emily taught music. Their time at the pensioned was cut short when Elizabeth Branwell, their aunt who joined the family after the death of their mother to look after the children, died of internal obstruction in October 1842. Charlotte returned alone to Brussels in January 1843 to take up a teaching post at the pensioned. Her second stay at the pensioned was not a happy one; she became lonely, homesick, and deeply attached to Constantin. She finally returned to Haworth in January 1844 and later used her time at the pensioned as the inspiration for some of The Professor and Villette.

In May 1846, Charlotte, Emily, and Anne published a joint collection of poetry under the assumed names of Currer, Ellis, and Acton Bell. Although the book failed to attract interest (only two copies were sold), the sisters decided to continue writing for publication and began work on their first novels. Charlotte continued to use the name 'Currer Bell' when she published her first two novels. Of this, later wrote:

"Averse to personal publicity, we veiled our own names under those of Currer, Ellis, and Acton Bell. The ambiguous choice being dictated by a sort of conscientious scruple at assuming Christian names positively masculine, while we did not like to declare ourselves as women. Without at that time suspecting that our mode of writing and thinking was not what is called 'feminine'—we had a vague impression that authoresses are liable to be looked on with prejudice; we had noticed how critics sometimes use for their chastisement the weapon of personality, and for their reward, a flattery, which is not true praise."

The critics deemed her novels coarse. Much speculation took place as to who Currer Bell really was, and whether Bell was a man or a woman.

Charlotte's brother, Branwell, the only son of the family, died of chronic bronchitis and marasmus exacerbated by heavy drinking in September 1848, although Charlotte believed his death was due to tuberculosis. Emily and Anne both died of pulmonary tuberculosis in December 1848 and May 1849, respectively.

Charlotte and her father were now alone. In view of the enormous success of Jane Eyre, she was persuaded by her publisher to visit London occasionally, where she revealed her true identity and began to move in a more exalted social circle, becoming friends with Harriet Martineau, Elizabeth Gaskell, William Makepeace Thackeray and G. H. Lewes. Her book had sparked a movement in regards to feminism in literature. The main character, Jane Eyre, in her novel Jane Eyre, was a parallel to herself, a woman who was strong. However, she never left Haworth for more than a few weeks at a time as she did not want to leave her aging father's side.

Charlotte, Photograph, 1854In June 1854, Charlotte married Arthur Bell Nicholls, her father's curate, and became pregnant very soon thereafter. Her health declined rapidly during this time, and according to Gaskell, her earliest biographer, she was attacked by "sensations of perpetual nausea and ever-recurring faintness." Charlotte and her unborn child died March 31, 1855. Her death certificate gives the cause of death as phthisis (tuberculosis), but many biographers suggest she may have died from dehydration and malnourishment, caused by excessive vomiting from severe morning sickness. There is also evidence to suggest that Charlotte died from typhus she may have caught from Tabitha Ackroyd, the household's oldest servant, who died shortly before her. Charlotte was interred in the family vault in The Church of St. Michael and All Angels, Haworth, West Yorkshire, England.

The Life of Charlotte, the posthumous biography of Charlotte by fellow novelist Elizabeth Gaskell, was the first of many biographies about Charlotte to be published. Though frank in places, Gaskell suppressed details of Charlotte's love for, a married man, as being too much of an affront to contemporary morals and as a possible source of distress to Charlotte's still-living friends, father and husband. Gaskell also provided doubtful and inaccurate information about Patrick, claiming, for example, that he did not allow his children to eat meat. This is refuted by one of Emily 's diary papers, in which she describes the preparation of meat and potatoes for dinner at the parsonage, as Juliet Barker points out in her recent biography, "The 's".

Chapter 3

Charlotte Bronte: Chronology

1816 Charlotte was born on April 21 at Thornton in Yorkshire.

1820 Charlotte's father appointed perpetual curate of Haworth.

1821 September 15, Charlotte's mother dies.

1824 Charlotte and sisters Maria, Elizabeth, and Emily become students at the Clergy Daughters' School, Cowan Bridge.

1825 May, Maria dies; June, Elizabeth dies; Charlotte and Emily return home.

1829 Charlotte begins to write the first accounts of what is to become the saga of Glasstown and Angria.

1831 January, Charlotte enrolls at Miss Wooler's School, Roe Head.

1832 May, completes schooling and returns home to tutor sisters.

1835 July, returns to Roe Head as a teacher.

1838 May, resigns position and returns home.

1842 February, Charlotte and Emily enroll in the *Pensioned,* Brussels; November, Aunt Elizabeth Branwell's death brings girls home.

1843 January, Charlotte returns to Brussels to teach English and to study.

1844 January, leaves Brussels; sisters attempt without success to start school.

1846 May, *Poems by Currer, Ellis and Acton Bell* published; *The Professor* completed and offered repeatedly for publication, but without success; August, Charlotte begins *Jane Eyre.*

1847 October, *Jane Eyre* published and acclaimed; December, *Wuthering Heights*, by Emily, and *Agnes Grey*, by Anne Barone, published.

1848 June, *The Tenant of Wildfell Hall*, by Anne, published. September 24, Branwell, the only son of the family, dies; December 19, Emily dies.

1849 May 28, Anne dies. October, *Shirley* published.

1853 January, *Villette* published.

1854 June 29, Charlotte marries A. B. Nicholls.

1855 March 31, Charlotte dies.

1857 March, Mrs. Gaskell's *Life of Charlotte* published; June, The Professor published posthumously.

1925 *The Twelve Adventurers and Other Stories*, a collection of Charlotte's juvenilia, published posthumously.

1931-38 The nineteen volumes of *The Shakespeare Head* —the most complete edition of the works of Charlotte, Emily, Anne, and Branwell—published.

1933 *Legends of Angria*, a collection of Charlotte 's juvenilia, published posthumously.

1971 *Five Novelettes*, a collection of Charlotte 's juvenilia, published posthumously.

Chapter 4

Charlotte Bronte: A Modern Woman

Without a doubt, Charlotte was progressive in her beliefs. In a time when women were considered little more than social adornments and bearers of offspring, Charlotte bravely contradicted society through her writing. Her novels speak volumes for the oppressed woman; thus establishing Charlotte as one of the first modern women of her time. To refer to Charlotte Brontë as a feminist would, however, be an insufferable misrepresentation. Unlike George Sand, who by appearances and her standard of living epitomized the nineteenth-century feminist, Charlotte Brontë withdrew from a society that would not entirely accept her, and expressed her stifled ideals through her words. Slight in size, perpetually modest, Brontë's suppressed spirit gave way to her literary fantasies. She often likened herself to others in her oppressed situation; the ugly daughter or poor spinster, which she equated to slaves imprisoned by circumstances beyond their control.

The options for the proper yet impoverished woman during the time were limited a governess or teacher, roles Charlotte Brontë considered forms of bondage, as well. She believed that a governess had no existence, and was not considered a living or rational being except in connection with the wearisome duties she was forced to perform. Marriage was always a viable solution, yet Charlotte Brontë would only marry a man she respected, no matter his status or fortune. She resigned to live in the role society placed upon her, yet no one, not even a stringent society, could hamper her burgeoning emotions. It was through her words that Charlotte Brontë created a woman of free thought, intellect, and strong moral character; the same traits Charlotte herself possessed.

It was a dreary existence on the Yorkshire moors for the Brontë children. Charlotte was an intelligent youth, who took an early interest in politics. Her interest, solely on her own accord, was self-taught by reading the newspapers her father left lying about. By the age of nine, she knew more about politics than most grown men.

The Brontë children were all avid readers, and since they were isolated children, plagued often by illness, death, and desolation, they frequently retreated into a world of literary fantasy, spawned by the works of Sir Walter Scott, as well as other romantic authors of the time. Spurred by their vivid imaginations, the children invented role-playing games, at times with the aide of wooden toys, other times in provisional costumes. While many children of the time spent their leisure in such pursuits, it was the manner in which the girls specifically played that provides insight into the strength of their spirit, particularly Charlotte, who was mature beyond her years, and was perceived as a mother figure to her surviving siblings.

It was during these imaginative dramas that the girls portrayed legendry figures, figures of strength throughout history: Bonaparte, Caesar, Hannibal, and the Duke of Wellington. Such were no ordinary games of make believe, but elabourate, well-written dramas. It was the archetypical male hero who interested girls, not weak or impressionable females. Even female historical figures that appeared strong, such as Cleopatra, did not interested Charlotte, for Cleopatra used her sexuality to attain greatness, instead of achieving it on her own.

Charlotte rejected the use of sexuality to attract men in any form, and criticized women who resorted to this female characteristic as lacking self-respect, a fate she deemed worse than death.

It was Charlotte who provided the *noms de plume* that were deliberately ambiguous in gender for her and her sisters (Gilbert and Guber, 347-51). It is a fact that woman authors during the time were not received as seriously as men; however, as Currier Bell, Charlotte had the freedom to create her characters the way she wanted. Concealed by anonymity, she created s with genuine ideas and erudite views, who, above all, respected themselves, and werent afraid to declare it. For Charlotte Brontë, it was the ideal emotional outlet.

A woman who revealed an independent spirit was rare, if non-existence during Charlotte Brontë's time. Such feelings were typically concealed beneath a stoic exterior, suppressing the creative, emotional, and spiritual self. Such suppression had dangerous consequences an unhappy, unfulfilled life. Charlotte Brontë wrote that imagination was a restless faculty which needed to be heard and exercised. "Are we to be quite deaf to her cry and insensate to her struggles?".

Charlotte Brontë withdrew into the world she created. It was through her writing that she was allowed to breathe life into her suppressed self and dreams. Charlotte Brontë spoke of the evils of the condition of women, deep-rooted within the structure of the social system. Charlotte Brontë urged women not to linger on such problems; though the literary world must be grateful she did not heed her own advice. It was through her discontent that the characters of Jane Eyre and Lucy Snowe were born.

Jane Eyre, arguably Charlotte Brontë's *tour de force*intermibles autobiographical elements with romantic notions of the period. In the character Jane, Charlotte Brontë created a slight woman, in all respects plain, modest, morally strong and intelligent. Like the author, Jane's isolation created her persona, providing her with the necessary survival skills. Jane does not need a man to make her feel worthy; instead, she carries her self-worth in her mind and determination. Through Jane, Brontë exhibits resentment toward a society that has scorned her, while maintaining a detachment toward humanity as a whole.

When Jane ultimately falls in love, she embraces the notion of love itself, not the label or profits derived from it. However, Jane will not sacrifice her morals or self-respect for any man. In essence, she will not sacrifice herself. It is imperative to her to remain true to herself. Nothing can tempt Jane in this respect: wealth, status, or love.

I care for myself. The more solitary, the more friendless, the more unsustained I am, the more I will respect myself.

Like Jane, Charlotte herself was determined to marry a man she respected. In fact, she refused several offers of marriage that would have afforded her a life of ease, simply because the offers did not come from men she deemed her equal, or rather she felt them intellectually and morally deficient. She believed that a good woman, like any decent man, could not live without self-respect. She believed passion a temporary emotion that could easily give way to disgust, or worse, indifference. "God help the woman who is left to love passionately and alone".

Jane returns to Rochester and finally offers her unconditional love to him when he essentially has nothing left. Blind and penniless, Rochester can only offer himself, proving that for Brontë love transcends the societal expectations of marriage, and is based instead on mutual respect and love.

At the time, *Jane Eyre* was considered a radical book that deposed authority, violated human code, and fostered rebellion and Chartism in the homes of society. A reviewer in *The London Quarterly Review* stated that *Jane Eyre* was the personification of an unregenerate and undisciplined spirit, and that the character of Jane was destitute of all attractive, feminine qualities. A governess, the reviewer reminds her reader, is not a real woman, but a burden to society. No real woman would create a character as unseemly as *Jane Eyre*; if she did, she has "long forfeited the society of her own sex". Currier Bell was thus believed to be a man, who had no concept of the role of women in society.

In *Villette*, Charlotte draws directly from her earlier days in Brussels, and her one-sided love for a married professor. Instead of creating a romantic portrait filled with passion and childish love, Brontë takes her unrequited love in stride and creates Lucy Snowe, one of the most altruistic, honest, and independent s in English Literature. With Lucy, pedigree, social position and recondite intellectual acquisitions are compared to third-class lodgers. Indeed the portrait is similar to the character of Jane Eyre &mdas; both s' intelligence and moral judgment is superior to those around them, even the heroes of the novels.

In Rochester, Brontë created a hero much like that of other literary heroes of the day: rich, dashing, and romantic, adding to the gothic style of the novel. Yet in *Villette,* a more mature author created the antithesis of the literary hero. Paul Emmanuel lacks all romance, is instead pure flesh and blood, and humanly flawed. Yet, through his flaws, Lucy recognizes a generous soul, and together they form a bond of mutual respect. Brontë is reminding her readers, or rather enlightening them to the fact that women of self-respect and intellect can seek their place in the world, without the assistance of men.

Brontë, in her subtlety, wrote of simple women, who relied upon the respect of themselves, rather than society, to provide fulfillment in their lives. Through her characters, Brontë gave the gift of the modern woman, a woman determined to make her own way, and live her life by her own set of standards, dictated not by society but by herself, and herself alone.

Chapter 5

The Bronte Family

WHEN Mrs. Gaskell published The Life of Charlotte Brontë, she was forty-seven, and had already written Mary Barton; Cranford and Ruth. In six years, there were to follow Sylvia's Lovers and that story in which is embalmed the charm of all things fading—Cousin Phillis. The biography was worthy of its author. Here was presented, not less truthfully than exquisitely, all that it was essential to know of the sad story of Charlotte Brontë's life, and, interwoven in its texture, and consummately in place, the beautiful piece of prose in which Ellen Nussey told of Anne Brontë's death.

It was surprising that this masterpiece, at its first appearance, should have been marred by indiscretions of revelation, relating, in part, to the father of the sisters, to whose paternal care the book paid tribute, and who was still alive, an octogenarian. The explanation was, partly, that Mrs. Gaskell was a novelist whose first obligation was truth to character, and who was interested in the subordinate personages of her narrative mainly in so far as they illustrated the figure of its. Partly, that the task she had set herself—to tell soon and fully Charlotte Brontë's life-story—was not one that could possibly have been executed without giving some temporary offence. Yet, the main lines of the story were seized and held with the unerring hand of genius, and; in the amended version, we now possess a book that, both in its candour and in its restraint, remains the true record for posterity.

Of the substantial accuracy of its picture of the Brontë household, there is no longer any question. Some of the original domestic details now banished from the volume may not have been correct; but such stories as attached themselves to Patrick Brontë do not gather round a man of an exacting character. His custom of dining alone in a house with two sitting rooms is sufficiently significant. "No one," writes Mary Taylor to Ellen Nussey, a year after Charlotte's death, "ever gave up more than she did and with full consciousness of what she sacrificed." Family affection for his offspring, on the one side, of course, there was, and, on the other, deep filial piety and that cherishing fondness which springs from piety; but it is a main element in Charlotte Brontë's later history that talk in the lonely house must often have been "but a tinkling cymbal."

Patrick Brunty or Brontë, as, at Haworth, he came finally to write the name, was, so far as we know, a pure Irishman. He was born in Emdale, county Down, in 1777, and, in 1802, presumably with the aid of some slender savings, he entered St. John's College, Cambridge. After taking his degree, he held various curacies, settling down finally, in 1820, in the incumbency of Haworth. But the troubles of life were not over; for, in less than two years, his always delicate wife, Maria Branwell, whom he had married in 1812, had died, leaving him the care of six children, Maria, Elizabeth, Charlotte, Patrick Branwell, Emily Jane and Anne, of whom the eldest was eight and the youngest not yet two years of age. In this difficulty, his wife's sister Elizabeth Branwell took up her residence with him at Haworth, remaining there as mistress of his house until her death. Thus, the household was constituted until Charlotte Brontë was twenty-six.

For so large a family, the house in the graveyard was a confined habitation: it stood at the top of the steep and drab village, its front windows looking on the church and the graves, and its back on the wide-stretching moors over which the tiny girls loved constantly to ramble. Their father was not a learned man; but he knew enough to teach infants, and it was a mistake that, in order to provide them with more systematic instruction, he should have sent four of them to a clergy daughters' boarding school. This was an absurdly cheap subsidised institution, for no other was within his means; and the disastrous experiment, afterwards forming the basis of the account of Lowood in Jane Eyre, came to an end within a year. Charlotte Brontë believed that the precarious health of her two elder sisters had suffered from the experience. In any case, the first tragedies of her home were the early deaths of the much-loved Maria and Elizabeth.

The household, thus reduced in numbers, remained at Haworth for the next six years, occupied with reading, rambling, household management and, above all, with literary invention. In 1831, when Charlotte was nearly fifteen, was again sent to a boarding school, this time to Miss Wooler's at Roe Head, where she made the acquaintance of Ellen Nussey and Mary Taylor, who became her lifelong friends. Miss Wooler was kind and competent, and eighteen fairly happy months of pupilage resulted, three years later, in Charlotte's returning as an instructress, while Emily and Anne also became pupils in the same school. But Charlotte was not born to be a teacher of young girls, and, after another interval of three years, she returned to Haworth, fretted in mind and spirit. Yet, something had to be done to replenish the family exchequer on which the one, and thoroughly unsatisfactory, brother was beginning to make a series of claims.

Emily had attempted and failed to live the life of an assistant schoolmistress under peculiarly exacting conditions, and there was nothing left for Charlotte and Anne except to become governesses in private families. But, though the gentle Anne was, apparently, a good governess, retaining one post for four years, the experiences of neither of the pair met their wishes, and it occurred to Charlotte and Emily that they should qualify for the three setting up school by themselves. For this, some knowledge of foreign languages was indispensable, and, in February 1842, the two sisters, aged, respectively, twenty-five and twenty-three, had found their way as pupils into a foreign school, the pensioned Héger, rue d'Isabelle, Brussels. The short year spent there was made especially interesting on account of the lectures of the professor of literature, Constantin Héger, a man of thirty-three who, obviously, added to some of the usual Napoleonisms of the professeur des jeunes filles

(Napoleonisms to which Charlotte Brontë was not blind) a genuine force of character, something of the genius of exposition and a touch of that ironic or semi-humours malice which is the salt of personality. But this brightening episode was not to last, and, in eight months, the sisters were hurrying home too late to attend the deathbed of their aunt Branwell.

The home was reorganised, Emily being left to keep house. Branwell, who had failed in several occupations, found a post as tutor in the same family where Anne was governess, and Charlotte Brontë allowed herself to be tempted to return to Brussels, in January 1843, as instructress in English. She was now verging on twenty-seven, and at Brussels were the surroundings that had broken the dull monotony of her life. Hitherto, this monotony had been endurable; henceforth, it was no longer so. As she taught in the school of the Hégers, at times instructing Constantin Héger and his brother-in-law in English, and hearing from him constantly of the high things in literature and life, there was set up that rapport of intelligence, and, more than this, that interplay where soul responds to soul, of which, hitherto, she had known nothing. In a year, she was back in the lonely house, herself now twice lonely "for remembering happier things."

All had not gone well in her absence. The brother was hastening down a career that ended in an early grave. The plan of a school had come to nothing; the tone of the communications she sent to her adored professor, too exalt led to the ending of all communication; and in the letters she wrote to Brussels in these barren years we can hear the cry of a stifled heart. In March, 1845, she writes to Ellen Nussey: "I can hardly tell you how time gets on at Haworth.

There is no event whatever to mark its progress. One day resembles another: and all have heavy lifeless physiognomies... There was a time when Haworth was a very pleasant place to me: it is not so now. I feel as if we were all buried here... Write very soon dear Ellen. There was one way of escape and one only—for "the imagination is not a state," as Blake tells us, "it is the human existence itself."

Chpater 6

Contemporary Responses to Jane Eyre

Background

Just as Emily Dickinson's life gave rise to the Myth of the Recluse, so the home life gave rise to the Myth of the Lonely Geniuses and to stories which sentimentalized the three sisters and demonized their home life. For instance, there is the story that their father, a minister, fired his gun in the house. Another story runs that while his wife, who had born six children in seven years, lay dying, he destroyed her only silk dress. Stories like these are now regarded as false.

Nonetheless, it is true that their home life was difficult. Their mother died when Charlotte, Emily, Anne, and their brother Branwell were children; the two oldest sisters, Maria and Elizabeth, died young. Branwell was a drug addict and an alcoholic whom Charlotte, Emily, and Anne nursed through his collapses, his psychosis, and his final days. The devoted sisters found support and companionship in one another; at night, they read their novels and their poems to one another. Their society did not encourage women to fulfill their talents.

The twenty-year old Charlotte wrote to Robert Southey, the poet laureate, for his opinion about writing. His response shows the barriers facing women writers: "Literature cannot be the business of a woman's life, and it ought not to be. The more she is engaged in her proper duties, the less leisure will she have for it, even as an accomplishment and a recreation."

Conventional wisdom held that men and women had separate "spheres" and duties, with woman's sphere being the house, family, and self-sacrifice. The popular image for the ideal woman was "the Angel in the House," who was expected to be devoted and submissive to her husband. The Angel was passive and powerless, meek, charming, graceful, sympathetic, self-sacrificing, pious, and above all—pure. The phrase "Angel in the House" comes from the title of an immensely popular poem by Coventry Patmore (1854), in which he holds his angel-wife up as a model for all women. Granting this view of women, it is not surprising that the sisters adopted pseudonyms to hide their sex when they published their poems and novels. They chose names which were not obviously masculine: Acton Bell (Anne), Currer Bell (Charlotte), and Ellis Bell (Emily).

Chapter 7

The Sisters and Their Works

As the three famous Brontë sisters grew up, they wrote stories even as young girls. They developed their characters and plotlines over the years, and these three works would later become either their best or only works; Charlotte with Jane Eyre, Emily with Wuthering Heights, and Anne with Agnes Grey. Focusing on the key works of Charlotte and Anne, readers get a glimpse into the writers' opinions of being a governess and perhaps life in general. Of the three sisters, Emily produced the least amount but was also the first to pass away. All three did see some of their poetry published before taking to their final resting place, but Emily published only one novel. Anne only published two, but the second novel The Tenant of Wildfell Hall was a much larger work than her first. Charlotte saw three of her novels published, Shirley, Villette, and Jane Eyre, and the fourth, The Professor, was released after her death. Charlotte was obviously the more productive one, but she lived to be 39, while Anne died at 29 and Emily at 30.

Charlotte and Anne spent a great deal of their adult lives as governesses, while Emily tried the profession once for six months. Looking exclusively at Agnes Grey and Jane Eyre then, one can see that the writers used much of their own lives and experiences in their works. The protagonists of both books become governesses at a young age, and if Jane and Agnes had never gone out on their own to pursue this personal independence, their stories would have ended quite differently. Jane would probably have died an old spinster at Lowood, and Agnes would have been so sheltered as an adult in her parents' house that she would never want leave, becoming a somewhat less eccentric Miss Havisham.

The protagonists have similar parentage. Jane and Agnes' fathers were clergyman, as was the Brontës' father. Both mothers married their fathers in spite of what their families said, and both women were disowned, given no dowry and cut off from any fortune. As a result, both families started off at a certain high point of poverty.

The protagonists grew up in quite different ways, however. Charlotte opted for the more dramatic history of her character and Jane's parents died in her infancy, which was a common plotline in novels at the time for the protagonists to be orphaned and alone in the world. Jane was raised by family, although Mrs. Reed was only family by marriage. The house was a nightmare for her, and surprisingly the Lowood School was a step up. While she was dragged down to absolute poverty due to the excessive thriftiness of Mr.. Brocklehurst, she was treated with respect when her peers saw her fit for respecting her by her actions.

In contrast, Agnes grew up in an entirely different household. The Grey family lived comfortably until they met with some financial hardships after an investment gone sour. The family made some drastic economies, but throughout the ups and downs of their pocketbooks, the family stayed together and there is no doubt that Agnes was well loved. She was not spoiled, but she had not experienced anything near the same hardships as Jane had.

Despite the differences of their upbringing, Jane and Agnes became governesses much the same way. Jane, already with experience as an instructor at Lowood, became restless after her dear friend marries and moves away. She decided to advertise for a governess position, and when one was found it was not long before she whisked off to brighter conquests. Agnes, quite ready to get away from the family that thinks her useless, wanting to help them in their financial struggles, and knowing that no gentleman should ever want to marry a girl from a poor family, inquired about becoming a governess. She practically begged her parents for permission, trying to prove to them that she was not the helpless kitten that they think her to be. "How delightful it would be to be a governess!

To go out into the world; to enter upon a new life; to act for myself; to exercise my unused faculties; to try my unknown powers; to earn my own maintenance...; to show papa what his little Agnes could do; to convince mamma and Mary that I was not quite the helpless, thoughtless being they supposed..." (1). She eventually gained their approval, and "many weeks" later, she found a position through a distant relative. A short time later, Agnes went off to her future endeavour.

Both women independently sought to better themselves and their situations by seeking independent employment and achieved it. Both protagonists start the journeys of their lives as they leave on their literal journeys to their new homes, and everything before that point is a means of introducing the reader to the protagonist in order to know their personalities. But in comparison, Jane already had a great deal of what could be considered training. The only environment she knew for eight years was that of a school, and spent the last two years as an employee teaching at it. She already had knowledge and experience in teaching children. On the opposite side, Agnes came directly from the sheltered environment of her family, never even having been sent away to school. On the surface, Jane Eyre appears to be the more optimistic of the two novels of the experiences of being a governess. But in fact, both give realistic pictures of the profession, displaying both the positive and negative aspects. In a sort of ironic twist, both protagonists get the appropriate first charge as result of their upbringing.

Jane had a terrible childhood that only improved slightly when drastic measures were taken by concerned persons to better Lowood. Jane's first (and only) charge was sweet little Adèle, the daughter of a French actress and rescued from poverty by her current guardian. Her only fault was her typical childish nature and resulting from Mr.. Rochester spoiling her. In fact, Jane's heart may have warmed to her even more once she learned they had similar backgrounds. The only disadvantages to the situation were the howlings and eccentricities of supposedly Grace Poole and the moody nature of her master.

However, not all was sunshine for the life of a governess in this atmosphere. Charlotte gives her readers a glimpse into the opinions of those who despise the women that govern them. While her master was entertaining guests for a short time, one evening Jane was forced to listen to the party ridicule the profession, all bragging about what they did to their governesses and how many they went through in a year, started by the intolerable Miss Ingram. Jane proved herself to be a much better person than these members of the elite class by simply sitting there and refusing to acknowledge their comments in any way, other than the uncontrollable blush.

The Ingram family could very well have been the Bloomfields in a past life. Agnes' first charge was an unwholesome group of small children, spoiled so much by their parents that Agnes had no choice to use some excessive force. Regardless of whether or not Agnes had actually done something, the little spawns of Satan would run to their mamma and Agnes would get a lecture. Even at this young age, they were much like the grown Ingram children; they bragged directly to Agnes about how they had already gone through one governess and what they had done to her. The Bloomfield household was quite different from the happy home Agnes had come from.

The experience was not completely disheartening or scarring. Once Agnes was dismissed by the Bloomfields and spent a few months vacation with her family, she pursued another position. After much searching and deliberation, and putting her own advertisement in like Jane did in the first place, she acquired a position in the Murray household. These children were older and much well behaved. The children were spoiled due to their comfortable living in the upper class, Miss Murray perhaps being the worst of them, but they were not so much that they had become intolerable wretches. They caused a bit of emotional trauma to Agnes, but not so much as to cause so much stress and anxiety that she must convalesce at her family's home for months. This position also gave her the opportunity to meet the man she would later marry.

How the two novels finish makes them drastically different from each other. Even though Agnes had fallen in love with a young clergyman, she returned home after Miss Murray became Lady Ashby and moved with her mother to a town near the ocean to start a school. She then encountered her love, Edward Weston, and they get married and live happily ever after.

Jane's future after relinquishing her position was much more complex. Both women end their careers because of a marriage, but it was Jane's own marriage in her story. She fell in love with her master, they were to get married until they find out he was already married to the crazy woman in the attic, she ran away, almost died from starvation and illness, was taken in by kind people who later turn out to be her family, took a position as a school mistress for a short time, came into her fortune, refused St. John's proposal, went back to find her battered beloved Rochester, married him, and lived happily ever after.

In the novels of this time, the authors frequently told what would happen in following years in just a few pages in order to finalize the story and tie up any loose ends. Usually in these final pages, nothing shocking happens or no new information is given that is drastically essential to the story. Jane Eyre is very much like this. After she marries Rochester, not everything else said is surprising or dramatic. The reader can easily expect what happens next and could almost foresee the outcome without the fine details.

Agnes Grey, on the other hand, is quite different. With only two pages left, the reader only just finds out at this point that Agnes' clergyman Mr.. Weston has transferred to a position nearby. In the only chapter left in the book, Weston professes his love for her, they ask her mother's permission to marry (Mr.. Grey has long since been dead), she approves, they marry, have a few children, and live happily ever after, all in two pages. This outcome is a huge surprise, considering Anne gives her readers very little to believe that Weston has the same feelings for Agnes as she does for him before this final chapter. Since this is such an unusual ending, one could classify this as a quirk of Anne Brontë, the way she ends her stories. In The Tenant of Wildfell Hall, however, she ends the large text in the usual way just as her sister ended Jane Erye.

Although different printings of books vary page numbers, it is clear that Jane Eyre is much longer than Agnes Grey is. Not only this can be seen by how long it takes a reader to read from start to finish, Charlotte gives a great deal more information and develops situations more than Anne develops. Also, while both novels do an excellent job of telling their stories, a great deal more happens in Jane Eyre. Agnes' childhood up until the turning point, where she leaves for her first position lasts less than the first chapter, while Jane's fills ten chapters.

Even though Agnes has, two positions as her career as a governess, what happens to Jane after she relinquishes her position is a great deal more and takes a long period of time. If the Brontës were writing these novels for a final class project, Anne would have received a B+ and Charlotte would have exerted herself far beyond any grade. It would be interesting to see what would happen if Agnes and Jane were picked up from their places, perhaps at the age of 18 so they could still grow up to be the same persons they are, and switch them. Agnes would live in Gateshead and Jane would start in Wellwood.

Rochester would never have fallen in love with Agnes. He loved her blunt and quizzical ways, a nature quite different from Agnes. He would have probably found her terribly dull and continue with his life just as he had before she had come. Though he and her beloved Weston share the same first name, Agnes would never have met Weston and hence never have fallen in love with him. Since Adèle is well behaved, Agnes would never need to leave unless Rochester pursued Miss Ingram. If he had never tried his test with her and had actually married her, Adèle would probably still be sent off to school, especially since Miss Ingram despised her so, and Agnes would find other employment. Agnes might not have even lasted that long, being frightened off by Gateshead's dark secrets.

Jane would never have gone beyond the Bloomfields. With her dark interior and exterior, her somber ways and Lowood education with a bit of Brocklehurst influence, she would have the little beasts sitting politely in their seats and reciting lines of Shakespeare by the end of the first week. If instead, her inner weakness made her falter and she found herself unable to control the children, she would still have the strength to confront her employers with the truth of the situation. They being the Bloomfields, they would blame everything on her, just as they blamed everything on Agnes, and Jane would do the nineteenth-century rendition of telling them off and then return to her room to start packing. If Jane continued on Agnes' path to the Murrays at Horton Lodge, she would find it a pleasant situation.

She would get along as well with her pupils in their spoiled nature as Agnes did, but their mind games would be useless. Miss Murray might still try to play on Jane's affections, but it would be useless considering Jane would have to secret feelings for Mr..Weston. Upon meeting him, she would think him a good man, respect him for his dedication to God and loyalty to the sick and elderly, even find him pleasant in conversation, but she would not have any feelings for him. Her and Rochester's personalities fit together, and Weston is nothing like Rochester.

Miss Murray would still marry Lord Ashby, so Jane would probably look for another position. In conclusion, Charlotte may have toned down her experience for the sake of the complexity of the novel, considering she never in real life fell in love with her master and then went on to marry him only to find out he was married to the wild beast in the attic. Anne's portrayal would be the more realistic of the two, considering Agnes' story is not beyond the realms of reality. Through these two works, however, one can get a sense of the Brontës' experience as governesses and their opinions of the profession.

Contemporary Response to *Jane Eyre*

When *Jane Eyre* published in 1847, it became a bestseller. The reviews were favorable. There was much speculation about whether the writer was a man or a woman and whether the Bells were really three persons, two persons, or just one person. When it became known that a woman had written such a passionate novel and seemed so knowing sexually, the reviews became more negative.

The reviewer for the *Atlas* praised the novel: "This is not merely a work of great promise; it is one of absolute performance. It is one of the most powerful domestic romances, which have been published for many years. It has little or nothing of the old conventional stamp upon it... but it is full of youthful vigour, of freshness and originality, of nervous diction and concentrated interest. The incidents are sometimes melodramatic, and, it might be added, improbable; but these incidents, though striking, are subordinate to the main purpose of the piece, which is a tale of passion, not of intensity, which is most sublime. It is a book to make the pulses gallop and the heartbeat, and to fill the eyes with tears (1847).

The reviewer for the *Rambler* expressed a criticism that was made against all the novels—coarseness. The reference to "grosser and more animal passions" is a roundabout way of saying "sex."

Jane Eyre is, indeed, one of the coarsest books, which we ever perused. It is not that the professed sentiments of the writer are absolutely wrong or forbidding, or that the odd sort of religious notions which she puts forth are much worse than is usual in popular tales. It is rather that there is a tendency to relapse into that class of ideas, expressions, and circumstances, which is most connected with the grosser and more animal portion of our nature; and that the detestable morality of the most prominent character in the story is accompanied with every sort of palliation short of unblushing justification (1848).

The conservative Eliza Rigby, writing for the *Quarterly Review,* assumed a connection between unrestrained passion and political rebellion. Jane Eyre is throughout the personification of the unregenerate and undisciplined spirit, the more dangerous to exhibit from that prestige of principle and self-control which is liable to dazzle the eye too much for it to observe the inefficient and unsound foundation on which it rests. It is true Jane does right, and exerts great moral strength, but it is the strength of a mere heathen mind, which is a law unto itself. No Christian grace is perceptible upon her.

Altogether, the autobiography of Jane Eyre is preeminently an anti-Christian composition. There is throughout in it a murmuring against the comforts of the rich and against the privations of the poor, which, as far as each individual is concerned, is a murmuring against God's appointment. There is a proud and perpetual assertion of the rights of man, for which we find no authority either in God's word or in God's providence. There is that pervading tone of ungodly discontent which is at once the most prominent and the most subtle evil which the law and the pulpit, which all civilized society in fact, has at the present day to contend with. We do not hesitate to say that the tone of mind and thought, which has overthrown authority and violated every human and divine code abroad and fostered Chartism and rebellion at home, is the same that has also written *Jane Eyre* (1847).

Underlying this harsh criticism is a fear of social unrest. In 1847, the working classes were organizing political protests in England, as well as on the Continent. The Chartists, regarded by the affluent classes as revolutionaries threatening the foundation of government and order, were demanding such rights as the vote for working men, a shorter workweek, and a secret ballot. In 1848, political protest erupted in so many revolutions on the Continent that historians call it the Year of Revolutions.

Point of View in *Jane Eyre*

Jane Eyre is written from the first person point of view or "I." When the novel was initially published, the subtitle was *An Autobiography,* and Currer Bell was identified as the editor rather than as the author. The subtitle was dropped in subsequent editions of the novel.

In general, a first person point of view has the advantages of being a constant point of view and helping to make the work consistent; also, it tends to give authority and credibility to the narrative, since the person telling the story observed and/

or was involved in all the incidents. Its drawbacks are that the story is limited to what the narrator saw or heard and to the narrator's interpretation of the other characters. Because the action is completed before, the story begins, the narrative may not be as vivid as fiction using other points of view, and the characters and action may seem more distant.

Jane Eyre has the virtues of this method; most readers accept Jane's interpretation and explanations of herself, the other characters, and events. However the problem of too great an aesthetic distance does not arise. Jane's emotional intensity and openness cause the reader to identify with her, so that her experiences and feelings temporarily become those of most readers.

Conflicts and Struggles

This novel presents a number of conflicts and struggles within Jane and between Jane and other characters, conflicts that must be resolved for her to achieve self-fulfillment and happiness:

- Reason and common sense range against feeling and imagination. Jane must learn to subordinate her passions to her reason. She must also learn to control imagination, which may take the form of superstition, as when she is locked in the Red Room. When she is a child, her passions erupt unchecked, with both positive and negative results.
- Jane's need for love is so great that, according to Charles Burkhart, "Love is a religion in *Jane Eyre*." A scrutiny of Jane's romantic relationships raises the question of whether they are really power struggles for control and, perhaps, show some sadomasochistic tendencies.
- She must also learn to adapt her desire for experience and independence to her dependent position.
- An orphan, she suffers the humiliations of being dependent on the charity of wealthy relatives. However, as an adult she supports herself as a teacher and a governess, she insists on her status as a lady

and struggles with feelings of inferiority. She alternates between submission and rebellion, between passivity and self-assertion, between restraint and freedom.

- Jane's quest for self-fulfillment is tied to her spiritual growth. When divine love and human love prove incompatible, Jane is forced to choose between them.

Other Characteristics

Jane as child and adult is the outsider who searches for family and place. She can also be seen as the other.

It has been suggested that at least part of the appeal of *Jane Eyre* comes from its fulfilling common fantasies and wishes. According to this theory, we feel that we are orphans, that the family we are living with is not our real family; we want to punish the parents (and other authority figures) who thwarted childhood desires by saying "no" to us; we desire wealth and the perfect mate. *Jane Eyre* fulfills these desires and dreams, and it justifies the punishment of cruel authority figures like Aunt Reed and Mr.. Brocklehurst, who deserve what they get. Think about this theory as you read the novel and decide whether you agree with it.

The image clusters running through this novel are fire, the moon, the weather, windows, and mirrors. Jane's paintings serve to characterize her and her situation.

Innovations

It is hard for the modern reader to see the innovative aspects of this novel because they have become familiar to us. Unlike her sisters, Charlotte rejected the convention of the beautiful. While writing *Jane Eyre,* she told them, "I will show you a as plain and as small as myself." She succeeded in her goal and established a trend of ordinary-looking or unattractive s. Also *Jane Eyre* is one of the first novels to present a child's experiences as the child saw and felt them and to trace that child's development into adulthood.

Chapter 8

Introduction to Gothic Fiction

"Goth" is a term that was applied to various Germanic tribes who ransacked southern Europe from 376-410 CE. Because the Goths were credited with bringing about the fall of Rome and its classical culture, Renaissance and Enlightenment critics later applied the term "Gothic" negatively, to mean "medieval" or that which was considered barbaric. Medieval or "Gothic" architecture, for example, did not follow the classical ideals of simplicity, unity, and symmetry—instead, soaring towers, pointed vaults or arches, flying buttresses, gargoyles and other intricate or "wild" elements prevailed in churches, castles, and monasteries. "Gothic" gradually lost its negative connotation and was used to refer to an ancient past, often in a nostalgic way.

The Gothic movement in literature, like Romanticism, is viewed as a reaction to Enlightenment rationalism, a return to the primitive. The 18th century was an "Age of Reason" concerned with classical principles and scientific progress. The novel, a young genre, was predominantly realistic and didactic. Appearing near the end of the 18th century, however, Gothic novels drew upon the conventions of the medieval (chivalric) romances that told of knights battling with magic and monsters. Gothic novels presented a protagonist's immersion into a dark, horrific realm of some kind and reintroduced supernatural elements into fiction.

Gothic texts characteristically deal with difficult-to-express issues and anxieties. Boundaries or limits (political, philosophical, sexual, etc.) are both established and challenged in Gothic fiction. Blurring or disruptions of borders are common (e.g., inside/outside, illusion/reality, masculine/feminine, material/spiritual, good/evil), and the tensions between the scientific and the supernatural are often prominent. Originally called "Gothic romances," Gothic novels were consumed by a popular audience—often women—and initially considered to be of low literary quality.

The Gothic novel's "golden age" is generally cited as lasting from 1764-1840; however, the Gothic influence remains visible not only in literature, but also in film, television, music, and even dance.

Conventions of the Gothic Novel:

- Wild landscapes
- Remote or exotic locales
- Dimly lit, gloomy settings
- Ruins or isolated crumbling castles or mansions (later cities and houses)
- Crypts, tombs
- Dungeons, torture chambers
- Dark towers, hidden rooms
- Secret corridors/passageways
- Dream states or nightmares
- Found manuscripts or artifacts
- Ancestral curses
- Family secrets
- Damsels in distress
- Marvellous or mysterious creatures, monsters, spirits, or strangers
- Enigmatic figures with supernatural powers
- Scientific tone (fantastic events observed empirically)
- Specific reference to noon, midnight, twilight (the witching hours)
- Use of traditionally "magical" numbers such as (3, 7, 13)
- Unnatural acts of nature (blood-red moon, sudden fierce wind, etc.)

The Ghost Story and the Horror Story:

The ghost story and the horror story are influenced by Gothic novels and appear early in the 19th century. Both stories have elements of horror, but while a ghost story usually deals with the reappearance of the repressed and must have a ghost (hence the name), a horror story does not; a confrontation with something unknowable/unexplainable is at the core of the horror story. Both types of stories explore the limits of what people are capable of doing/experiencing (e.g., fear, violence, madness) in a world where the "normal" rules of cause and effect do not necessarily apply. The stories present an attempt to find adequate descriptions/symbols for deeply rooted energies and fears related to death, afterlife, punishment, darkness, evil, violence, and destruction. Traditionally. considered as existing in another location or plane (e.g., Dante's *Inferno*), Hell has been re-envisioned as residing in the mind or consciousness.

Chapter 9

Various Approaches to Jane Eyre

A Marxist Approach to *Jane Eyre*

Based on the ideas of Karl Marx, this theoretical approach asks us to consider How a literary work reflects the socioeconomic conditions of the time in which it was written? What does the text tell us about contemporary social classes and how does it reflect classism? *Jane Eyre* depicts the strict, hierarchical class system in England that required everyone to maintain carefully circumscribed class positions. Primarily through the character of Jane, it also accents the cracks in this system, the places where class differences were melding in Victorian England. For example, the novel questions the role of the governess: Should she be considered upper class, based on her superior education, or lower class, because of her servant-status within the family? What happens when relationships develop between people of different classes, such as Rochester and Jane?

Jane's ambiguous class status becomes evident from the novel's opening chapter. A poor orphan living with relatives, Jane feels alienated from the rest of the Reed family. John Reed tells Jane she has "no business to take our books; you are a dependent... you ought to beg, and not to live here with gentleman's children like us." In this quote, John claims the rights of the gentleman, implying that Jane's family was from a lower class, and, therefore, she has no right to associate on equal footing with her wealthy cousins. Jane's lack of money leaves her dependent upon the Reeds for sustenance. She appears to exist in a no-man's land between the upper- and servant classes. By calling her cousin John a "murderer," "slave-driver," and "Roman emperor," Jane emphasizes her recognition of the corruption inherent in the ruling classes. As she is dragged away to the red-room following her fight with John Reed, Jane resists her captors like a "rebel slave," emphasizing the oppression she suffers because of her class status. When Miss Abbot admonishes Jane for striking John Reed, Jane's "young master," Jane immediately questions her terminology. Is John really her "master"; is she his servant? Emphasizing the corruption, even despotism of the upper classes, Jane's narrative makes her audience aware that the middle classes were becoming the repositories of both moral and intellectual superiority.

Jane's experiences at Thornfield reinforce this message. When Jane first arrives, she is happy to learn that Mrs. Fairfax is a housekeeper, and not Jane's employer, because this means they are both dependents and can therefore, interact as equals. Mrs. Fairfax discusses the difference between herself, as an upper-servant, and the other servants in the house; for example, she says Leah and John are "only servants, and one can't converse with them on terms of equality; one must keep them at due distance for fear of losing one's authority."

As a governess, Jane is in the same category as Mrs. Fairfax: neither a member of the family nor a member of the serving classes. The ambiguity of the governess is especially pronounced, as we see with the example of Diana and Mary Rivers: the well-educated daughters of upper-class parents who have fallen on hard financial times, the Rivers are better educated than their employers, though treated with as little respect as the family cook. Victorian society brutally maintained the boundaries between governesses and the upper-class families, practically prohibiting marriages between the two groups and attempting to desexualize governesses, who were often accused of bringing a dangerous sexuality into the family. Blanche, for example, calls governesses "incubi," and Lady Ingram believes that liaisons should never be allowed between governesses and tutors, because such relationships would introduce a moral infection into the household.

The relationship between Jane and Rochester also emphasizes class issues. In a conversation preceding their betrothal, Rochester treats Jane like a good servant: Because she has been a "dependent" who has done "her duty," he, as her employer, wants to offer her assistance in finding a new job. Jane confirms her secondary status by referring to Rochester as "master," and believing "wealth, caste, custom," separate her from him. She fears he will treat her like an "automaton" because she is "poor, obscure, plain and little," mistakenly believing the lower classes to be heartless and soulless. Claiming the aristocratic privilege of creating his own rules, Rochester redefines Jane's class status, by defining her as his "equal" and "likeness."

Before she can become Rochester's wife, Jane must prove her acceptability based on class. Does she have an upper-class sensibility, despite her inferior position at Thornfield? For example, when Bessie sees Jane at Lowood, she is impressed because Jane has become "quite a lady"; in fact, her accomplishments surpass that of her cousins, yet they are still considered her social superiors based solely on wealth. The conversation emphasizes the ambiguities of Jane's family's class status and of the class system in general: Should a lady be judged based on academic accomplishments, money, or family name? The novel critiques the behaviour of most of the upper-class characters Jane meets: Blanche Ingram is haughty and superficial, John Reed is debauched, and Eliza Reed is inhumanely cold. Rochester is a primary example of upper-class debauchery, with his series of mistresses and his attempt to make Jane a member of the harem.

In her final view of Thornfield, after Bertha has burned it down, Jane emphasizes the stark contrast between her comforting, flowering, breathtaking dream of Thornfield, and the reality of its trodden and wasted grounds. The discrepancy emphasizes that the world's vision of the upper classes does not always capture the hidden passions that boil under the veneer of genteel tranquility.

One of Jane's tasks in the novel is to revitalize the upper classes, which have become mired in debauchery and haughtiness. Just as Rochester sought Jane for her freshness and purity, the novel suggests that the upper classes in general need the pure moral values and stringent work ethic of the middle classes. At novel's end, Rochester recognizes the error in his lifestyle, and his excessive passions have been quenched; he is reborn as a proper, mild-mannered husband, happily dependent on his wife's moral and intellectual guidance.

A Jungian Approach to *Jane Eyre*

The famous psychologist Carl Jung was interested in *the collective unconscious,* or the primordial images and ideas that reside in every human being's psyche. Often appearing in the form of dreams, visions, and fantasies, these images provoke strong emotions that are beyond the explanation of reason. In *Jane Eyre,* the bounds of reality continually expand, so that dreams and visions have as much validity as reason, providing access to the inner recesses of Jane's and Rochester's psyches. Their relationship also has a supernatural component.

Throughout the novel, Jane is described as a "fairy." Sitting in the red-room, she labels herself a "tiny phantom, half fairy, half imp" from one of Bessie's bedtime stories, a spirit-creature that comes out of "lone, ferny dells in moors." As fairy, Jane identifies herself as a special, magical creature, and reminds the reader of the importance that imagination plays in her life. Jane's dreams have a prophetic character, suggesting their almost supernatural ability to predict the future. In a dream foreshadowing the direction of her relationship with Rochester, she is "tossed on a buoyant but unquiet sea." Jane's dream warns her that their relationship will be rocky, bringing chaos and passion into her life. Similarly, her dreams of infants are prophetic, indicating impending trouble in her life.

Not only is Jane a mythical creature, but the narrative she creates also has a mythic element, mixing realism and fantasy. We see the first instance of this as Jane sits nervously in the red-room and imagines a gleam of light shining on the wall; for her, this indicates a vision "from another world. Generally, supernatural occurrences such as these serve as transition points in the novel, signaling drastic changes in Jane's life. As Jane's departure from Gateshead was marked by her pseudo-supernatural experience in the red-room, her movement away from Lowood also has a paranormal component. Meditating upon the best means for discovering a new job, Jane is visited by a "kind fairy" who offers her a solution. This psychic counselor gives her very specific advice: Place an advertisement in the local newspaper, with answers addressed to J.E. and do it immediately. The fairy's plan works, and Jane soon discovers the job at Thornfield.

As a gypsy woman, Rochester aligned himself with mystical knowledge. During her telling of her fortune, Rochester seems to have peered directly into Jane's heart, leaning her deep into a dream-state she likens to "a web of mystification." He magically weaves a web around Jane with words, and appears to have watched every movement of her heart, like an "unseen spirit." During this scene, he wears a red cloak, showing that he has taken over the position of Red Riding Hood that Jane held earlier. The potion he gives Mason also has mystical powers, giving Mason the strength he lacks for an hour or so, hinting at Rochester's mysterious, possibly supernatural powers.

In emphasizing the uniqueness of Jane and Rochester's love, Brontë gives their meetings a mythical feel, so that they are depicted as archetypes of true lovers. Her association of Rochester's horse and dog with the mythical Gytrash places their initial meeting in an almost fairytale-like setting. Later, Rochester reveals that at this initial meeting, he thought Jane was a fairy who had bewitched his horse, and he repeatedly refers to her as a sprite or elfin character, claiming the "men in green" are her relatives. The lovers' reunion at the end of the novel also has a psychic component. As she is about to accept St. John's wishes, Jane experiences a sensation as "sharp, as strange, as shocking" as an electric shock. Then she hears Rochester's voice called her name. The voice comes from nowhere, speaking "in pain and woe, wildly, eerily, urgently." So powerful is this voice that Jane cries, "I am coming," and runs out the door into the garden, but she discovers no sign of Rochester. She rejects the notion that this is the devilish voice of witchcraft, but feels that it comes from benevolent nature; not a miracle, but nature's best effort to help her, as if the forces of nature are assisting this very special relationship. She introduces the ideal of a telepathic bond between the lovers. This psychic sympathy leads Jane to hear Rochester's frantic call for her, and for Rochester to pick her response out of the wind. In fact, he even correctly senses that her response came from some mountainous place. Through the novel's supernatural elements, Jane and Rochester become archetypes of ideal lovers, supporting Jane's exorbitant claim that no one "was ever nearer to her mate than I am." These mythic elements transform their relationship from ordinary to extraordinary.

A Postcolonial Approach to *Jane Eyre*

As a theoretical approach, post-colonialism asks readers to consider the way colonialist and anti-colonialist messages are presented in literary texts. It argues that Western culture is Eurocentric, meaning it presents European values as natural and universal, while Eastern ideas are, for example, inferior, immoral, or "savage." A postcolonial approach to *Jane Eyre* might begin by considering the following questions: What does the novel reveal about the way cultural difference was represented in Victorian culture? How did Britain justify its colonialist project by imaging the East as "savage" or uncivilized? What idea does the text create of "proper" British behaviour? Tentative answers to these questions can be discovered by examining the novel's representation of foreign women, especially Bertha Mason, and the colonialist doctrines of Jane and of St. John Rivers.

One of the colonialist goals of this novel is to create a prototype of the proper English woman, someone like Jane who is frank, sincere, and lacking in personal vanity. This ideal is created by Jane's attempt to contrast herself with the foreign women in the text. For example, both Céline Varens and her daughter are constantly criticized in the novel for their supposed superficiality and materialism. According to Rochester, Céline Varens charmed the "English gold" out of his "British breeches," a comment that emphasizes his supposedly British innocence and her wily French ways. Supporting this idea, Jane comments that Adèle has a superficiality of character, "hardly congenial to an English mind." Jane's final ethnocentric comments in relation to little Adèle are significant: "a sound English education corrected in a great measure her French defects." Only through a good English lifestyle has Adèle avoided her mother's tragic flaws: materialism and sensuality, characteristics the novel specifically associates with foreign women. Jane's comments imply that the English, unlike their French neighbors, are deep rather than superficial, spiritual rather than materialistic.

But Jane's position is more conflicted than Rochester's: As a woman she is also a member of a colonized group, but as a specifically British woman, she is a colonizer. When she claims Rochester gives her a smile such as a sultan would "bestow on a slave his gold and gems had enriched," she emphasizes the colonized status of all women. Insisting that he prefers his "one little English girl" to the "Grand Turk's whole seraglio," Rochester points to Jane's powerlessness, her reduction to sex slave. Rather than becoming slave, Jane insists she will become a missionary, preaching liberty to women enslaved in harems. Her comments show the dual position of European women: both colonized and colonizers. While Rochester reduces her to a colonized "doll" or "performing ape," her comments show her Eurocentric understanding of Eastern culture: She implies that she'll be the enlightened Englishwoman coming to the rescue of poor, abused Turkish women. All women are enslaved by male despotism, but the British woman claims a moral and spiritual superiority over her Eastern sisters.

This difference becomes intense in Jane's representation of Bertha Mason. Bertha's vampiric appearance suggests she is sucking the lifeblood away from the innocent Rochester, who tells Jane he was as innocent as she is until he turned twenty-one and was married to Bertha: His goodness was taken by this savage woman. An insane Creole woman, Bertha represents British fears of both foreigners and women. The "blood-red" moon, a symbol of women's menstrual cycles, is reflected in her eyes, suggesting her feminine, sexual potency. Unlike Jane, Bertha refuses to be controlled; a woman whose stature almost equals her husband's, she fights with him, displaying a "virile" force that almost masters Rochester. Post-colonial critics argue that Bertha, the foreign woman, is sacrificed so that British Jane can achieve self-identity.

Their arguments suggest Rochester is not as innocent as he claims; as a colonialist, he was in the West Indies to make money and to overpower colonized men and women. Notice how both Jane and Rochester emphasize his ability to control Bertha's brother, Richard. Much of Rochester's critique of Bertha hinges on her sexuality and exotic excess. When he first met her, Rochester's senses were aroused by her dazzle, splendor, and lusciousness. But he later found her debauchery to be his "Indian Messalina's attribute." Thus, the characteristics that first attract her to him, her sensual excesses, soon repulse him.

The representation of Bertha presents native peoples in the colonies as coarse, lascivious, and ignorant, thus justifying St. John's missionary role: Bertha is a foreign "savage" in need of British guidance and enlightenment. Just as Jane retrains the minds of her lower class students in England, St. John will reform the values of the pagans in India. Both characters perpetuate a belief in British, Christian-based moral and spiritual superiority.

But St. John's inability to "renounce his wide field of mission warfare" shows that his colonialist impulse is not based on compassion or mutual understanding, but on violence—violating the minds of native peoples, if not their bodies. For twenty-first-century readers, St. John's missionary zeal is morally suspect, because it shows his participation in the colonialist project, which resulted in violence against and violation of native peoples. St. John's cold heartedness suggests the brutality and self-serving function of colonialism. Jane claims St. John "forgets, pitilessly, the feelings and claims of little people, in pursing his own large views"; imagine the damage he will inflict on any native people who resist him. Like Jane, they will be repressed by his merciless egotism. St. John spends the rest of his life labouring for "his race" in India. A great warrior, St. John sternly clears the "painful way to improvement" for the natives, slaying their prejudices of "creed and caste," though obviously not his own. In his zealous Christianity, he sees the Indians as an inferior race and hopes to implant British values in their supposedly deficient minds.

Chapter 10

Jane Eyre: Plot Overview

Jane Eyre is an orphan is being raised by Mrs. Reed, her cruel, wealthy aunt. A servant named Bessie provides Jane with some of the few kindnesses she receives, telling her stories and singing songs to her. One day, as punishment for fighting with her bullying cousin John Reed, Jane's aunt imprisons Jane in the red-room, the room in which Jane's Uncle Reed died. While locked in, Jane, believing that she sees her uncle's ghost, screams and faints. She wakes to find herself in the care of Bessie and the kindly apothecary Mr.. Lloyd, who suggests to Mrs. Reed that Jane be sent away to school. To Jane's delight, Mrs. Reed concurs.

Once at the Lowood School, Jane finds that her life is far from idyllic. The school's headmaster is Mr.. Brocklehurst, a cruel, hypocritical, and abusive man. Brocklehurst preaches a doctrine of poverty and privation to his students while using the school's funds to provide a wealthy and opulent lifestyle for his own family. At Lowood, Jane befriends a young girl named Helen Burns, whose strong, martyr like attitude toward the school's miseries is both helpful and displeasing to Jane. A massive typhus epidemic sweeps Lowood, and Helen dies of consumption. The epidemic also results in the departure of Mr.. Brocklehurst by attracting attention to the insalubrious conditions at Lowood. After a group of more sympathetic gentlemen takes Brocklehurst's place, Jane's life improves dramatically. She spends eight more years at Lowood, six as a student and two as a teacher.

After teaching for two years, Jane yearns for new experiences. She accepts a governess position at a manor called

Thornfield, where she teaches a lively French girl named Adèle. The distinguished housekeeper Mrs. Fairfax presides over the estate. Jane's employer at Thornfield is a dark, impassioned man named Rochester, with whom Jane finds herself falling secretly in love. She saves Rochester from a fire one night, which he claims was started by a drunken servant named Grace Poole. But because Grace Poole continues to work at Thornfield, Jane concludes that she has not been told the entire story. Jane sinks into despondency when Rochester brings home a beautiful but vicious woman named Blanche Ingram. Jane expects Rochester to propose to Blanche. But Rochester instead proposes to Jane, who accepts almost disbelievingly.

The wedding day arrives, and as Jane and Mr.. Rochester prepare to exchange their vows, the voice of Mr.. Mason cries out that Rochester already has a wife. Mason introduces himself as the brother of that wife—a woman named Bertha. Mr.. Mason testifies that Bertha, whom Rochester married when he was a young man in Jamaica, is still alive. Rochester does not deny Mason's claims, but he explains that Bertha has gone mad. He takes the wedding party back to Thornfield, where they witness the insane Bertha Mason scurrying around on all fours and growling like an animal. Rochester keeps Bertha hidden on the third story of Thornfield and pays Grace Poole to keep his wife under control. Bertha was the real cause of the mysterious fire earlier in the story. Knowing that it is impossible for her to be with Rochester, Jane flees Thornfield.

Penniless and hungry, Jane is forced to sleep outdoors and beg for food. At last, three siblings who live in a manor alternatively called Marsh End and Moor House take her in. Their names are Mary, Diana, and St. John (pronounced "Sinjin") Rivers, and Jane quickly becomes friends with them. St. John is a clergyman, and he finds Jane a job teaching at a charity school in Morton. He surprises her one day by declaring that her uncle, John Eyre, has died and left her a large fortune: 20,000 pounds. When Jane asks how he received this news, he shocks her further by declaring that her uncle was also his uncle: Jane and the Riverses are cousins. Jane immediately decides to share her inheritance equally with her three newfound relatives.

St. John decides to travel to India as a missionary, and he urges Jane to accompany him—as his wife. Jane agrees to go to India but refuses to marry her cousin because she does not love him. St. John pressures her to reconsider, and she nearly gives in. However, she realises that she cannot abandon forever the man she truly loves when one night she hears Rochester's voice calling her name over the moors. Jane immediately hurries back to Thornfield and finds that it has been burned to the ground by Bertha Mason, who lost her life in the fire. Rochester saved the servants but lost his eyesight and one of his hands. Jane travels on to Rochester's new residence, Ferndean, where he lives with two servants named John and Mary.

At Ferndean, Rochester and Jane rebuild their relationship and soon marry. At the end of her story, Jane writes that she has been married for ten blissful years and that she and Rochester enjoy perfect equality in their life together. She says that after two years of blindness, Rochester regained sight in one eye and was able to behold their first son at his birth.

Chapter 11

Character Analysis

Jane Eyre

The protagonist and narrator of the novel, Jane is an intelligent, honest, plain-featured young girl forced to contend with oppression, inequality, and hardship. Although she meets with a series of individuals who threaten her autonomy, Jane repeatedly succeeds at asserting herself and maintains her principles of justice, human dignity, and morality. She also values intellectual and emotional fulfillment. Her strong belief in gender and social equality challenges the Victorian prejudices against women and the poor.

Edward Rochester

Jane's employer and the master of Thornfield, Rochester is a wealthy, passionate man with a dark secret that provides much of the novel's suspense. Rochester is unconventional, ready to set aside polite manners, propriety, and consideration of social class in order to interact with Jane frankly and directly. He is rash and impetuous and has spent much of his adult life roaming about Europe in an attempt to avoid the consequences of his youthful indiscretions. His problems are partly the result of his own recklessness, but he is a sympathetic figure because he has suffered for so long as a result of his early marriage to Bertha.

St. John Rivers

Along with his sisters, Mary and Diana, St. John (pronounced "Sinjin") serves as Jane's benefactor after she runs away from Thornfield, giving her food and shelter. The minister at Morton, St. John is cold, reserved, and often controlling in his interactions with others. Because he is entirely alienated from his feelings and devoted solely to an austere ambition, St. John serves as a foil to Edward Rochester.

Mrs. Reed

Mrs. Reed is Jane's cruel aunt, who raises her at Gateshead Hall until Jane is sent away to school at age ten. Later in her life, Jane attempts reconciliation with her aunt, but the old woman continues to resent her because her husband had always loved Jane more than his own children.

Bessie Lee

The maid at Gateshead, Bessie is the only figure in Jane's childhood who regularly treats her kindly, telling her stories and singing her songs. Bessie later marries Robert Leaven, the Reeds' coachman.

Mr.. Lloyd

Mr.. Lloyd is the Reeds' apothecary, who suggests that Jane must be sent away to school. Always kind to Jane, Mr.. Lloyd writes a letter to Miss Temple confirming Jane's story about her childhood and clearing Jane of Mrs. Reed's charge that she is a liar.

Georgiana Reed

Georgiana Reed is Jane's cousin and one of Mrs. Reed's two daughters. The beautiful Georgiana treats Jane cruelly when they are children, but later in their lives, she befriends her cousin and confides in her. Georgiana attempts to elope with a man named Lord Edwin Vere, but her sister, Eliza, alerts Mrs. Reed of the arrangement and sabotages the plan. After Mrs. Reed dies, Georgiana marries a wealthy man.

Eliza Reed

Eliza Reed is Jane's cousin and one of Mrs. Reed's two daughters (along with her sister, Georgiana). Not as beautiful as her sister, Eliza devotes herself somewhat self-righteously to the church and eventually goes to a convent in France where she becomes the Mother Superior.

John Reed

John Reed is Jane's cousin, Mrs. Reed's son, and brother to Eliza and Georgiana. John treats Jane with appalling cruelty during their childhood and later falls into a life of drinking and gambling. John commits suicide midway through the novel when his mother ceases to pay his debts for him.

Helen Burns

Helen Burns is Jane's close friend at the Lowood School. She endures her miserable life there with a passive dignity that Jane cannot understand. Helen dies of consumption in Jane's arms.

Mr.. Brocklehurst

The cruel, hypocritical master of the Lowood School, Mr.. Brocklehurst preaches a doctrine of privation, while stealing from the school to support his luxurious lifestyle. After a typhus epidemic sweeps Lowood, Brocklehurst's shifty and dishonest practices are brought to light and he is publicly discredited.

Maria Temple

Maria Temple is a kind teacher at Lowood, who treats Jane and Helen with respect and compassion. Along with Bessie Lee, she serves as one of Jane's first positive female role models. Miss Temple helps clear Jane of Mrs. Reed's accusations against her.

Miss Scatcherd

Jane's sour and vicious teacher at Lowood, Miss Scatcherd behaves with particular cruelty toward Helen.

Alice Fairfax

Alice Fairfax is the housekeeper at Thornfield Hall. She is the first to tell Jane that the mysterious laughter often heard echoing through the halls is, in fact, the laughter of Grace Poole—a lie that Rochester himself often repeats.

Bertha Mason

Rochester's clandestine wife, Bertha Mason is a formerly beautiful and wealthy Creole woman who has become insane, violent, and bestial. She lives locked in a secret room on the third story of Thornfield and guarded by Grace Poole, whose occasional bouts of inebriation sometimes enable Bertha to escape. Bertha eventually burns down Thornfield, plunging to her death in the flames.

Grace Poole

Grace Poole is Bertha Mason's keeper at Thornfield, whose drunken carelessness frequently allows Bertha to escape. When Jane first arrives at Thornfield, Mrs. Fairfax attributes to Grace all evidence of Bertha's misdeeds.

Adèle Varens

Jane's pupil at Thornfield, Adèle Varens is a lively though somewhat spoiled child from France. Rochester brought her to Thornfield after her mother,, abandoned her. Although was once Rochester's mistress, he does not believe himself to be Adele's father.

Varens

Varens is a French opera dancer with whom Rochester once had an affair. Although Rochester does not believe 's claims that he fathered her daughter Adèle, he nonetheless brought the girl to England when abandoned her. Rochester had broken off his relationship with after learning that was unfaithful to him and interested only in his money.

Sophie

Sophie is Adèle's French nurse at Thornfield.

Richard Mason

Richard Mason is Bertha's brother. During a visit to Thornfield, his mad sister injures him. After learning of

Rochester's intent to marry Jane, Mason arrives with the solicitor Briggs in order to thwart the wedding and reveal the truth of Rochester's prior marriage.

Mr.. Briggs

John Eyre's attorney, Mr.. Briggs helps Richard Mason prevent Jane's wedding to Rochester when he learns of the existence of Bertha Mason, Rochester's wife. After John Eyre's death, Briggs searches for Jane in order to give her inheritance.

Blanche Ingram

Blanche Ingram is a beautiful socialite who despises Jane and hopes to marry Rochester for his money.

Diana Rivers

Diana Rivers is Jane's cousin, and the sister of St. John and Mary. Diana is a kind and intelligent person, and she urges Jane not to go to India with St. John. She serves as a model for Jane of an intellectually gifted and independent woman.

Mary Rivers

Mary Rivers is Jane's cousin, the sister of St. John and Diana. Mary is a kind and intelligent young woman who is forced to work as a governess after her father loses his fortune. Like her sister, she serves as a model for Jane of an independent woman who is also able to maintain close relationships with others and a sense of meaning in her life.

Rosamond Oliver

Rosamond is the beautiful daughter of Mr.. Oliver, Morton's wealthiest inhabitant. Rosamond gives money to the school in Morton where Jane works. Although she is in love with St. John, she becomes engaged to the wealthy Mr.. Granby.

John Eyre

John Eyre is Jane's uncle, who leaves her his vast fortune of 20,000 pounds.

Uncle Reed

Uncle Reed is Mrs. Reed's late husband. In her childhood, Jane believes that she feels the presence of his ghost. Because he was always fond of Jane and her mother (his sister), Uncle Reed made his wife promise that she would raise Jane as her own child. It is a promise that Mrs. Reed does not keep.

Chapter 12

Major Themes

Love versus Autonomy

Jane Eyre is very much the story of a quest to be loved. Jane searches, not just for romantic love, but also for a sense of being valued, of belonging. Thus Jane says to Helen Burns: "to gain some real affection from you, or Miss Temple, or any other whom I truly love, I would willingly submit to have the bone of my arm broken, or to let a bull toss me, or to stand behind a kicking horse, and let it dash its hoof at my chest" (Chapter 8). Yet, over the course of the book, Jane must learn how to gain love *without* sacrificing and harming herself in the process.

Her fear of losing her autonomy motivates her refusal of Rochester's marriage proposal. Jane believes that "marrying" Rochester while he remains legally tied to Bertha would mean rendering herself a mistress and sacrificing her own integrity for the sake of emotional gratification. On the other hand, her life at Moor House tests her in the opposite manner. There, she enjoys economic independence and engages in worthwhile and useful work, teaching the poor; yet she lacks emotional sustenance. Although St. John proposes marriage, offering her a partnership built around a common purpose, Jane knows their marriage would remain loveless.

Nonetheless, the events of Jane's stay at Moor House are necessary tests of Jane's autonomy. Only after proving her self-sufficiency to herself can she marry Rochester and not be asymmetrically dependent upon him as her "master." The marriage can be one between equals. As Jane says: "I am my husband's life as fully as he is mine.... To be together is for us to be at once as free as in solitude, as gay as in company.... We are precisely suited in character—perfect concord is the result" (Chapter 38).

Religion

Throughout the novel, Jane struggles to find the right balance between moral duty and earthly pleasure, between obligation to her spirit and attention to her body. She encounters three main religious figures: Mr.. Brocklehurst, Helen Burns, and St. John Rivers. Each represents a model of religion that Jane ultimately rejects as she forms her own ideas about faith and principle, and their practical consequences.

Mr.. Brocklehurst illustrates the dangers and hypocrisies that Charlotte Brontë perceived in the nineteenth-century Evangelical movement. Mr.. Brocklehurst adopts the rhetoric of Evangelicalism when he claims to be purging his students of pride, but his method of subjecting them to various privations and humiliations, like when he orders that the naturally curly hair of one of Jane's classmates be cut so as to lie straight, is entirely un-Christian. Of course, Brocklehurst's proscriptions are difficult to follow, and his hypocritical support of his own luxuriously wealthy family at the expense of the Lowood students shows Brontë's wariness of the Evangelical movement. Helen Burns's meek and forbearing mode of Christianity, on the other hand, is too passive for Jane to adopt as her own, although she loves and admires Helen for it.

Many chapters later, St. John Rivers provides another model of Christian behaviour. His is a Christianity of ambition, glory, and extreme self-importance. St. John urges Jane to sacrifice her emotional deeds for the fulfillment of her moral duty, offering her a way of life that would require her to be disloyal to her own self.

Although Jane ends up rejecting all three models of religion, she does not abandon morality, spiritualism, or a belief in a Christian God. When her wedding is interrupted, she prays to God for solace (Chapter 26). As she wanders the heath, poor and starving, she puts her survival in the hands of God (Chapter 28). She strongly objects to Rochester's lustful immorality, and she refuses to consider living with him while church and state still deem him married to another woman. Even so, Jane can barely bring herself to leave the only love she has ever known. She credits God with helping her to escape what she knows would have been an immoral life (Chapter 27).

Jane ultimately finds a comfortable middle ground. Her spiritual understanding is not hateful and oppressive like Brocklehurst's, nor does it require retreat from the everyday world as Helen's and St. John's religions do. For Jane, religion helps curb immoderate passions, and it spurs one on to worldly efforts and achievements. These achievements include full self-knowledge and complete faith in God.

Social Class

Jane Eyre is critical of Victorian England's strict social hierarchy. Brontë's exploration of the complicated social position of governesses is perhaps the novel's most important treatment of this theme. Like Heathcliff, in *Wuthering Heights*, Jane is a figure of ambiguous class standing and, consequently, a source of extreme tension for the characters around her. Jane's manners, sophistication, and education are those of an aristocrat, because Victorian governesses, who tutored children in etiquette as well as academics, were expected to possess the "culture" of the aristocracy. Yet, as paid employees, they were more or less treated as servants; thus, Jane remains penniless and powerless while at Thornfield. Jane's understanding of the double standard crystallizes when she becomes aware of her feelings for Rochester; she is his intellectual, but not his social, equal. Even before the crisis surrounding Bertha Mason, Jane is hesitant to marry Rochester because she senses that she would feel indebted to him for "condescending" to marry her. Jane's distress, which appears most strongly in Chapter 17, seems to be Brontë's critique of Victorian class attitudes.

Jane herself speaks out against class prejudice at certain moments in the book. For example, in Chapter 23 she chastises

Rochester: "Do you think, because I am poor, obscure, plain, and little, I am soulless and heartless? You think wrong!—I have as much soul as you—and full as much heart! And if God had gifted me with some beauty and much wealth, I should have made it as hard for you to leave me, as it is now for me to leave you." However, it is also important to note that nowhere in *Jane Eyre* are society's boundaries bent. Ultimately, Jane is only able to marry Rochester as his equal because she has almost magically come into her own inheritance from her uncle.

Gender Relations

Jane struggles continually to achieve equality and to overcome oppression. In addition to class hierarchy, she must fight against patriarchal domination—against those who believe women to be inferior to men and try to treat them as su Three central male figures threaten her desire for equality and dignity: Mr.. Brocklehurst, Edward Rochester, and St. John Rivers. All three are misogynistic on some level. Each tries to keep Jane in a submissive position, where she is unable to express her own thoughts and feelings. In her quest for independence and self-knowledge, Jane must escape Brocklehurst, reject St. John, and come to Rochester only after ensuring that they may marry as equals. This last condition is met once Jane proves herself able to function, through the time she spends at Moor House, in a community and in a family. She will not depend solely on Rochester for love and she can be financially independent. Furthermore, Rochester is blind at the novel's end and thus dependent upon Jane to be his "prop and guide." In Chapter 12, Jane articulates what was for her time a radically feminist philosophy:

Women are supposed to be very calm generally: but women feel just as men feel; they need exercise for their faculties, and a field for their efforts as much as their brothers do. They suffer from too rigid a restraint, too absolute stagnation, precisely as men would suffer; and it is narrow-minded in their more privileged fellow-creatures to say that they ought to confine themselves to making puddings and knitting stockings, to playing on the piano and embroidering bags. It is thoughtless to condemn them, or laugh at them, if they seek to do more or learn more than custom has pronounced necessary for their sex.

Fire and Ice

Fire and ice appear throughout *Jane Eyre*. The former represents Jane's passions, anger, and spirit, while the latter symbolizes the oppressive forces trying to extinguish Jane's vitality. Fire is also a metaphor for Jane, as the narrative repeatedly associates her with images of fire, brightness, and warmth. In Chapter 4, she likens her mind to "a ridge of lighted heath, alive, glancing, and devouring." We can recognize Jane's kindred spirits by their similar links to fire; thus, we read of Rochester's "flaming and flashing" eyes (Chapter 25). After he has been blinded, his face is compared to "a lamp quenched, waiting to be relit" (Chapter 37).

Images of ice and cold, often appearing in association with barren landscapes or seascapes, symbolize emotional desolation, loneliness, or even death. The "death-white realms" of the arctic that Bewick describes in his *History of British Birds* parallel Jane's physical and spiritual isolation at Gateshead (Chapter 1). Lowood's freezing temperatures—for example, the frozen pitchers of water that greet the girls each morning—mirror Jane's sense of psychological exile. After the interrupted wedding to Rochester, Jane describes her state of mind: "A Christmas frost had come at mid-summer: a white December storm had whirled over June; ice glazed the ripe apples, drifts crushed the blowing roses; on hay-field and corn-field lay a frozen shroud... and the woods, which twelve hours since waved leafy and fragrant as groves between the tropics, now spread, waste, wild, and white as pine-forests in wintry Norway. My hopes were all dead" (Chapter 26).

Finally, at Moor House, St. John's frigidity and stiffness are established through comparisons with ice and cold rock. Jane writes, "By degrees, he acquired a certain influence over me that took away my liberty of mind.... I fell under a freezing spell" (Chapter 34). When St. John proposes marriage to Jane, she concludes, "as his curate, his coMr.ade, all would be right.... But as his wife—at his side always, and always restrained, and always checked—forced to keep the fire of my nature continually low, to compel it to burn inwardly and never utter a cry, though the imprisoned flame consumed vital after vital—this would be unendurable" (Chapter 34).

Substitute Mothers

Poet and critic Adrienne Rich has noted that Jane encounters a series of nurturing and strong women on whom she can model herself, or to whom she can look for comfort and guidance: these women serve as mother figures to the orphaned Jane.

The first such figure that Jane encounters is the servant Bessie, who soothes Jane after her trauma in the red-room and teaches her to find comfort in stories and songs. At Lowood, Jane meets Miss Temple, who has no power in the world at large, but possesses great spiritual strength and charm. Not only does she shelter Jane from pain, she also encourages her intellectual development. Of Miss Temple, Jane writes: "she had stood by me in the stead of mother, governess, and latterly, companion" (Chapter 10). Jane also finds a comforting model in Helen Burns, whose lessons in stamina teach Jane about self-worth and the power of faith.

After Jane and Rochester's wedding is cancelled, Jane finds comfort in the moon, which appears to her in a dream as a symbol of the matriarchal spirit. Jane sees the moon as "a white human form" shining in the sky, "inclining a glorious brow earthward." She tells us: "It spoke to my spirit: immeasurably distant was the tone, yet so near, it whispered in my heart—"My daughter, flee temptation." Jane answers, "Mother, I will" (Chapter 27). Waking from the dream, Jane leaves Thornfield.

Jane finds two additional mother figures in the characters of Diana and Mary Rivers. Rich points out that the sisters bear the names of the pagan and Christian versions of "the Great Goddess": Diana, the Virgin huntress, and Mary, the Virgin Mother. Unmarried and independent, the Rivers sisters love learning and reciting poetry and live as intellectual equals with their brother St. John.

Symbols

Symbols are objects, characters, figures, or colours used to represent abstract ideas or concepts.

Bertha Mason

Bertha Mason is a complex presence in *Jane Eyre*. She impedes Jane's happiness, but she also catalyses the growth of Jane's self-understanding. The mystery surrounding Bertha establishes suspense and terror to the plot and the atmosphere. Further, Bertha serves as a remnant and reminder of Rochester's youthful libertinism.

Yet Bertha can be interpreted as a symbol. Some critics have read her as a statement about the way Britain feared and psychologically "locked away" the other cultures it encountered at the height of its imperialism. Others have seen her as a symbolic representation of the "trapped" Victorian wife, who is expected never to travel or work outside the house and becomes ever more frenzied as she finds no outlet for her frustration and anxiety. Within the story, then, Bertha's insanity could serve as a warning to Jane of what complete surrender to Rochester could bring about.

One could also see Bertha as a manifestation of Jane's subconscious feelings—specifically, of her rage against oppressive social and gender norms. Jane declares her love for Rochester, but she also secretly fears marriage to him and feels the need to rage against the imprisonment it could become for her. Jane never manifests this fear or anger, but Bertha does. Thus Bertha tears up the bridal veil, and it is Bertha's existence that indeed stops the wedding from going forth. And, when Thornfield comes to represent a state of servitude and submission for Jane, Bertha burns it to the ground. Throughout the novel, Jane describes her inner spirit as fiery, her inner landscape as a "ridge of lighted heath" (Chapter 4). Bertha seems to be the outward manifestation of Jane's interior fire. Bertha expresses the feelings that Jane must keep in check.

The Red-Room

The red-room can be viewed as a symbol of what Jane must overcome in her struggles to find freedom, happiness, and a sense of belonging. In the red-room, Jane's position of exile and imprisonment first becomes clear. Although Jane is eventually freed from the room, she continues to be socially ostracized, financially trapped, and excluded from love; her sense of independence and her freedom of self-expression are constantly threatened.

The red-room's importance as a symbol continues throughout the novel. It reappears as a memory whenever Jane makes a connection between her current situation and that first feeling of being ridiculed. Thus, she recalls the room when she is humiliated at Lowood. She also thinks of the room on the night that she decides to leave Thornfield after Rochester has tried to convince her to become an undignified mistress. Her destitute condition upon her departure from Thornfield also threatens emotional and intellectual imprisonment, as does St. John's marriage proposal. Only after Jane has asserted herself, gained financial independence, and found a spiritual family—which turns out to be her real family—can she wed Rochester and find freedom in and through marriage.

Chapter 13

Summary and Analysis

Volume I, Chapter 1 Summary:

Jane Eyre narrates from the home of the well-off Reed family, Gateshead Hall. Refused permission by her aunt, Mrs. Reed, to play with her with cousins Eliza, John, and Georgiana10-year-old Jane reads Bewick's "History of British Birds." The bullying John interrupts her reading and says that, since she was orphaned and is dependent on his family, she has no right to read their books. He strikes her with the book and they fight, but Jane acquits herself well and scares him off. The other children alert Mrs. Reed, who locks Jane away in the "red-room."

Analysis: Immediately the reader is positioned on Jane's side through careful novelistic craftsmanship. From the first page, Jane is oppressed, sent off while her cousins play. We learn through exposition from John that she is a penniless orphan, dependent on the heartless Reed family; indeed, social class will play an important role in the rest of the novel. She is also a sensitive girl given to flights of fancy while reading, but she also displays her strength in her defence against John. All the elements are in place for a classic "Bildungs roman," the literary genre originating in the German literally as "novel of formation" or, as it is generally known, the "coming-of-age" story. In the Bildungs roman, classic examples of which are Goethe's The Sorrows of Young Werther, Mark Twain's Huckleberry Finn, and J.D. Salinger's The Catcher in the Rye, the young protagonist matures through a series of obstacles and defines his or her identity.

Volume I, Chapter 2 Summary:

Jane resists physically and verbally as the servants Bessie and Miss Abbot lead her to the red-room, named for the colour of most of its drapery and furniture. The room also contains a miniature version of Mr.. Reed, who has been dead nine years; his actual body lies in a vault under the Gateshead chur Before they lock her up, the servants reprimand her for her disobedience and warn her against angering God. Jane catches her ghostly reflection in the mirror and, thinking about her miserable condition and about her dead uncle, recalls how he took the orphaned Jane in and made Mrs. Reed promise to take care of her. Suddenly, a ray of light enters the room, and Jane cries out, believing the light is a ghost. She alerts Bessie, Miss Abbot, and Mrs. Reed, but they accuse her of trickery and refuse to free her. After they leave, Jane faints.

Analysis: The red-room has both deathly associations (red as the colour of blood, the room's containing a miniature version of the dead Mr.. Reed, and Jane's belief that she sees a ghost in it) and is a clear symbol of imprisonment. Throughout the novel, Jane will be imprisoned in more metaphorical ways, particularly relating to class, gender, and religion. Ironically, although John is the root cause of Jane's imprisonment here, the three aggressors in this chapter are all women, and Jane's one savior, it appears, was her uncle.

The chapter also introduces Gothic details with the ghost Jane thinks she sees and the revelation that Mr.. Reed's body lies beneath the chur The Gothic novel, popularized in the 18th-century, utilizes supernatural, suspenseful, and mysterious settings and events to create an atmosphere of horror and morbidity. The Gothic novel is also characterized by damsels in distress (and women are frequently the protagonists); though Jane faints here, common for Gothic women, she proves herself strong-willed and determined to fight back against her oppressors.

Volume I, Chapter 3 Summary:

Jane wakes up, dimly aware of voices and of someone's supporting her. She soon realises she is in her bed and sees

Bessie and Mr.. Lloyd, the apothecary. He gives instructions for Jane's care and departs, and Bessie, more concerned than before over Jane's health, leaves soon after. Jane sleeps and awakens the next day feeling terrible. The family is away, and under Bessie's care she takes Gulliver's Travels, but is unable to thrill to its fantastical tales as she normally does. She cries after Bessie sings her a sad song (a popular one composed by Edward Ransford, 1840) about an orphan.

Mr.. Lloyd returns and, once Bessie is gone, Jane tries to tell him about the ghost of Mr.. Reed she saw. He does not believe her, and whenever she brings up the abuses she suffers at Gateshead, he observes that she is lucky to live in such a beautiful house. She would not like to live with her poor relatives, regardless of them being kind. She however would like to go to school.

The family returns, and Mr.. Lloyd speaks with Mrs. Reed and apparently recommends sending Jane to school. Later, while pretending to be asleep, Jane overhears Miss Abbot discussing how Mrs. Reed was glad to get rid of Jane, and about her parent's history. Her mother married her poor clergyman father against the wishes of her friends and family, and was financially cut off by her disapproving father, and the two died of typhus while visiting poor people in a manufacturing town after a year of marriage.

Analysis: The conflicts of social class, which were suggested in Chapter I by John's taunting of Jane, deepen here. Jane has the odd situation of being poor within a rich family. As such, her notions of poverty are skewed; as she admits, children "have not much idea of industrious, working, respectable poverty for me was synonymous with degradation." Her parents, too, ran into problems with class, as her rich mother's marriage to her poor father directly resulted in both their deaths.

Adding insult to injury, Bessie's song drums home Jane's status as a "poor orphan child." Jane, of course, is poor in both pitiable and pecuniary terms, without anyone to love her and without any money for self-sufficiency.

Volume I, Chapter 4 Summary:

Time passes and Jane regains her strength, but the subject of her unhappiness is never broached, and the family treats her even more poorly than before. Jane challenges Mrs. Reed one day, questioning what her late husband would think of her behaviour. Jane is excluded from family celebrations around the holidays, finding solace only in the doll with which she sleeps and in Bessie's kindly goodnight kisses. In mid-January, Mr.. Brocklehurst, whose Lowood school Jane learns she will attend, visits Gateshead and interrogates Jane about her religious beliefs, warning her she must repent and cleanse her "wicked heart." Mrs. Reed hopes Jane's time at Lowood will reform her, particularly her tendency to lie, an accusation that stings Jane. After Mr.. Brocklehurst leaves, Jane defends her honesty to her aunt and launches a series of recriminations. Mrs. Reed seems stunned and leaves, but Jane's victorious feelings soon give way to remorse. She feels better later when Bessie, who informs her that she will leave in a couple of days for the school, confides that she prefers Jane to the other children.

Analysis: Jane's love for her doll constitutes one of the major themes of the novel, that "human beings must love something." However, being loved is just as important, and the only affection Jane receives is from Bessie, who acts as a surrogate mother figure.

Religion makes its first formal appearance in the novel through Mr.. Brocklehurst. Already, we can see the religious hypocrisies Brontë exposes; he believes the deceitful Mrs. Reed over Jane, and relishes the seemingly heartless reformations that take place at school.

Fire and ice are running motifs throughout the novel; the former is associated with Jane and with positive creation, while the latter is associated with her antagonists and with negative destruction. Brontë is often subtle with these symbolic attachments; Mrs. Reed's eyes, for instance, are compared twice to ice in this chapter: "her cold composed grey eye her eye of ice continued to dwell freezingly on mine."

Volume I, Chapter 5 Summary:

Jane leaves Gateshead by coach alone for Lowood. She is introduced to some of the school's daily routines, which consist largely of Bible recitations, regular academic lessons, and abominable meals and sleeps in a room filled with other girls. The next day she meets the kindly, beautiful superintendent, Miss Temple, and another girl, Helen Burns, who informs Jane that all the student are "charity-children" orphans whose tuition is largely made up for by benefactors. One of the nastier teachers, Miss Scatcherd, mistreats Helen in class, though the stoic Helen impressively bears her punishment.

Analysis: Immediately we see that Lowood's religious education does not necessarily mean the orphans should be treated well. Their food is inedible, their lodgings are cramped, and some of the teachers are cruel. Brontë drops a few hints about the suspicious goings-on when Helen reveals that "benevolent-minded ladies and gentlemen" make up the tuition and that Mr.. Brocklehurst is the treasurer of the house.

Another possible surrogate mother figure arrives in the form of Miss Temple. Her name, with its religious overtones, indicates that she is the only teacher at Lowood who truly upholds the Christian ethic.

Volume I, Chapter 6 Summary:

Jane is introduced to her regular tasks at Lowood, namely sewing. Miss Scatcherd continually berates and even whips Helen, who never makes any response. Jane learns more about Helen, who espouses a doctrine of endurance, since the Bible, "'bids us return good for evil.'" Helen also refuses to call Miss Scatcherd cruel; she believes she has numerous character flaws that Miss Scatcherd is correct to point out. Although Helen is very fond of Miss Temple and finds she learns more from her, her mild-mannered teaching style does not force Helen to be actively good; rather, she is passively good, and she believes "'there is no merit in such goodness.'" Jane disagrees with Helen's philosophy; she feels one should repay goodness with goodness and cruelty with cruelty. She tells Helen about the Reed family, but Helen insists in a long speech that one must forgive one's enemies.

Analysis: Helen presents to Jane her Christian philosophy of forgiveness and endurance: one must bear the sins of others, turn the other cheek, and love thy enemy. Jane, of course, is at odds with this idea, believing that standing up for herself frequently means fighting back. We have already witnessed several situations in which she availed herself of these tactics, particularly the fight with John and her lashing out at Mrs. Reed. The former led to her imprisonment in the red-room, while the latter was a short-lived victory that soon turned into remorse. While Helen's Christianity is not useful for Jane, neither is Jane's attitude of self-defence; she must find and develop her own brand of spirituality.

Volume I, Chapter 7 Summary:

Jane passes a difficult first quarter at Lowood, with both the snowy weather and strict environment contributing to her misery. Mr.. Brocklehurst visits Miss Temple's classroom and instructs her not to indulge the girls in the slightest way; their privations will remind them of the Christian ethic. He spots a girl with curly hair and deems it unacceptable for an evangelical environment, as are all the topknots on the girls' heads. Jane, nervous that Mr.. Brocklehurst will convey Mrs. Reed's warnings about her behaviour to Miss Temple, accidentally drops her slate. Mr.. Brocklehurst chastises her in front of the class and three visiting fashionable ladies (Mr.. Brocklehurst's relatives), telling everyone to ignore her rest of the day, as she is a liar. Jane must stand on a stool in front of the class all day, with her only solace coming as Helen furtively smiles at her.

Analysis: Helen's philosophy of Christian forgiveness is tested as Mr.. Brocklehurst unjustly punishes Jane. Though Jane does not fight back, she inwardly seethes and thinks, "I was no Helen Burns."

Mr.. Brocklehurst's Christianity shows more hypocritical flaws. Though he claims that privation leads to purity, his relatives are dressed to the nines. He even wants to cut off one girl's naturally curly hair, demonstrating his lust for absolute power over others.

Volume I, Chapter 8 Summary:

Jane filled with self-pity by the time school dismissed. Helen assures her that not everyone hates her; in fact, they sympathize with her maltreatment. Jane feels she needs love from others to survive, but Helen thinks she puts too much stock in love from others; the rewards of spirituality and the glorious afterlife should be our ballast. Miss Temple finds them and takes them to her room, where she asks Jane to tell her side of the story concerning Mrs. Reed. Jane also does mentions Mr.. Lloyd's visit to her when sick. Miss Temple believes her and says she will write Mr.. Lloyd for corroboration; when he does, Jane's name will be cleared. She treats the girls to tea and snacks as Miss Temple and Helen discuss intellectual matters.

The bedtime bell breaks the heavenly atmosphere, as Miss Scatcherd reprimands Helen for messiness. The next day Helen must wear the word "Slattern" on a paper crown around her forehead; at the end of the day, Jane tears it off for her and burns it while crying. A week later Miss Temple announces to the school that Jane's name is cleared, and she is reaccepted into the community. The incident prompts Jane to work harder in class, and Lowood, despite its failings, grows on her.

Analysis: Jane explicates her need for love from others, while Helen outlines her belief that spirituality is enough. While it is clear that Jane will not accept these notions, Helen is correct in noting that Jane needs to be less reliant on others. Jane will have to find a combination of self-reliance and love from others.

As we have seen before, ice is a motif in Jane Eyre for cruel, negative destruction, and here fire fans out as a symbol of goodness and creation. The fire in Miss Temple's room warms the girls, as does Miss Temple's kindness, conversation, and treats. More interestingly, Jane burns Helen's shameful "Slattern" crown in fire; even when destructive, fire is a sort of positive destruction that obliterates evil in the world.

Volume I, Chapter 9 Summary:

As spring comes, Lowood becomes a more pleasant place. However, more than half the girls, including Helen, who suffers from consumption, have gotten sick from neglectful care, some even fatally. Jane, one of the healthy, enjoys the outdoors, all the more so because Mr.. Brocklehurst no longer visits the school. Jane is shocked to learn that Helen is on her deathbed, but she is not allowed to visit her in Miss Temple's room. Still, Jane sneaks in at night. Helen accepts her impending death and place in heaven, and tells Jane not to grieve for her. Jane sleeps with her, and Helen dies during the night. Her grave is unmarked at first, but fifteen years later, a marble tablet is placed over it inscribed with the Latin word "Resurgam," or "I will rise again."

Analysis: Jane's devotion to Helen is moving, and Helen lives out her Christian beliefs to her dying day. Jane continues to question Helen's unshakable faith she wonders, though does not speak aloud, if heaven truly does exist. Helen completes her representation as a Christ figure for Jane, dying so Jane can learn more of what it means to be Christian; though Jane is not willing to accept fully everything Helen espouses, the "Resurgam" tablet (placed by Jane, it seems) indicates that she has incorporated her beliefs into her own ideology.

Volume I, Chapter 10 Summary:

The typhus fever incites an investigation into Lowood's unhealthy environment, and outraged benefactors bring it up to speed and share administrative responsibility with the disHonoured Mr.. Brocklehurst. Jane excels as a student under the wing of Miss Temple for six years and as a teacher for two. Miss Temple marries and departs from Lowood, leaving Jane empty and searching for a "new servitude,'" a new job serving someone else. She places an advertisement for being a governess in a newspaper and gains employment for a Mrs. Fairfax at a manor named Thornfield near the manufacturing town of Millcote. Before she leaves, she is overjoyed by a visit from Bessie, now married and with two children. Bessie brings news of the Reeds and of a Mr.. Eyre who, seven years ago, came to Gateshead looking for Jane before he sailed to the Portuguese island of Madeira looking to make his fortune as a wine-merchant. Bessie and Jane part ways the next day.

Analysis: This brief transitional chapter jumps eight years through Jane's life, during which she matures greatly from an angry girl bent on self-survival into a mostly independent young woman seeking to serve others. The mention of Mr.. Eyre's visit to Gateshead also suggests he will reappear in some form later on, adding suspense to the narrative.

Volume I, Chapter 11 Summary:

Jane arrives at Thornfield and meets the elderly, welcoming Mrs. Fairfax, who Jane later learns is not the owner, but the housekeeper, of the manor. Two servants and Adèle Varens, the girl Jane will tutor and the ward of Mr.. Rochester, the manor's owner, live with her. The next day Jane explores the grounds and meets the young Adèle, a garrulous native French speaker who also speaks English. Rochester, according to Mrs. Fairfax, is a "'peculiar'" man who frequently travels. While exploring the house, Jane hears a loud, odd laugh. Mrs. Fairfax chastises Grace; a seamstress employed in the house, for "too much noise,'" and bids her to "'Remember directions!'"

Analysis: The introductory chapter to Thornfield plants a few narrative seeds. First, there is an obvious correspondence between Jane and Adèle, both orphans, although Adèle's living conditions are far better. Rochester's background is mysterious, made more so by Adèle's belief that he "'has not kept his word'" to her by constantly abandoning her and Mrs. Fairfax's opaque label that he is "'peculiar.'" The ghostly laugh at the end of the chapter, emanating from an area "like a corridor in some Bluebeard's castle," also ratchets up the Gothic suspense of the novel, as do Mrs. Fairfax's curious commands to Grace.

Volume I, Chapter 12 Summary:

Life at Thornfield proves pleasant, and Adèle is an affectionate and able, if somewhat spoiled, student. Still, when Jane walks around the attic of Thornfield she yearns for more experience in the world. Here she frequently hears Grace's bizarre laugh and "eccentric murmurs" and observes other strange behaviour. One day in January while she is delivering a letter she helps a gruff, nearly middle-aged man who falls from his horse and sprains his ankle; a dog travels with him. He asks her several questions about Rochester before leaving. When she returns to Thornfield, she sees the same dog from before. She discovers that it is, indeed, the dog from the road, and it belongs to Rochester, who has just sprained his ankle while riding his horse.

Analysis: Jane's craving for experience apart from stereotypical female experience is explained in a lengthy passage: "It is narrow-minded in their more privileged fellow-creatures men to say that women ought to confine themselves to making pudding and knitting stockings, to playing on the piano and embroidering bags." She goes on, and the conflict is clear; Jane desires a life of action and independence unavailable to her as a woman.

Rochester is further cloaked in mystery in Jane's meeting with him by his refusal to identify himself to her and by his somewhat standoffish manner. Still, Jane asserts some power at the beginning of their relationship, since Rochester is placed in a weakened position his sprained ankle from the fall and is reliant on Jane for aid. Another physical impediment forcing Rochester's dependence on Jane will arise later in the novel.

Volume I, Chapter 13 Summary:

With Rochester home, Thornfield becomes a noisier, busier place, much to Jane's liking. He invites Jane and Adèle to dine with him and Mrs. Fairfax. Adèle immediately asks if he has a gift for Jane, Jane asserts that the best gift he can give her is praise of Adèle's progress. Rochester interrogates her about her background with hostility, though he is full of praise for Jane's watercolour sketches Adèle has shown him. After dinner, Jane and Mrs. Fairfax discuss Rochester. His older brother died nine years ago, whereupon Rochester inherited the estate, though he avoids the place as much as possible; Mrs. Fairfax's justification that perhaps Rochester finds the place "'gloomy'" does not satisfy Jane, and Mrs. Fairfax is evasive about Rochester's other "'Family troubles.'"

Analysis: The mystery concerning Rochester deepens, and this constitutes the major dramatic thrust of the novel. Gothic novels usually have a romantic component that revolves around passionate, unrequited love; Rochester's dark, brooding, nature and secretive past makes him an ideal candidate for such a love.

Part of Jane's struggle with Rochester will be assertion of her independence and equality. As we can already see, Rochester only begrudgingly admits Jane's positive qualities, criticizing her even when praising her watercolours. Nevertheless, he seems to regard her as his intellectual equal.

Volume I, Chapter 14 Summary:

Jane sees little of Rochester the next few days as he deals with business and acquaintances. His moods shift rapidly, but Jane cannot figure out their source. One night he gives Adèle her long-awaited gift and is more genial while talking with Jane. Jane keeps looking at him, a fact he notes; he asks if she finds him handsome, but she answers "No." He claims he does not mean to condescend to her, but that his air of superiority comes from his being much older and more experienced. Jane does not believe age and experience should automatically confer authority. He opens up more as they discuss sin and redemption, and he promises to explain more about Adèle's mother in the future.

Analysis: Regardless of what Rochester says about his superiority in regards to experience with Jane, it is clear from his lengthy, involved discussion with her that he views her, at least, as his intellectual equal. Though she has a fraction of his worldly experience, Jane acquits herself well with the complicated topics Rochester brings up, and even earns his approval at points for her thoughts. Their flirtation also unofficially begins, as Jane admits to herself that though "most people would have thought him an ugly man," he carries himself with a charismatic, detached confidence.

Volume I, Chapter 15 Summary:

One afternoon, while Adèle plays elsewhere, Rochester explains that he was once passionately devoted to her mother, a French opera-dancer named Céline Varens, and that, despite her superior beauty, she seemed to return his ardor. He spent a fortune treating her to a luxurious life in Paris until he discovered he was being cuckolded in a rather humiliating fashion. Rochester shot the other man in his arm and thought he was done with the affair, but Céline claimed that the six-month-old Adèle was his daughter. A few years later Céline abandoned Adèle and Rochester, though he is positive Adèle is not his, took responsibility for the destitute girl. Rochester is still clearly affected by the episode.

Jane has more sympathy and affection for Adèle after learning of her background. As for Rochester, these revelations and his confidence in Jane make him handsomer and more amiable to her, and she is worried he will soon leave Thornfield, as Mrs. Fairfax says he always does. In the middle of the night, she thinks she hears movement outside her door, then hears a "demoniac" laugh. She finds a candle burning in the hallway, sees Rochester's door is open, and finds his curtains on fire. The smoky air stupefies him, but she wakes him by extinguishing the flames and dousing him with water. She relates what she knows, and he goes into the attic. He returns a few minutes later and says the cause was Grace, as Jane suspected from the laugh. He tells her not to speak about the matter to anyone, and then thanks her sincerely for saving his life; he is reluctant for her to leave him. Jane is unable to sleep that night, thinking instead pleasurably of the "hills of Beulah" which, unfortunately, she is not able to rea.

Analysis: "Beulah" means "marriage" in Hebrew; at Volume I's poetic end, then, Jane is entertaining thoughts of marrying Rochester. However, she feels there is a "counteracting breeze" that makes this impossible. All the allusions to the odd goings-on in the attic come to a head here. Rochester is obviously trying to sweep this episode under the rug, as his desire to pin its blame on Grace comes across as disingenuous. However, there is nothing disingenuous about his thanks to Jane for having saved his life, and his reluctance for her to leave tells something about his wounded heart. After his bitter betrayal by Céline, he is yearning for a constant love based on more than mere physical attraction, and Jane seems to provide that.

Volume II, Chapter 1 Summary:

The day after the fire in Rochester's bedroom, Jane is shocked to see Grace, who presumably tried to murder Rochester last night, mending the curtains. Grace tells Jane that Rochester fell asleep while his candle was lit, but he awoke before the fire spread too far. Both Jane and Grace seem to know more than each lets on, and they test the other's story; Jane accordingly changes part of her story. Jane is flummoxed by Grace's account and by Rochester's desire for Jane not to tell her side of it.

Jane learns that Rochester has left for a social engagement at someone's estate, most likely for a week or more, and that he is a favourite of the ladies there, particularly the young and beautiful Blanche Ingram. Jane feels foolish for having thought she, a plain, poor governess, was of interest to Rochester. She quickly sketches an ugly portrait of herself and paints a gorgeous picture of what she imagines Miss Ingram looks like as a reminder of their different positions in life.

Analysis: The chapter is split into two sections: the plot developments surrounding the fire, and Jane's preoccupation with Rochester.

It is clear that Grace is probably not the culprit behind the curtains, or else Rochester would have fired her. If anything, she knows something about it that she must withhold from Jane, and the odd laugh Jane heard is most likely behind the mystery.

Jane's sense of inadequacy compared to Blanche Ingram pivots around appearance but more around class. Though Rochester is not handsome, his class and noble manners make him attractive, but Jane's personality, for all its sparkle, cannot make up for her relative poverty, especially compared to the beautiful and wealthy Miss Ingram.

Volume II, Chapter 2 Summary:

After two weeks, Rochester sends word that he will be returning in a few days with guests. The servants busily prepare the house for his arrival. Jane notices that Grace spends nearly all her time on the third-floor. Jane overhears the servants discussing Grace's high salary and the difficulty of her job, but they stop when they see Jane.

Rochester arrives with Miss Ingram and several other men and women. Jane and Adèle keep out of their way as they socialize and dine. Rochester appears to prefer the company of Miss Ingram to that of the other ladies. Jane and Adèle are invited to socialize the next night after dinner. Jane aloofly observes the scene, paying special attention to Miss Ingram, as Adèle charms the crowd. Miss Ingram and the others speak dismissively of Jane and governesses in general. Miss Ingram goes on to criticize male vanity; beauty should be the domain solely of women, and her future husband will not be her aesthetic equal. She then plays piano, commanding Rochester to sing. He does, beautifully, and Jane leaves inconspicuously. Rochester meets her outside and beseeches her to return, as she seems "'depressed,'" but Jane declines. He nearly bids her goodnight with a term of endearment before stopping himself.

Analysis: Although Miss Ingram's beauty and confident manner take center stage in the drawing room, the attraction between Rochester and Jane is evident after Jane leaves, especially in his parting words to her. Miss Ingram demonstrates the snobbery and classism that strikes at the heart of Jane's curious position that she holds both at Thornfield and previously at Gateshead: poverty in the midst of great wealth. The flip comments of the society ladies about their governesses and their casual ignorance of Jane in the room make Jane a virtual prisoner of her social standing. Yet another prisoner lurks at Thornfield: Grace. In her third-floor hideaway, she is "as companionless as a prisoner in his dungeon." "Prisoner" is a loaded word for Jane Eyre, suggesting imprisonment far beyond physical confines. However, the mysterious events and hints surrounding Grace suggest she may not be companionless, after all.

Volume II, Chapter 3 Summary:

Thornfield is a vibrant, fun place with the visitors. One night they play charades; Rochester pairs off with Miss Ingram.

Miss Ingram's mother says Jane "'looks too stupid'" to play. Rochester and Miss Ingram pantomime a marriage ceremony among other scenes until one of the gentlemen solves the charade: Bridewell (a London prison). Jane watches the two of them flirt after their mutual success, unable to still her growing love for Rochester. However, she is not jealous of Miss Ingram, whom she views as disingenuous, dim, and rude, and she believes Miss Ingram's attempts to woo Rochester fail. Rochester's desire to marry for social connections also surprises Jane, though she does not hold it against him.

One day while Rochester is out on business, a handsome man named Richard Mason arrives looking for Rochester, whom he knew from the West Indies. That night an elderly fortune-teller comes to Thornfield; after much debate, they allow her to tell the fortunes of the young ladies in private. Miss Ingram is first, and afterwards she dismisses the teller as a charlatan, though Jane sees that Miss Ingram is disturbed by whatever her fortune was. The three other young ladies have their fortunes told, and report, with glee, that the woman seemed to know everything about them. The fortune-teller insists she will not leave until she has read Jane's fortune.

Analysis: The marriage pantomime has obvious parallels to Jane's romantic anxieties. While she cannot believe Rochester actually prefers Miss Ingram to her, she does believe he can only marry someone of Miss Ingram's elevated social position. Jane is no bride, but a "Bridewell," imprisoned by her social class and confined to limited romantic possibilities.

The Gothic element of the novel continues with the fortune-teller. Brontë creates suspense both by ending the chapter on a cliffhanger what will Jane's fortune reveal and by not revealing the nature of Miss Ingram's disturbing fortune.

Volume II, Chapter 4 Summary:

Jane joins the fortune-teller in the library. The fortune-teller, who admits she has an inside source in Grace, tells Jane several truths, focusing on her feelings toward Rochester. The fortune-teller predicts that Rochester will marry Miss Ingram;

her previous implication to Miss Ingram that she wants Rochester only for his money is what disturbed the young lady. She gives Jane her own fortune, which revolves around Jane's power of reasoning over her emotions.

Suddenly, the old woman reveals her disguise: it is Rochester. Jane, who had suspected something was amiss from the start, that perhaps the woman was Grace in disguise, is not too upset. When she tells him that Mason has come to Thornfield, Rochester is shocked and nearly faints. He asks Jane to go into the dining room and find out what Mason is doing. She reports that the party, Mason including, is socializing. Rochester, after assuring himself of Jane's loyalty, asks her to whisper an invitation to Mason to see Rochester. She does so, and goes up to bed; late at night, she hears Rochester cheerfully show Mason to his room.

Analysis: The Gothic element of fortune-teller mingles with the novel's Gothic romance once Rochester reveals his disguise; mysticism and the supernatural give way to Rochester's burgeoning love for Jane. The reader is also delighted to see that he is aware of Miss Ingram's mercenary designs on his estate. Rochester's ability to disguise himself also speaks of his hidden, secretive identity.

In a novel that otherwise focuses on Jane's internal world, Brontë keeps the action moving by constantly introducing new pieces of the mystery of Rochester's past; here, Rochester's feelings concerning Mason apparently reverse completely without any explanation.

Volume II, Chapter 5 Summary:

During the night, Jane hears a shrill cry from the third story, then someone shouting for Rochester's help. Jane hears the sounds of someone opening a door and running upstairs. Jane leaves her room, as has everyone else. Rochester descends from the third story and reassures everyone that a servant has merely had a nightmare. Everyone retires to bed, but Jane goes back and dresses. She thinks she is the only one who heard the words after the scream and is certain Rochester's story is false.

After Jane waits for an hour in her room for another sound, Rochester asks her to come with her upstairs. He has her bring a sponge and some salts, and then shows her the tapestry-room Mrs. Fairfax had once shown her. He opens a door hidden behind the tapestry, from which again emanates the curious laughter Jane sometimes hears, speaks with whom ever is inside, and then emerges and closes the door. Rochester then shows Jane what he has brought her up for: a dazed Mason lies on a chair in the tapestry-room, soaked in blood. Rochester promises him that Jane will fix him up and he will be fine by morning. He directs Jane to tend to him without any conversation between the two.

Jane is frightened by the baffling circumstances, especially by the thought of Grace in the next room. After two hours, Rochester returns with a surgeon, Carter. Mason says that "'she'" bit him when "'Rochester got the knife from her.'" Rochester blames Mason for going to see "'her'" without him; had he waited until tomorrow, Rochester would have accompanied him. After Carter does more work on him, Mason stands up, and the party helps Mason into a carriage waiting outside. Rochester instructs Carter to take him home; he will visit in a day or two.

After they leave, Rochester takes Jane on a walk around the garden. Rochester assures her that neither he nor she is in any danger; the only thing he has to fear is Mason's saying a certain thing. He asks her to consider the following "hypothetical" situation: a young man, in a foreign land, made an error not a crime or an illegal act that has haunted him forever. No measures he took to deal with it alleviated his misery. He traveled copiously, hoping that would help him, but not until he returned home and met someone new did he feel better. He wants to marry this woman, but feels convention is against him. Is this man, who seeks repentance and salvation in this woman, justified in overturning custom, he asks? Rochester then admits he is the man, and says the woman is after a long pause Miss Ingram.

Analysis: It is unclear what prompts Rochester to change his tack with Jane; obviously, he is discussing her in his hypothetical story before revealing that Miss Ingram, supposedly, is his object of desire. Jane describes Rochester's face as "losing all its softness and gravity, and becoming harsh and sarcastic" when he names Miss Ingram. There is little doubt that Rochester prefers Jane to Miss Ingram, so to bolster the romantic plot of Jane Eyre, Brontë continues piling on to the mystery of the room on the third story. Whoever is in there and how it relates to the "error" Rochester committed in his youth is preventing Rochester's marrying Jane, much more so than the presence of Miss Ingram does.

Volume II, Chapter 6 Summary:

Robert Leaven, the coachman at Gateshead for years who is now married to Bessie, visits Jane. He brings news that John Reed, who was in gambling debt, died last week, perhaps of suicide. The shock gave Mrs. Reed a stroke; she has since recovered slightly and asked for Jane. Rochester grants his permission for Jane to leave for a week and gives her some money. Jane arrives at Gateshead in the early evening and reunites with Bessie, who tells her that Mrs. Reed is expected to last another week or two. She also talks with Eliza and Georgiana, who are as cold as ever, though they no longer hurt Jane's feelings. The girls are reluctant to let Jane see their ailing mother, but Bessie arranges a meeting.

Mrs. Reed, her mind clearly elsewhere, does not realise who Jane is, and speaks harshly of Jane's character. Jane prompts her to discuss her feelings about Jane, and Mrs. Reed reveals that she always disliked Jane's mother, her husband's sister, since Mr.. Reed always favored her and, subsequently, the orphaned Jane. Mrs. Reed is also under the impression that John is still alive. Jane leaves her bedside.

For ten days, Jane does not see Mrs. Reed again, and busies herself with sketching. One day she sketches a portrait of Rochester that attracts the attention of the Reed girls, whom she also sketches. The episode fosters new intimacy between Jane and Georgiana, who is hung up on her former life in high society London. Eliza maintains her distance from both of them; one night she lashes out at Georgiana for her immaturity and slothfulness, and says they will have nothing to do with each other after their mother's death.

Jane visits Mrs. Reed one afternoon while no one is around and reveals her identity. Mrs. Reed apologizes for not bringing her up as one of her own, and for spitefully withholding from her a three-year-old letter from her uncle, John Eyre, who wanted Jane to come to him at Madeira. Though Jane says she offers her forgiveness, Mrs. Reed is unable to let go of her hatred for Jane, and she dies that night.

Analysis

Jane's ample growth is demonstrated when she returns to Gateshead. Whereas John Reed fell into a dissolute lifestyle, Georgiana became a spoiled debutante, and Eliza became an aloof, emotionless woman, Jane has dedicated her life to helping others with humility. The initial cold reception from the Reed girls, then, does not disturb Jane as it once might have, nor does Mrs. Reed's unforgiving hatred on her deathbed.

In fact, Jane tells her aunt that "'you have my full and free forgiveness: ask now for God's; and be at peace.'" Jane seems to have found a third way with religion, far from the evangelical posturing of Mr.. Brocklehurst and removed from the all-encompassing and self-destructive tolerance of Helen Burns. Jane is forgiving for the past ills done her by Mrs. Reed; they did not destroy her, but only made her stronger. Helen, on the other hand, seems to have been destroyed by her utter forgiveness. The meek, in Jane's eyes, shall not inherit the earth, but neither do the powerful.

In the midst of this emotional chapter, Brontë throws in a twist with the letter from John Eyre. He hints at having accumulated a fortune, so Jane's economic status is again complicated: a poor tutor who squabbles with her wealthy employer over a few pounds before she leaves for Gateshead, she may finally be due some money.

Volume II, Chapter 7 Summary:

Jane leaves Gateshead after a month, helping the Reed daughters longer than expected; she mentions that after this Georgiana married a wealthy man and Eliza became a nun. Jane returns to Thornfield and is surprised to see Rochester, who has just returned from London, where he bought a new carriage most likely to prepare for his wedding. Rochester is in an infectiously good mood, but Jane worries that after his marriage to Miss Ingram he will no longer need her services. However, the wedding is never mentioned and no preparations are made, and Jane hopes it has been called off.

Analysis: Rochester's impending marriage is vague. Not only does Rochester avoid answering questions about it, he only says that his carriage "'will suit Mrs. Rochester exactly.'" The name could apply to any woman who marries him and, as such, leaves open the possibility that he intends to marry Jane.

Volume II, Chapter 8 Summary:

The summer is glorious at Thornfield. One evening Jane runs into Rochester in the gardens. He reveals that he will marry Miss Ingram in a month and Jane must leave Thornfield; he already has another governess position lined up for her in Ireland. A devastated Jane says she does not want to leave Thornfield or Rochester, but Miss Ingram's presence makes it necessary.

Rochester suddenly reverses position, asking her to stay, but Jane will not do so if she means so little to him that he is willing to marry someone else inferior to him. Rochester asks her to marry him, but she does not believe he is serious. He is aware that Miss Ingram only wants him for his money, and he does not love her. After Jane is convinced of his earnestness, she accepts. Rain forces the overjoyed lovers inside, where they retire to their separate quarters; Rochester checks on Jane three times during the storm to make sure she is all right.

Analysis: The long build-up to Jane and Rochester's romance culminates in Rochester's marriage proposal, but a greater change comes about within Jane. Oppressed much of her life because of her poverty, she asserts her validity as a person to Rochester, regardless of her material wealth: "'Do you think, because I am poor, obscure, plain, and little, I am soulless and heartless? You think wrong! I have as much soul as you, and full as much heart!'"

Jane has so much soul and heart, in fact, that she is not necessarily willing to submit her desires to those of someone else. While her search for being loved drives Jane Eyre, Jane understands that attachment to others comes at a price, and she will not sacrifice her autonomy: "'I am a free human being with an independent will; which I now exert to leave you.'" Her relationship with Rochester, however, promises the opportunity for a balance of love and independence.

Volume II, Chapter 9 Summary:

The next morning, Jane feels she looks prettier. Rochester compliments her, says they will marry in four weeks, and says he is sending for jewels from London for her, though Jane makes him rescind the order she will feel uncomfortable wearing such ostentation. He also vows to take her traveling with him around Europe and pledges his love to her, and confesses that he feigned interest in Miss Ingram to make Jane jealous.

Jane gets ready for a drive to Millcote with Rochester, and he tells Mrs. Fairfax about their upcoming marriage. Mrs. Fairfax expresses her shock to Jane, and warns her to be on her guard, as wealthy men rarely marry their governesses. Adèle wants to go to Millcote with them, and Jane convinces Rochester to bring her along. They ride off, and Rochester jokes to Adèle that he is bringing Jane with him to the moon, and makes a veiled reference to their marriage that Adèle does not understand.

In Millcote, the clothing and jewelry Rochester lavishes on Jane embarrasses her. She tells Rochester that she will not be his "English Céline Varens," but will continue to work as Adèle's governess and maintain her financial independence. She also declines his dinner invitation, though she spends time with him in the evening as he sings and plays piano. He sings a love song and advances toward her, but she refuses to submit to his charms. Jane maintains this distance between them as she falls deeper in love with Rochester, believing it will serve them better.

Analysis: Jane discusses her shock at hearing Rochester call her "Mrs. Rochester": "'Because you gave me a new name Jane

Rochester; and it seems so strange.'" She reminds us that the title of the book is Jane Eyre, and that this name will always define her identity as an independent woman. "Eyre" is a 14th-century word that means "a circuit traveled by an itinerant justice in medieval England or the court he presided over," and derives from the Old French word "errer," "to travel." If this etymology was Brontë's intention, then the name is ironic. While Jane travels far mentally as she develops into a woman she is an avid reader, an artist, a musician her physical journeys are quite circumscribed compared to those of the globe trotting Rochester.

Jane asserts her desire for both economic and emotional independence. She wants to earn her keep at Thornfield, and her teasing of Rochester, as she calls it, is to ensure she does not completely submit her will to his.

Volume II, Chapter 10 Summary:

A month passes, and the household has finished preparing for Jane and Rochester's marriage tomorrow. Jane is disturbed by something she saw last night. She waits for Rochester to return from business and tells him about it. Last night, with a strong wind blowing, she seemed to hear a howling sound while she lay in bed. She then had a series of nightmares revolving around her care of a little child. She woke up in the night to see a strange woman who, after looking through her closet, ripped Jane's wedding veil. The woman then looked at Jane, who fainted.

Rochester tries to convince Jane the episode was a dream, but she is adamant it was not the wedding veil is ripped in two. Rochester is horrified, and grateful that nothing more harmful happened to Jane. He tells her the woman must have been Grace, and says he will one day explain why he keeps her in the house. Jane appeases him, though she is not satisfied with the explanation. Jane sleeps in Adèle's room that night, though she does not fall asleep.

Analysis: It should be obvious by now that the woman who entered Jane's room is related to the laughter from the third story and from the fire in Rochester's room (especially because the woman uses a candle as she investigates Jane's closet). It is also clear from the ripped wedding veil that the woman harbors hostility toward the wedding, and that Rochester is still covering something up by claiming the woman was Grace.

Jane's devotion to children, both in her dream and when sleeping with Adèle, also speaks, as she says, to her departure from her childhood identity of Jane Eyre and her ascent into married adulthood as Jane Rochester.

Volume II, Chapter 11 Summary:

Jane prepares for the marriage ceremony in the morning, and she and Rochester head to the nearby chur Jane notices two strangers enter the church before they do. The priest begins the ceremony, but when he asks Rochester if he will take Jane as his wife, one of the strangers objects to the marriage. The man, Briggs, a solicitor from London, comes forward and claims that Rochester already has a living wife from a previous marriage 15 years ago. He has a witness to attest to the wife's being alive three months ago: Mason. Mason steps forward and reveals that Rochester's wife is living at Thornfield, and that he is her brother. Rochester confesses that the accusation is true, and that his insane wife, Bertha Mason, who he married not knowing of her family's history of madness, lives upstairs in his attic under careful watch of Grace. He invites everyone to see Bertha and judge for themselves whether or not he was justified in seeking remarriage.

The party goes to Thornfield and up to the attic. In the room where Mason was stabbed and bitten, Grace cooks food while the crazed Bertha runs around like an animal. Bertha lunges at Rochester and bites him, and he wrestles her into submission and ties her to a chair. They all leave the room. Briggs informs Jane that her uncle is on his sickbed but wanted to prevent the marriage, which Mason told him about. He suggests Jane stay in England until she hears more from her uncle. Briggs and Mason leave, and Jane goes into her room alone, reflecting on the sudden change of fortune. She feels she cannot love Rochester anymore; even though she does not consider it a betrayal, he is no longer who he once was to her. She thinks of a prayer to God, unable to summon the energy to speak them.

Analysis: The loose ends are tied up with the revelation of Rochester's marriage to Bertha: the laughter from the third story, Rochester's early error in life and desire for a new wife, Mrs. Fairfax's warning to Jane to be on her guard, the fire in Rochester's room, and the interloper in Jane's room. Just as Jane has trouble deciding how to judge Rochester, the reader, too, is in a difficult position, especially since the times are different now. Obviously, in modern times Rochester would simply divorce his insane wife and be done with her; in Victorian England, such an arrangement was not so easy, and his imprisonment of Bertha would not be considered quite so barbaric.

Jane narrates the bad turn of events with relentless imagery of ice: "A Christmas frost had come at midsummer; a white December storm had whirled over June; ice glazed the ripe apples" As before, ice symbolizes destruction, cruelty, hopelessness, and death. In this moment of despair, Jane reaches out to God. While she does not have blind faith in Him (as evidenced by her inability to speak the prayer), God is her last salvation and her last chance (so she believes) to be loved by another.

Volume III, Chapter 1 Summary:

Jane wrestles over whether to leave Thornfield or not. Rochester asks her forgiveness, and Jane privately grants it to him, though not outwardly. Moreover, she does not let him kiss her, as he already has a wife. Rochester apologizes for bringing Jane to Thornfield and for concealing his wife from her. He will send Adèle off to school and have Grace stay at Thornfield to watch over Bertha. Jane refuses to go off with him and cries, saying that though she loves him, she must leave him.

Rochester explains the conditions surrounding his marriage to Bertha. His greedy father wanted to leave his entire estate to Rochester's older brother, Rowland. So that Rochester was not completely poor, he arranged for a marriage to the daughter of his old acquaintance, Mr.. Mason; Rochester would gain 30,000 pounds from the union. After college, Rochester went to Jamaica to meet the beautiful and desirable Bertha

Mason, though he spent little time alone with her. They were quickly married, and soon after he learned that Bertha's mother was in an insane asylum and her younger brother was mad, too; Rochester suspects that her older brother, Mason, will also one day go mad. Over the four years he lived with Bertha in Jamaica, she grew increasingly insane and violent. In the meantime, Rochester's father and brother died, leaving him with their fortune. Feeling hopeless, Rochester took Bertha to Thornfield, where he hired Grace to take care of Bertha in the attic cell. Rochester then sought out another wife in his travels around Europe, though he found no one suitable until he met Jane, whom he was attracted to from the start, although he could not tell if she returned the affection.

Jane is torn, but she declares she still must leave him. Rochester points out that she has no family who will be offended by her marriage to him, and it occurs to her that no one else in the world cares for her except for herself. Rochester, incensed and desperate, cannot convince her to stay with him. She leaves him in the room alone.

Jane cannot sleep at night, and instead packs up and furtively leaves Thornfield, resisting the temptation to express her love to Rochester and stay. She gets a ride on a coach to a distant town called Whitcross.

Analysis: Although Jane's departure from Thornfield is her third major exit from a place after Gateshead and Lowood, it is by far her hardest decision. If she stays, she enjoys the love of a man whom she admits she worships, as well as the luxury that his wealth affords (but this is of secondary concern to Jane).

However, if she stays, she feels she will lose self-respect, and more than the love of others, Jane's quest is for self-love and independence. As she puts it to herself, "I care for myself. The more solitary, the more friendless, the more unsustained I am, the more I will respect myself."

Why will marriage destroy Jane's independence? Jane continually uses the excuse of Rochester's marriage to Bertha, but this is most likely not the true reason after all, she was at times hesitant about marriage before she learned about Bertha.

Rather, we can view Rochester's marriage to Bertha as a symbol for the inequalities of Victorian marriage especially in the way it imprisons (literally, in Bertha's case) the female. Jane is worried about similar imprisonment, particularly from Rochester's higher social standing and the proprietary feelings he has for her (note his frequent pet names for her).

Rochester's marriage to Bertha has other implications. Bertha has been identified as a Creole, meaning she is white but was born in the British-colonized West Indies, or she has some actual black ancestry. If we read Bertha's status as a metaphorically imprisoned "colony" of the British empire, then it is safe to assume that Brontë saw the same issues of colonization in marriage.

Volume III, Chapter 2 Summary:

The coach drops Jane off at the desolate crossroads of Whitcross; the nearest town is ten miles away. Finding nature her only ally, she heads deep into the heath and seeks protection under a crag. She tries to sleep, but longs for Rochester. After finding evidence of God in the majesty of nature, she sleeps. The next day, she sets out on the road and finds a village. She looks around for work, but there is none available, and she is reduced to begging for food.

As night falls, Jane walks toward a lit house in the distance among the marshes. She looks through the windows and sees two young ladies, Diana and Mary, and their elderly servant, Hannah. She listens in on their conversation, and discovers they are awaiting someone named St. John, and that the woman's husband and the ladies' father recently died. Jane knocks on the door and begs Hannah to let her stay for the night, but Hannah fears Jane will bring others with her. St. John arrives at the same time and rescues her, bringing her into the house. After being revived with bread and milk, she gives her name but can give no further details, and says she puts herself in their hands. The members of the household privately discuss the matter, then put Jane to bed.

Analysis: Jane, seeking autonomy throughout the novel, finally receives it and promptly abandons it. Freed from the bonds of marriage at Thornfield, she learns that truly independent living means sleeping outdoors, scavenging for food, and giving up all dignity. She leans more heavily on God in this chapter, and, indeed, it is a religious man, St. John, who proves her salvation. At the chapter's end, Jane relinquishes whatever independence she previously claimed: "'I will trust you. If I were a master less and stray dog, I know that you would not turn me from your hearth tonight: as it is, I really have no fear. Do with me and for me as you like" She willfully succumbs to the identity of a stray dog, putting her faith in others rather than in herself.

Volume III, Chapter 3 Summary:

Jane spends the next three days in bed at the house, attended to by Hannah and occasionally seeing Diana and Mary. On the fourth day, Jane gets out of bed and goes downstairs to the kitchen. She assures Hannah she is not a beggar, and discovers that the house is called Marsh End or Moor House, and that the ladies' brother, the parson St. John Rivers, lives in his parish in nearby Morton. Jane reprimands Hannah for trying to turn her out the other night and for reproaching Jane for her poverty, but she quickly forgives the elderly woman. Hannah fills Jane in on the history of Marsh End, which has been in the Rivers family for generations. Since the children's father has recently died, the ladies are staying at the house for a few weeks.

Diana, Mary, and St. John soon return, and the sisters direct her to keep out of the kitchen and sit into the parlor. St. John is there, and Jane examines his classically handsome face. Jane tells them that she has no home or friends, and refuses to reveal her last residence. Instead, she provides a bare bones history of her life. She admits that the name "Jane Elliott" she gave them is a pseudonym, but will not tell them her real name. She asks to stay with them until she finds work, and they agree to help her.

Analysis: Brontë draws an obvious contrast between the altruistic, kindly Rivers children Diana, Mary, and St. John and the spoiled, cruel Reed children Eliza, Georgiana, and the far from holy John. That St. John is a parson indicates Jane's view of religion will undergo further revision as she seeks a Christian model applicable to her life.

In fact, Jane cites Christianity in her defensive speech to Hannah: "'Some of the best people that ever lived have been as destitute as I am; and if you are a Christian, you ought not to consider poverty a crime.'" Once again, Jane is out of sorts financially. Whereas before she was consistently a poor figure in a rich environment (in the Reed house and at Thornfield), she is here identified as a beggar. Although she has indeed been begging, Jane resists this definition, seeking an identity divorced from money.

Volume III, Chapter 4 Summary:

Jane gets to know and like her hosts and the house more over the next few days; she is especially drawn to Diana's charisma. She does not see much of St. John, and when she does, he is generally reserved and brooding. One day she hears him preach in his church, and his stern Calvinist oration about predestination has a profound, thrilling effect on her, although it leaves her saddened. Despite his eloquence, she feels he has not "found that peace of God which passeth all understanding" anymore than Jane has.

After a month, Diana and Mary prepare to return to their positions as governesses elsewhere in England. Jane asks St. John if he knows of any work for her. He informs her that after his sisters leave, he will shut up the house, and that his relative poverty means he can offer her only one job: that of headmistress for a girls' school he is establishing in Morton. Jane gladly accepts, but St. John suspects that Jane will grow bored of the job and soon leave. Before the sisters leave, St. John tells them that their uncle John is dead. They are relieved by this news, and Diana explains that their uncle and father quarreled, and the upshot was that their father lost most of his fortune while their uncle profited greatly. The uncle has left almost all his 20,000 pounds to his one other relation, while giving a pittance to the Rivers children. Over the next few days, all the inhabitants of the house leave.

Analysis: Jane finds greater intimacy with the residents at Marsh End, and there is a reason for this not yet revealed in the narrative. The astute reader will notice some connections between the fortune left by the Rivers's uncle and that of Jane's own uncle John.

St. John's calculated, somewhat cold Calvinism is not an ideal Christian model for Jane, as she finds in it "a strange bitterness; an absence of consolatory gentleness." While Helen Burns's doctrine of tolerance and forgiveness was too meek for Jane, St. John's is far too intolerant and unforgiving.

Volume III, Chapter 5 Summary:

Jane is installed in her cottage and has finished the first day of school. Her students are largely uneducated, but many are eager learners. She has sunk into some self-pity over her situation, but resolves to work hard and help the students. She maintains that she is better off being free and in somewhat difficult conditions than staying with Rochester as a beloved slave in luxury. St. John opens up and tells her that a year ago he was unhappy as a priest and was looking for a more exciting lifestyle. But he heard a call from God to be a missionary, and he will soon leave Europe to proselytize in the East. A beautiful, angelic young lady, Rosamond Oliver, interrupts them; her father has told her St. John's new school has opened, and she wants to know how the first day was. Jane realises that Miss Oliver is the wealthy benefactress of the school. Miss Oliver invites St. John to visit her father, but he stolidly declines. They part ways.

Analysis: Jane has come full circle; she was once a neglected, poor orphan at Lowood and is now headmistress of her own school. Following in the mold of the kindly Miss Temple, she resolves to help her students who, while not orphans, are poor and largely uneducated. In fact, Jane nearly turns to snobbishness when describing the students, and must remind herself that "these coarsely clad little peasants are of flesh and blood as good as the scions of gentlest genealogy."

Such a scion comes in the form of the stunning Miss Oliver, the first example in the novel of someone who is rich, beautiful, and good-natured.

Volume III, Chapter 6 Summary:

Jane adjusts to the rigors of teaching, and over time finds her students able and amiable. She becomes a well-liked fixture in the community. Still, she often dreams at night of being with Rochester. Miss Oliver frequently visits her, and Jane can see the effect she has on St. John, who does his best to conceal his feelings though he clearly desires her, he has devoted himself to his religion. Jane visits her and Mr.. Oliver one evening at her home, Vale Hall. Jane discovers that Mr.. Oliver wants his daughter to marry St. John. One day, while Jane is working on a portrait of Miss Oliver she has been asked to do, St. John visits. The portrait takes him, and Jane tells him of Miss Oliver's affection for him. He confesses that he loves her, too, and finds her beautiful, but thinks she is not a good match for him as a missionary, a calling he will not relinquish. St. John then sees something on the edge of the blank paper between the portrait and the cardboard backing Jane is not sure what it is, furtively rips it off, and leaves.

Analysis: St. John is much like Jane; unwilling to give up his independence for love, he would rather seek his own calling in life than be beholden to someone else, even someone he might love passionately. Without much fanfare, Jane is, indeed, finding her calling as she teaches girls who are much like she once was. Without romance on her mind, except for the occasional nightmares about Rochester, she is learning to love and be loved in a stable, affirming community.

Volume III, Chapter 7 Summary:

It snows heavily. St. John comes in, covered in ice. He tells her a story of a poor curate who, twenty years ago, fell in love with a rich man's daughter and married her; her friends disowned her after the wedding. They both died within two years, leaving behind a daughter, who was raised by her aunt-in-law, Mrs. Reed of Gateshead. St. John recounts the rest of Jane's life up until her departure from Thornfield, after which everyone searched for her to no avail. He has just received a letter from Briggs telling him these details. It also appears that Rochester has left Thornfield, most likely for somewhere else in Europe.

The reason Briggs sought Jane, St. John says, is because Jane's uncle, Mr.. John Eyre of Madeira, has died and left her his great fortune of 20,000 pounds. Jane is stunned, but also questions why Briggs reached her through St. John. St. John reveals that his full name is St. John Eyre Rivers, that his mother's brother is Jane's uncle that Jane's legal name scrawled on the sheet of paper before tipped him off and that they are cousins. Jane is as overjoyed to discover she has cousins as she is by the fortune. Jane decides to split the fortune four ways among the cousins and live to at Moor House with Diana and Mary, but St. John urges her to reconsider; the fortune was left solely to her, and she should not feel obliged to share it. Jane says having close relations is more important to her than the money; she also discards the notion of ever marrying. St. John pledges to treat her as his sister, and Jane says she will stay on as headmistress until he finds a replacement. Eventually, Jane persuades her cousins to share her fortune.

Analysis: Various clues from before including that of Jane's wealthy uncle John, the fortune the Rivers children were cut out of by their uncle John, and the scrap of paper St. John tore from Jane's paper come together in a satisfying way that allows the reader to overlook one of the more improbable events: that Jane, purely by accident, came across her long-lost cousins.

Although the fortune is a deus ex machina plot twist that, as Jane says, gives her a victory she "never earned and does not merit," she has, in many ways, earned it. By being selfless, humble, and eschewing the fortune Rochester would have given her in return for her virtual servitude, Jane is most deserving of a gift that will finally give her true independence.

Volume III, Chapter 8 Summary:

Jane finishes her duties at the school before Christmas, but promises to visit weekly and teach her students. Jane cleans Moor House in preparation for Diana and Mary's arrival. Jane observes St. John's taciturn, reserved nature, and understands why he and Miss Oliver would not make a good mat Still, even he cannot dampen the joy of his sisters' homecoming. They all soon hear that Miss Oliver is to marry the wealthy Mr.. Granby. St. John is stoic and claims that he is glad, as it has cleared the way for his mission. While Jane loves living with her female cousins, St. John continues to treat Jane coldly, treating her more as a servant than as a relative. Jane continues to think of Rochester and writes to Mrs. Fairfax for news, but receives nothing.

One spring day, St. John tells Jane that he will leave for his mission in India in six weeks, and asks Jane to come with him as his helper. He says she is intended to be a "'missionary's wife,'" and he will claim her "'not for my pleasure, but for my Sovereign's service.'" Jane resists, saying she is unfit for the position, but he insists she has the right qualities. She tells him she will go as his adopted sister, but not as his wife. St. John says she could only do this as his real sister; otherwise, their union must be consecrated by marriage. Jane grows irritated, and says she scorns his conception of marriage. St. John drops the proposal for now, and says he will leave for Cambridge tomorrow for two weeks, during which time Jane can reconsider. When he says goodnight to Jane, he insists that he is not offended, but Jane wishes "he had knocked me down."

Analysis: Autonomy again appears as Jane's main desire. Though the idea of being a Christian missionary appeals to her and would add structure to her life and continues her notion of servicing others she is unwilling to be imprisoned in yet another marriage. While she disdained Rochester's marriage because, although she would be loved, she feared a status of inferiority, she refuses St. John's proposal because love would not even enter the equation.

Jane thus rejects St. John's model of Christianity, as she formerly rejected Helen Burns's and Brocklehurst's. While St. John's Christianity is neither overly meek nor hypocritical and corrupt, his is too dutiful and not emotional enough. As Jane said earlier, he has not found his peace with God, and his religious zeal seems more mechanical rather than human.

Volume III, Chapter 9 Summary:

St. John waits a week to leave for Cambridge, treating Jane coldly in the interim. However, she refuses to buckle by marrying him, and he rejects taking her along as his unmarried assistant. Jane admits she will seek out Rochester, and St. John leaves. Jane reveals St. John's plans to Diana, and Diana approves of Jane's decision. Later, St. John is his usual polite, aloof self to Jane while reading from Revelations and through it he hints that Jane will end up in Hell for her refusal to join him. The next morning, he leaves for Cambridge, and in a sincere moment again tells Jane she should reconsider her decision while he is gone. She is so moved by his warmth that she is tempted to yield to his desires. She has a mystical vision and hears Rochester's voice declare "Jane! Jane! Jane!" She announces that she is coming for Rochester. She does not find him, of course, and tells St. John to leave her alone. In her room alone, she prays and feels rejuvenated.

Analysis: The continuing debate between Jane's need for autonomy and her desire to succumb to St. John's powers continue, but the outcome is rarely in doubt. Instead, Jane's love for Rochester deepens, and she now has the tools needed for a liberated marriage: self-esteem, the love of others (including relatives), financial independence, and an identity she has carved out on her own. While St. John would most likely batter these traits as he leads Jane through his missionary work in India, a marriage to Rochester would no longer squelch these qualities.

With such assurance, Jane can now also turn to religion in a positive, healthy manner, one different from all other models she has observed: "I...prayed in my way a different way to St. John's, but effective in its own fashion. I seemed to penetrate near a Might Spirit; and my soul rushed out in gratitude at His feet." Jane's spirituality that has neither the hypocritical postures of Brocklehurst's evangelism, the meekness of Helen Burns's forgiveness, nor the detachment of St. John's proselytizing, but attains a transcendence of love and connection lacking in the philosophies of those three.

Volume III, Chapter 10 Summary:

The next morning, St. John leaves a note for Jane requesting her decision when he returns from Cambridge. But Jane's mind is on Rochester, and she leaves that afternoon for

Thornfield. Two days later she arrives, only to find the house has burned down. At a nearby inn, she talks with the innkeeper who was Rochester's father's butler, who tells her that one night Bertha Mason had escaped from Grace's watch and set fire to the governess's old bed. Rochester got all his servants out of the house, but Bertha jumped to her death from the roof. Rochester was blinded by a falling beam during the fire, and is relegated to Ferndean, a nearby manor house. Jane asks him to drive her to Ferndean immediately.

Analysis: While the fire at Thornfield destroyed both Rochester's estate and his eyesight, fire continues to be a positive force, even through destruction, in at least one respect: it has killed Bertha Mason, thus opening the door for Rochester's remarriage to Jane. In another sense, the fire levels the playing field more between Jane and Rochester; while she has recently gained her own fortune, he has lost much of his.

That Rochester's eyesight is gone seems no impediment to the love between him and Jane, since it was never founded upon physical attraction. As the innkeeper says about Rochester and Jane, "'nobody but him thought her so very handsome.'"

Volume III, Chapter 11 Summary:

Jane travels to the desolate Ferndean. She sees Rochester come out the front door and reject his servant John's help to reenter. He goes in on his own, and Jane knocks. John's wife, Mary, answers, and brings Jane in. Jane brings in a tray of candles to Rochester, and he eventually figures out who she is. He is overjoyed by her return, and she tells him that she is now independently wealthy and offers to stay with him as his nurse; she contends she does not care about marrying anyone. He thinks she would be revolted by his blindness and by the loss of one of his hands, but she is not. She starts tending to him, reviving his spirits, but teasingly refuses to tell him whom she has been with the past year.

The next day, Jane tells Rochester of the last year, and he insists he would not have treated her as his subjugated mistress, but as his equal. Rochester is obviously jealous of St.

John and disheartened by the news of his marriage proposal, but Jane assures him that she does not love her cousin, and that her heart belongs to Rochester. He asks her to marry him, and she agrees. He wants the ceremony to take place in three days. Rochester reveals a new spiritual side, and says that four nights ago he prayed to God for a reunion with Jane, and involuntarily recited Jane's name three times. Jane says that she heard his voice in her own mystical vision that night, and Rochester tells her that he seemed to hear her reply to him. Rochester thanks God for this gift. Jane helps him home.

Analysis: Jane's search for religion culminates with the mystical union between her and Rochester. Their bond is based on a profound, spiritual connection that passes through God.

Jane's independence is asserted here, both in her own words ("'I am an independent woman now'") and by a symbolic action at the end of the chapter. "I took that dear hand, held it a moment to my lips, then let it pass round my shoulder: being so much lower of stature than he, I served both for his prop and guide." Though Jane is of "much lower stature" than Rochester she comes from humbler origins she now has sufficient strength and independence to lead Rochester and, indeed, he is dependent on her for it. Her quest for autonomy is complete, and it does not exclude a happy marriage to someone she leaves.

Volume III, Chapter 12 Summary:

Jane and Rochester have a quiet marriage. She writes to Moor House and Cambridge and tells her cousins the news; the females are joyful, but she does not hear from St. John until six months later, and he does not mention the marriage. Finding Adèle unhappy at her strict boarding school, Jane enrolls her in a better school closer to home, and she blossoms there. After ten years of marriage, Jane is still enthralled with her union with Rochester. Two years into their marriage, Rochester's vision improved slightly in one eye, enough to see their newborn son. Diana and Mary are both married, while St. John tirelessly continues his missionary work in India and remains unmarried, as he always will, since he is a "faithful servant" to God.

Analysis: Two major themes Jane's desire for love and her search for religion mingle with her greatest preoccupation, her need for independence, in different ways. As we have already seen, she has blended love with independence in her marriage with Rochester: "To be together is for us to be at once as free as in solitude, as gay as in company."

However, Jane is also able to maintain a spiritual relationship with God without sacrificing her independence. St. John, on the other hand, is not, as his letter to Jane reveals: "'My Master,' he says, has forewarned me. Daily he announces more distinctly, surely I come quickly!' and hour I more eagerly respond, Amen; even so come, Lord Jesus!'" Brontë ends the novel on this note to underscore the connections between St. John's religious devotion and her concern with female subjugation. Unlike St. John, Jane fears yielding her will to her "Master" (or husband), and Brontë has used Bertha's imprisonment in the attic and Jane's imprisonment in the red-room as symbols for the ways in which Victorian society can confine women in marriage or in any other regard. Thus, Brontë concludes the novel on a critique of religion while demonstrating that marriage need not incorporate its restrictions of individual will.

Chapter 14

Study Questions

THE FUNCTION OF SETTINGS IN JANE EYRE

Q. How the settings revolve around Jane Eyre?

Or

Q. Do they seem to contribute in bringing reality to the novel?

Or

Q. Does the location play a significant role in making Jane meet her love life?

Throughout Jane Eyre, as Jane herself moves from one physical location to another, the settings in which she finds herself vary markedly. makes the most of this necessity by carefully arranging those settings to match the differing circumstances Jane finds herself in at ea As Jane grows older and her hopes and dreams change, the settings she finds herself in are perfectly attuned to her state of mind, but the walls, real and figurative, around her, always define her circumstances.

As a young girl, she is essentially trapped in Gateshead. This sprawling house is almost her whole world. Her life as a child is sharply delineated by the walls of the house. She is not made to feel wanted within them and continues throughout the novel to associate Gateshead with the emotional trauma of growing up under its "hostile roof with a desperate and embittered heart."

Gateshead is, so far as we can tell, a very nice house, though not much of a home. As John Reed delights in reminding her, she is a dependent; she could not and has not contributed in a manner commensurate with their standard of living. She may well be a relation, and likely their peer socially, but the unfortunate circumstances of her mother's unsanctioned marriage and her father's lack of wealth leave her vulnerable to this petty tyrant's whims, especially considering Mrs. Reed's predisposition to despising Jane. This is simply another circumstance over which she is has no control but which nonetheless shapes her existence.

Jane is, in short, a nine-year-old girl who has grown up in relative comfort physically but who is powerless in the extreme even for a culture that did not invest much power in grown women. Every aspect of life with the walls of Gateshead, as seen through Jane's eyes, confirms this.

Shortly after we meet Jane, she finds herself even more confined than she suggests that she was prior to the beginning of the novel. Her row with John Reed — which leaves her bleeding and frightened in the Red Room — results in her virtual ostracism from the rest of the family. Through no fault of her own, she tells us — and Jane is a credible narrator — she is a pariah. The walls of the nursery become her world, not just those of the house. She eats and sleeps there and passes her days without seeming to leave it. Jane is now all but officially a prisoner in her house.

When she finally leaves for Lowood, as she remembers later, it is with a "sense of outlawry and almost of reprobation." Lowood is, physically, as different from Gateshead as would be possible and still provide shelter from the elements. Whereas at Gateshead her physical needs were more than adequately met, while her emotional needs were ignored, Lowood is, for its inmates, an austere place of continual privation. And yet, here Jane finds people who will love her and treat her with respect. Miss Temple and Helen Burns are quite probably the first people to make Jane feel worthwhile since Mr.. Reed died.

Lowood is bounded by high walls that sharply define Jane's world. Except for Sunday services, the girls of Lowood never leave the confines of those walls. At Lowood, Jane learns that, female or not, knowledge is the key to power. By learning, Jane earns greater respect and, such as it was at Lowood, privilege. Eventually, she becomes a teacher there, a position of relative power, all the more so compared to what she left behind at Gateshead.

Jane stays inside the walls of Lowood for eight years. She has learned a great deal but all she finds herself able to hope for, when she does finally decide to leave, is "a new servitude." The idea that she might be free to roam in an unbounded world is not yet part of her experience — in a sense, it never will be.

Once again, Jane changes setting and circumstance and into a world that is completely new to her experience. Thornfield is in the open country and Jane is free from restrictions on her movements. Jane has always lived within physical walls and even as a teacher at Lowood had to get permission to leave. Jane describes looking our from the leads of Thornfield and wishing for "a power of vision" to see beyond the limits of the valley. She is still confined, in a sense, but now she is living with relative freedom. She is restless and longs for "more... acquaintance with variety of character" that she has access to, but she is also freer than she has ever been.

Jane is an adult but to live she must be employed. Except for the very wealthy, this is the condition of all adults. One is free even while one is not. Jane's restlessness is a product of idleness relative to her capabilities. She imagines that out there in the "busy world" that she has "heard of but never seen" that life is "quickened with... incident, life, fire, feeling." Now the walls around her are less real, but no less confining. And, as she will discover later, Jane is not equipped to live if utterly free. Thornfield, if it is a prison, has soft shackles.

Jane finally gets to see that "busy world." After Mr.. Rochester arrives, Thornfield becomes the first home that Jane has ever felt she had. Nevertheless, she is above being his mistress and leaves Thornfield. What she finds in the world she had heretofore only imagined is that she is ill-equipped to survive in utter freedom. At Thornfield, or even Gateshead, a mistake as simple as leaving her purse on a coach would not have meant she would be utterly destitute. The world outside any walls is not so forgiving. That world is not constituted to allow a woman with no salable skills or money to live and she lacks the knowledge necessary to try. She resolves to live with Nature, to "seek her breast and ask repose," but Want finds her "pale and bare" the very next day. She quickly ends up a common beggar, eating food given to her because "t' pig doesn't want it."

Still, Jane cries out to Providence to direct her, Aid to guide her and, it would seem, she is answered. She stumbles upon Moor House and is taken in. Soon she regains her health and is allowed to stay. The companionship of Mary and Diana is perhaps better suited to her intellect and temperament that any she has had before and the walls that she finds herself within are attractive. At Moor House, Jane is exposed to a way of living she had never quite seen before and, having seen the reality of the world she had previously only imagined, she is ready to accept it. Then, as she must do at some point, being who she is, she takes a job as a teacher — the only skill she has.

She finds another home, and again it suits her prospects. The cottage is "a little room with white-washed walls and a sanded floor" and a bed to sleep in. The coziness, yet simplicity of the arrangement matches the eventual offer from St. John to marry him and join him in his mission. These are a set of walls she understands and feels comfortable within. However, just as she could not abandon her sense of self to be a mistress to Mr.. Rochester, neither can she settle for a marriage to St. John that does not appeal to her.

In the end, she returns to Mr.. Rochester and, she thinks, to the walls that suit her best. Only the circumstances have changed. With Mr.. Eyre of Madeira's death, Jane is wealthy for the first time in her own right. When she gets there, she discovers that Thornfield has burned to the ground and Mrs. Rochester has died. All the walls that had confined her are gone. She has moved beyond the walls and can be the person that she truly is.

On Location with Jane Eyre

Q. Does location play an important role in creating some memories for Jane?

Or

Q. What was the final home for Jane?

Location is a very important factor in the novel Jane Eyre, written by Charlotte. The first place Jane stays is Gateshead Hall. While at Gateshead, Jane is treated unfairly and is punished for things she did not do. After the death of Jane's parents, her uncle, Mr.. Reed brought Jane into his house. On her uncle's deathbed, Mrs. Reed promises to treat Jane like one of her own children. Jane's aunt, Mrs. Reed, does not like Jane and has a very hard time doing this. She feels Jane was forced upon her family after the death of her parents. Against her husband's request, Mrs. Reed does not treat Jane like a human being and is constantly criticizing and punishing her. In one example, Jane was keeping to herself, reading a book when her cousin John Reed decided to annoy her. John then grabbed the book and threw it at her knocking her down and cutting her on the head, which bled and was very painful. Mrs. Reed then punished Jane by sending her into the red room, the room her uncle died in, for the entire night.

While in the red room Jane became terrified and thought she saw or heard the flapping of wings. The treatment Jane received caused her to become bitter and to truly dislike Mrs. Reed. Jane then goes on to live at Lowood School. While at Lowood Jane meets a young girl named Helen Burns. Helen taught Jane many things about life and religion. Jane recalls a time when Helen was scolded for not cleaning her nails or washing her face. Mrs. Scatherd, throwing out the fact that the water was frozen proceeded to punish Helen by smacking her on the back of the neck with a bundle of twigs. Jane is amazed at Helen's ability to accept the punishment, even though it was not Helen's fault.

Jane then asked Helen if she wanted to leave Lowood. Helen tells her no because she was sent to get an education. This shows how mature, intelligent, and religious Helen is and how she tries to teach Jane this. Mr.. Brocklehurst was visiting the school one day, and during his visit he criticized and scolded Miss. Temple for feeding the children extra food. During his tirade Jane dropped her slate and immediately was called up by Mr.. Brocklehurst. Mr.. Brocklehurst then went on to call Jane a liar and told all the teachers to watch her actions and punish her body in order to save her soul. This made Jane feel horrible but Helen then consoled her and she soon felt better.

These events at Lowood twisted and pulled Jane's emotions, and with the help of Helen Burns, Jane was able to realise what it meant to be a good and loving person. Jane then proceeds on to Thornfield Hall. At Thornfield Hall, Jane becomes the teacher or mistress of the young Adele. Jane then meets the owner of Thornfield Hall, Mr.. Rochester, on a barren road on a cold dark night. Jane frightens Mr.. Rochester's horse and he was thrown from his horse and wounded his leg. Once back at Thornfield Hall, Mr.. Rochester and Jane have a long detailed conversation, concerning Jane. Mr.. Rochester asked her about her education at Lowood, how long she had been at Thornfield, and about her other talents. Jane answered all of his questions and soon started to take a liking to Mr.. Rochester. Late one night, the sound of a hideous laugh and the smell of smoke awaken Jane.

When she goes to see what is bothering her she finds that Mr.. Rochester's bed has been set on fire with him sleeping in it. Jane woke up Rochester, and then he proceeds to put the fire out. Rochester then thanks Jane for saving his life and he then seems to become closer to her. Rochester and Jane then begin to pay special attention to each other until the time that he leaves to attend a house party. After three days Rochester returns, but he returns with many rich and wealthy people. These people were at Thornfield Hall for a house party that was going to be hosted by Rochester. Among the people there, there was a woman by the name of Blanche Ingram, the woman to whom Rochester was supposed to marry.

This upsets Jane because she knows that she has feelings for Rochester and she thought that Rochester might have feelings for her. A man by the name of Mason then interrupts the party and asks to see Rochester. As Rochester is talking to Mason. Jane can hear Rochester complimenting Mason. Rochester invites Mason to join the party and that he can stay with them during the night. During the night a loud scream that came from the room upstairs, awakens Jane. When Jane leaves her bedroom, she finds Rochester and he asks her to follow him. When they arrive upstairs they find that Mason has been wounded and is bleeding.

Once the doctor was called upon, Mason is taken to the doctor's house for treatment. After the doctor left, Rochester proposes to Jane, and she accepts. On the day of the wedding Mr.. Mason showed up again and stopped the wedding. He claimed that Rochester had married his sister and was still her husband. Rochester does not deny this fact and once again Jane feels alone and lonely, she feels cheated by Rochester, whom she once trusted, she feels helpless. Jane then advances on to Moor House. At Moor House Jane is at first disliked because of her begging and poor first impression, but Jane is soon taken into liking by all three members of the Rivers family, St. John, Diana, and Mary. While at Moor House, St. John gives Jane a teaching job at Morton. The job is a very frustrating job for Jane because many of the children were ignorant and refused to do their work.

During the time that Jane was at Moor House, she found out that she was the cousin to all three members of the Rivers family. This greatly pleased Jane because now she knew that she really has a family. Then one day St. John asked Jane to marry him. He said that God was calling Jane to be a missionary, and that she should go with him to India. Jane refused this offer. The next day St. John left for India, and Jane returned to Thornfield Hall, because she thought she heard Rochester's voice calling her.

Finally, Jane reaches her final home at Ferndean. She arrives after a long trip that took her back to Thornfield where she found it in ruins. Many questions enter Jane's mind but they receives answers by an innkeeper. She told Jane that after she left; Bertha set fire to the building and it soon was burned down to the ground and during the fire, a staircase fell on Mr.. Rochester. During the fall, Rochester lost one of his eyes and lost sight in his other eye due to swelling and inflammation. Soon after he also had to have his left hand amputated. The innkeeper then told Jane that Rochester was at Ferndean. She then left for Ferndean, when she arrived she was overwhelmed by the sight of her lost love. At first it took some time to convince Rochester that it was Jane Eyre, but he soon realised that it was her. Jane and Rochester were then married and she gave birth to a baby son. At the end of the novel, Jane and Rochester have been married for ten years and Rochester had partially gained his sight back. This was Jane's final home.

Jane Eyre: Submission or Revolt

Q. Does the novel represent the dual aspect of Submission and Revolt?

Or

Q. Does love of Jane prove to be a rebellion for her to conquer?

The single greatest conflict of Charlotte Brontë's Jane Eyre is Jane's struggle between submission and revolt. At times it is difficult for her to know which of those two actions to choose— she is a spirited woman who cannot accept oppression but sometimes has no choice but to submit. As a little girl she had no knowledge that there was a medium between the two. Eventually she learns moderation and she doesn't need to choose submission or revolt; she comes into her own money by the end and escapes from the oppression she suffered as a child.

Jane's oppression begins at Gateshead Hall while living with her Aunt Reed and cousins. For most of her time there, she chooses submission to all their cruelties because she has no choice really. She is a little child with no money and not living relatives that she knows about. John Reed is terrible to her; he teases Jane cruelly and tries to harm her. Jane sees "in him a tyrant: a murderer" in the instance when he yells at her for reading his books and then throws the book at her, drawing blood. This is when Jane decides not to remain passive and submit to these cruelties, but to revolt fully against him. She insults him back and physically fights with him. As a result of this, however, Jane is forced to submit to even greater oppression by Mrs. Reed; she is locked in the red-room like an animal. She tries to revolt, but she is unable to accomplish anything at all while locked in the room, except for becoming ill with fear of the room.

Before Jane leaves Gateshead for Lowood Institution, she chooses to verbally revolt against Mrs. Reed, as she was unable to before. She tells Mrs. Reed that she is "bad, hard-hearted" and "deceitful" and renounces her as a relation. Soon after, Jane is off to Lowood school where more adults tell her what to do.

Jane is not as oppressed at Lowood school, but she still is not allowed to do as she pleases, especially not at first. The teachers treat her well, especially Miss Temple, one of her closest friends there. However, after she has been there a few weeks, Mr.. Brocklehurst puts her in front of the class and denounces her as a liar. Helen Burns entreats Jane not to let it get her down because Brocklehurst "is not a god" and is disliked by everyone. It would seem that Helen advises Jane to submit to the treatment, but really she suggests that Jane have a "mental revolution" against the cruel things that Brocklehurst says. Even if everyone believed Jane a liar, what matters is if Jane believes herself she is a liar. She doesn't have to submit her mind to believe the bad things said about her.

The oppression at Lowood does not last a horribly long time because it is discovered that the children are not treated well there, and conditions are improved. Jane lives at the school submitting to their rules, yet happy, until the age of 18. She has no problem obeying the rules and is an exemplary student and teacher, but she submits to these because of the love of Miss Temple. She obeys out of love, not out of fear, as at Gateshead. When Miss Temple gets married and leaves the school, Jane feels restless and doesn't wish to submit to the world of Lowood. She rebels by advertising on her own for the position of governess and leaving the school to work at Thornfield.

At Thornfield, Jane does not face any serious oppression. Of course, being a paid employee, she must take orders from Rochester, her master. She submits to all these except for his wish to draw her out, to make her reveal herself. Jane uses that mental rebellion that she discovered earlier at Lowood; she never really does reveal her whole self to Rochester, even after they are engaged to be married.

Jane often revolts against Rochester's wishes. After they are engaged, he tries to bestow riches and jewelry upon her, but she puts her foot down. Jane says "Oh sir! — never mind the jewels!" and will not accept them. She was not a wildly ornate person before, and will not let him make her into one. Later, Jane has one of the most tempting times to submit to Rochester's wishes.

It is after the whole Bertha scandal comes out and Rochester asks her to stay as his mistress. He says they can live in his villa in the South of France, and though it is tempting, Jane says no way. She says "Mr.. Rochester, I will not be yours". Jane upholds her principles, her morals and her independence. Had she accepted his offer, she would have had no self-respect and since she is poor, would have been dependent on him for the rest of her life. She does not submit and leaves Thornfield before sunrise the next morning, and Rochester has no possibility of changing her mind.

Eventually, Jane ends up at the Moor House with St. John Rivers trying to control her. She is very passive with him and submits to his wish to teach her and to run the village school. Jane also submits to St. John's request of her to accompany him to India, but does not yield to his proposal of marriage. She rebels against his marriage proposal although it is very difficult for her.

After the Rivers incident, Jane gains a middle point between revolt and submission. She accepts her uncle's inheritance money and realises she is a totally independent woman. Jane has a need to find out what happened to Rochester and so goes back to Thornfield, finding out about the fire and Bertha's death. She and Rochester can again be reunited, this time in a way that is lawful and pleasing to Jane. The medium between rebellion and submission is choice, and that is what Jane exercises at the end, at Ferndean. For the moment, she need not rebel against nor submit to Rochester because she has her own independence and is in control of herself. Later, if she should need to yield or defy Rochester or anyone, she has the power of choice. Jane chooses what she wants, and that is to be with Rochester. She reaches her moderation point between submission and revolt.

A TALE OF TWO HEARTS

Q. Explain how aesthetically the love tale of two people is described in the novel?

Or

Q. Does it justify the love of Jane for already married person?

Or

Q. Does the novel use the narrative technique? If yes then how?

Or

Q. Is this novel a perfect example of Victorian Romanticism?

While an artist uses a variety of colours and brushes to create a portrait, Charlotte used contrasting characters and their vivid personalities to create a masterpiece of her own. In her novel Jane Eyre, uses narration and her characters to portray the struggle between a society's Victorian realism and the people's repressed urges of Romanticism.

In order to discern between the Victorian and Romantic themes, selects certain characters to portray the perfect stereotype of each theme. Mademoiselle Varens is the model of the Romantic attitude. Varens a "French opera-dancer" found herself as the "grande passion" of Mr.. Rochester. The amour between Rochester and Varens started in a "complete establishment of servants, a carriage, cashmere, diamonds, dentells, etc." and ended with Rochester "finding her out" with another man. Varens' irrationality did not only affect Rochester, but also her child: "she abandoned her child and ran away with a musician or singer." Varens, a woman in a daring profession, led a life of passion, freedom and irresponsibility.

Her life was ballad of adventure idolized by Romantics but frowned upon by society. Mrs. Reed is the perfect representative of Victorian realism. She had all the visual attributes found in a Victorian styled lady. She possessed gentry as the mistress of Gateshead Hall and her material wealth was made obvious by the luxuries found in her home –"a bed supported on massive pillows of mahogany, hung with curtains of damask"—and in her children "in their Muslim frocks and scarlet sashes." Besides wealth and gentility, Mrs. Reed also maintained Victorian characteristics of insularity and censoriousness.

"Eliza, John and Georgiana were now clustered round their mama in the drawing room: she lay reclined on the sofa by the fireplace and her darlings about her..."Mrs. Reed literally maintains insularity – snobbishly creating an island of her and her children, detaching themselves from Jane. Lastly, Mrs. Reed exercised censoriousness towards Jane on a continual basis until Jane was left with "a habitual mood of humiliation, self doubt and forlorn depression." Jane's state is the result of the Victorian need of moral severity, which was expressed by blame and disapproval. uses Varens and Reed to paint the contrast between the Romantics controlled by emotion, freedom and imagination and the Victorians who exhibit middle-class stuffiness and pompous conservatism.

But any author can capture the essence of two societies and illustrate the opposites in two opposing characters. 's talent lies in her ability to place the two contrasting attitudes in one person, allowing a conflict to grow, until a civil war is raging in a single person's mind. Jane Eyre and Mr.. Rochester were to be 's vessels of such confusion. Jane Eyre was a child of Romantic desires. As a little girl she often acted upon deeply irrational and emotional impulses. These tendencies were very obvious to those around her. Helen, a schoolmate, tells Jane: "Hush Jane! You think too much of the love of human beings, you are too impulsive, too vehement." Jane soon learned that emotions, rashness, and imaginative fancies were considered as faults by society. She learned that such tendencies must be erased or at least repressed. For a time, Jane successfully repressed such desires. "...School rulers, school duties, school habits and notions...such was what I knew of my existence." Jane Eyre soon became the model governess. By being confined to Lowood School for eight years, Jane learned to be docile, humble, and modest woman and lived a quiet moral life. But this mundane existence was not enough for the hidden Romantic longings locked deep in her soul. "I desire liberty, for liberty I gasped; for liberty I uttered a prayer." Although Lowood gave Jane the virtues expected by society, the same place was suffocating to Jane's spirit who needed more than moral primness. The oppression she felt on her soul caused Jane to leave Lowood in search of freedom.

Mr.. Rochester by surface was the typical Victorian gentleman. He was born of good name and owner of the Thornfield estate. He had inherited a wealth from his father, which he used to spoil his little ward Adele. Mr.. Rochester has all the upper-class privileges expected: social status, luxuries and snobiness, traits of well to do Victorian characters. But unlike his counterparts such as Mrs. Reed he lacks the deep conviction of moral and conservatism. In fact he has done many things that would make Mrs. Reed blush. "I sought my ideal of a woman amongst English ladies, French countesses, Italian signoras, and German grafinnien.

I could not find her." Underneath all the Victorian pageantry, Rochester has simple needs and desires that need to be satisfied. He looked for companionship in ladies similar to that of his own prestigious ranking, but could find no one to satisfy his "dream." Romantic tendencies cause Rochester to desperately look for love in the farthest corners of the earth. "For ten long years I roved about living in one capital then another; sometimes in St. Petersbourg; oftener in Paris." Rochester's aimless travels left him in the ties of nasty love affairs with mistresses; relationships starting with hope and ending in disappointment ("I now hate the recollection of the time I passed with, Giacinta, and Clara."). . Regardless of heartbreak, Rochester still searches for his female companion to quench his desires.

Jane's search for freedom and Rochester's search for any indication of a "realisation of his dream" led these two wanderers to each other.

"I never met your likeness Jane, you seem to submit, and you master me—a sense of pliancy and while I am twining the soft silken shein round my finger it sends a thrill up my arm to my heart. I am influenced—conquered; and the influence is sweeter than I can express..."Somehow Jane, a

repressed Romantic, and Rochester, a dream seeking Victorian, find themselves deeply in love. Rochester finally found his treasure in his little governess. Under the façade of docility and modesty, Jane hides a feisty spirit. Rochester says that Jane "seems to submit" but it is really himself who is the "conquered." Jane and Rochester's mild differences but underlying force to satisfy their soul's longings makes them the missing components to each other. Humanity has produced many writers, artists and musicians, but only select individuals become masters of their art. proved in Jane Eyre that she is a master of literature. She was able to bottle two conflicting attitudes of society into the characters of her novel. Through personalities like Mrs. Reed and Varens, readers were able to understand Victorian realism and the Romantic age. As the novel developed, it led readers to assume that any union between these themes is impossible. But 's writing was able to make these two fighting foes combine into the single personalities of Jane and Mr.. Rochester. 's talents lie in her ability to present two greatly contrasting attitudes through her narrations and characters and then successfully manipulate her fictional creations to compliment each other despite their differences.

Role of Women in Emma and Jane Eyre

Q. Why the novels of women novelist of 19th century Women-Oriented?

Or

Q. "The female protagonists hold much impression than the male" Discuss

Or

Q. Are the characters of Emma and Jane Eyre alike?

Throughout history, women have played important roles in society. Women have gone through much adversity to get where they are today. Jane Austen and Charlotte Brontë are some the pioneers of women's literature. Each shows their different aspects of a women's role in society in their books Emma by Austen and Jane Eyre by Brontë. In both of these books the author shows how a woman deals with societies' norms, values, and manners. Jane Eyre is an orphaned daughter of a poor family. She is brought up by her aunt Sarah Reed. Where she is teased and tortured by the aunt and the family. She is not very pretty and is barely on the social structure. On the other hand, Emma Woodhouse is a beautiful girl and is financially sound. Her maternal father raises her.

In Emma, Emma Woodhouse is in search of finding the appropriate man for herself is the main theme. As the reader goes deeper into the text, Emma slowly progresses into a self-deception. Having since childhood been obliged to manage her father, she still likes to manage things, and particularly people. She manages to manipulate everyone except Mr.. George Knightley. In Jane Eyre, Jane demonstrates a strong need to be herself, to take responsibility for her action. She is put to the test by her daily teasing and abuse from her cousins. When she is brought to a boarding school she soon distinguishes herself through her classes. Eventually ends up in Thornfield where she meets Edward Rochester.

While growing up in Gateshead Hall, Jane is treated less than a servant. Her cousins John, Eliza, and Georgiana Reed remind Jane she has no worth and is an unwelcome relative. Out of the three cousins John was one of the meanest, not only of Jane Eyre but of all living creatures. "John, no one thwarted, much less punished: though he twisted the necks of the pigeons, killed the little pea-chicks, set the dogs at the sheep, stripped the hothouse vines of their fruit, and broke the buds of the choicest plants in the conservatory" Jane becoming unable to withstand her treatment at Gateshead Hall she is sent to Lowood, a boarding school for the poor.

Before she leaves Gateshead, she tells her aunt how she feels. " I am not deceitful: if I were, I should say I loved you, but I declare I do not love you: I dislike you the worst of anybody in the world expect John Reed; and this book about the liar, you may give to you girl Georgiana, for it is she who tells lies, and not I." From that point forward, Jane realised her newfound power over other. She stands her ground and refuses to be walked over. In beginning of Emma, Emma is left alone with her father because her best friend Anne Taylor is being married to Mr.. Weston. Now that Emma's friends and relatives are all married for the first time she is left with herself. No longer having friends to talk to she relies on her imagination, realizing that she could match between Miss Taylor and Mr.. Weston and then stating that she matched them up. But George Knightley reasons with Emma that is unjust should not do.

This set the tone for the story by setting up the opposition between imagination and reasoning. Emma begins to shape her self-deception by meeting Harriet Smith, a pretty girl who is orphaned by her maternal parents. Emma shapes her self-deception by taking Harriet "under her wings". Emma takes on a snobbish look on the social structure. "A degree or two lower and a creditable appearance might interest me; I might hope to be useful to their families in some way or other. But a farmer can need none of my help, and is therefore in one sense as much above my notice as in every other he is below it."

In helping Harriet, Emma discourages her interest in Robert Martin because she belongs to a more conventional family than his. Emma then sets Harriet with Mr.. Philip Elton to be his future spouse. This planned fail because of Mr..Elton loved Emma instead of Harriet.

Jane Eyre soon arrives in Lowood, where she becomes friends with Helen Burns, a sickly child whose saint-like encouragement helps Jane with the hardships of school life. Here is where Jane's renewal in faith starts to develop. Helen who dies in Jane's arms tells Jane that they will meet again in heaven. Jane soon begins to thrive on her academic successes and becomes a teacher. Where she decides to take a job in Thornfield, where she is to teach a foster child Adéle Varens, who speaks French mixed with English. The owner of Thornfield, Edward Rochester often travels therefore Mrs. Fairfax, the housekeeper maintains the house will Rochester is gone. Jane and Rochester introduced each other when Rochester is the person whom Jane helped when she was on her way to mail a letter. Their relationship starts to build up from that point. Where Rochester proposes to Jane and she accepts.

In Emma, Emma rejects Mr.. Elton because she does not love him, and Emma is faced to tell Harriet. Her tears fell abundantly-but her grief was so truly artless, that no dignity could have made it more respectable in Emma's eyes-and she listened to her and tried to console her with all her heart and understanding. Really for the first time convinced that Harriet was the superior creature of the two-and resemble her would be more for her own welfare and happiness than all that genius or intelligence could do.Emma starts realised that she is not above Harriet any more. Emma has her encounter with Jane Fairfax, an elegant and accomplished person. Emma dislikes that Jane has met Frank Churchill. Where Emma has somewhat of crush for Frank Churchill even though they have never met before. For when the two meet Emma becomes inhibited by Churchill that is no longer attached to him.

In Jane Eyre, before the Rochester proposed to Jane she took a leave of absence to visit her aunt, Sarah Reed. Her aunt is ill and calling for Jane. For her daughters do not care for her anymore and did not visit. Jane offers to reconcile with her aunt but, her aunt rejects Jane. Jane's aunt resented that a long time ago, she promised to obey her dying husband's request to care of Jane and that Jane's uncle, John Eyre has been trying to locate her.

Soon after Sara Reed dies. On Jane's wedding day is ruin some news that Rochester is already married. They all go up to the top of Thornfield where they find Bertha Mason Rochester, a madwoman married to Edward Rochester. Jane being a witness to all this leaves Thornfield on a coach to the Moor House where she meets St. John Rivers, a Minster.

In Emma, Emma starts to have feeling for George Knightley. Emma observers that Harriet and Churchill have something developing between them and decides not to interfere. But in actuality Harriet is interested in someone above her. Emma finds out it is George Knightley. And Emma does anything to make Knightley marry her even if it is loose her friendship with Harriet. But eventually Harriet marries Robert Martin. Emma marries Knightley in "perfect happiness".

In Jane Eyre, Jane becomes good friends with St. John Rivers and his sister. One day St. John discovers that Jane has inherited twenty thousand pounds from her uncle and that St. John is a cousin of Jane. Jane gives half to St. John and his sister. St. John realised that she loves Jane and proposes to her but she does not accept for she is still in love with Rochester. Jane leaves St. John in return to Thornfield. Coming back to Thornfield Jane find out that it is burned down. She finds out the Bertha Mason Rochester set it on fire and jumped off the roof.

Austen in a way showed this as a rebirth for Rochester and Jane Eyre. Jane returns to Rochester even though he suffered an amputated hand and is blinded by the fire. Eventually they marry and Rochester regains his sight in one eye and produces a son.

In both of these books the author shows how a woman deals with societies' norms, values, and manners. Jane and Emma endure harsh realities in life. Jane had to be a strong character to go through what she did. Emma not as strong but the determination in finds a spouse. Even though Jane and Emma had different hardships the had similar characteristics. They both had wisdom, imagination, and character.

The Themes of Jane Eyre

Q. Describe the Themes Used in Jane Eyre

In the beginning of Jane Eyre, Jane struggles against Bessie, the nurse at Gateshead Hall, and says, I resisted all the way: a new thing for me..."(Chapter 2). This sentence foreshadows what will be an important theme of the rest of the book, that of female independence or rebelliousness. Jane is here resisting her unfair punishment, but throughout the novel she expresses her opinions on the state of women. Tied to this theme is another of class and the resistance of the terms of one's class. Spiritual and supernatural themes can also be traced throughout the novel.

Soon after Jane is settled at Lowood Institution she finds the enjoyment of expanding her own mind and talents. She forgets the hardships of living at the school and focuses on the work of her own hands. She is not willing to give this up when she is engaged to Rochester. She resists becoming dependent on him and his money. She does not want to be like his mistresses, with their fancy gowns and jewels, but even after she and Rochester are married, she wants to remain as Adele's governess. She is not willing to give up her independence to Rochester, and tries to seek her own fortune by writing to her uncle. In the end, when she does have her own money, she states, "I am my own mistress" (Chapter 37).

Jane not only shows the reader her beliefs on female independence through her actions, but also through her thoughts. Jane desires to see more of the world and have more interaction with its people. While she appreciates her simple life at Thornfield, she regrets that she does not have the means to travel. She relates her feelings to all women, not just those of her class, saying:

Women are supposed to be very calm generally. But women feel just as men feel; they need exercise for their faculties, and a field for their efforts as much as their brothers do. They suffer from too rigid a restraint, too absolute stagnation, precisely as men would suffer; and it is narrow-minded in their more privileged fellow-creatures to say that they ought to confine themselves to making puddings and knitting stockings, to playing on the piano and embroidering bags (Chapter 12).

It is also important here to talk about Bertha, for she is a female character who is often seen resisting. It may be wondered why Jane seems to have little sympathy for her, and part of the reason for this may be seen with how Bertha is portrayed. While Bertha is a woman, she is not presented as su She is described in animal-like terms, and is called 'it', not even 'she' in the beginning. Jane describes her meeting with Bertha as such:

In the deep shade, at the farther end of the room, a figure ran backwards and forwards. What it was, whether beast or human being, one at first sight could not tell: it grovelled, seemingly, on all fours; it snatched and growled like some strange wild animal: but it was covered with clothing; and a quantity of dark, grizzled hair, wild as a mane, hid its head and face (Chapter 26).

Jane is disadvantaged in many ways as she has no wealth, family, social position or beauty. Jane does have intelligence though, and her disposition is such to make Rochester fall in love with her. Here is seen resistance against class, as Rochester wishes to marry Jane in spite of the disapproval that will come from his class, and Jane also resists this disapproval and will marry him. However, Jane will not rebel against God or lose her self-respect and become Rochester's mistress when she finds out that he is already married.

There is also a spiritual theme running through the novel. When Jane is at Lowood she meets Helen Burns, the good and sacrificing girl whom Jane questions about God and Heaven right before she dies. This seems to begin Jane's relationship with religion that is traced more through the book. Jane calls on God after she finds out about Rochester's wife. She locks herself in her room, and states, "One idea only still throbbed lifelike within me – a remembrance of God: it begot an unuttered prayer...'be not far from me for trouble is near: there is none to help'" (Chapter 26). Again, when she is trying to resist succumbing to Rochester's passion and a dishonest marriage with him we see her turning to God. After Rochester's attempts, Jane tells him to "do as I do: trust in God and yourself. Believe in Heaven. Hope to meet again there" (Chapter 27).

The religion theme is perhaps most important in Jane's relationship with St. John. When Jane refuses his attempts to get her to marry him and go to India, he says that she is not refusing him, but God. When Jane does almost accept him it is because she suddenly feels much veneration for him and her reasons for not accepting him dissolve. She says, "Religion called – Angels beckoned – God commanded – life rolled together like a scroll – death's gates opening showed eternity beyond: it seemed, that for safety and bliss there, all here might be sacrificed in a second" (Chapter 35).

Here one of the supernatural aspects of the novel steps in, and Jane hears Rochester calling her from afar. Later it is related that Rochester could also hear her reply. This is only one example of the supernatural in the novel. Near the beginning of the novel Jane feels she sees a ghost while she is locked in the red-room, and she takes it as a message from another world. When Jane is walking to Hay and first hears Rochester's horse approaching, she expects to see a North-of-England spirit called a 'Gytrash' a lion-like creature with a huge head. When she sees Rochester the spell is broken, as she knows that nothing ever rides the Gytrash. When Jane first sees Bertha in her room by candlelight, she describes her in supernatural-like terms, thinking perhaps that she is a ghost.

Jane also relates a dream of a woman she knew in the past and how it was a presentiment of her sister's illness. Jane dreams of infants, as this woman did, and these dreams are followed by the attack on Mason and Robert's visit telling Jane that John Reed had died and that Mrs. Reed was on her deathbed. She again has dreams of infants before her failed wedding, and she has a dream of Thornfield as a ruin, which she later sees has become reality

Descriptions of Place in Jane Eyre

Q. Was the Victorian period man oriented? Explain
Or
Q. What made release her novel under the name of a man?
Or
Q. Briefly describe the five main settings of the novel?

Charlotte wrote the novel "Jane Eyre" during the Victorian period in 1847. She wrote under a man's name, Currer Bell, so that she would find it easier to get her book published. The book is about the life of a strong, brave, an independent woman who has many adventures along the way to happiness.

There are five main settings in the novel where Jane finds herself.

The first setting is Gateshead where she lives with her aunt by marriage. Her uncle Reed has died and the aunt, who is not a blood relative, treats her badly. Her cousins also treat her badly.

Therefore, the house has no comfort for her. In fact, at the age of ten, she prefers to leave it and go to boarding school. The reader can understand why she wishes to leave Gateshead because of the actions done to her and the feelings she has for the place. At one point aunt Reed has her locked in the Red Room as punishment for arguing with her cousin. uses sympathetic background to stress the fear that Jane feels locked away, "I heard the rain beating continuously on the staircase window, and the wind howling in the grove behind the hall; I grew by degrees cold as a stone, and then my courage sank."

The weather is in sympathy with her fearful feelings. The simile "cold as a stone" helps the reader to understand her.

Aunt Reed agrees to send Jane away to school and the future headmaster; Mr.. Brocklehurst visits Gateshead. Jane had looked forward to going to school for a better quality of life but after Mr..

Brocklehurst's visit she wonders if this will be true. He says to her, "Little girl, here is a book entitled the "Childs Guide", read it with prayer, especially the part containing "an account of the awfully sudden death of Martha G_, a naughty child addicted to falsehood and deceit."

Afterwards she goes into the garden and the setting reflects her mood writes, "I found no pleasure in the silent trees, the falling fir-cones, the congealed relics of autumn, russet leaves, swept by past wind in heaps, and now stiffened together."

The garden is cold and unpleasant as she thinks about her future at the hands of Mr.. Brocklehurst. The second setting that Jane finds herself in is Lowood, the boarding school for orphaned girls. The name Lowood is not pleasant and it's low lying place in the wood, which is damp and still, brings infections to the girls in winter. wrote that many girls died of chest complaints every winter at the school. The school and its surroundings are bleak and the girls are always hungry and abruptly treated. Jane's description of Lowood and the surroundings show her feelings for the place, "That beck itself was a torrent, turbid, and curbless: it tore asunder the wood, and sent a raving sound through the air, often thickened with wild rain or whirling sleet; and for the forest on its banks, that showed only ranks of skeletons."

She uses a metaphor to describe the trees as she calls them skeletons. The reader can understand her state of mind. The girls around her look like skeletons.

Jane survives Lowood because of the kindness of Miss Temple, a teacher, and her friend Helen Burns. She learns a lot and becomes a teacher herself but after eight tiresome years, she becomes interested in what the outside world has to offer. Jane is brave because she has no one outside who is interested in her but advertises in a newspaper as a governess. This shows her independence. Ladies of her age and standing usually looked for marriage to provide them with a home and very few went out to work. At the time that Jane is beginning to feel constricted by Lowood her description of the view outside of her window reflects her feelings, "My eye passed all other objects to rest on those most remote, the blue peaks: it was those I longed to surmount; all within their boundary of rock and heath seemed prison-ground, exile limits."

Thornfield is the third setting for Jane Eyre. Here she gets a reply from Mrs. Fairfax to work as a governess for Adele, Mr.. Rochester's ward. Jane has some good years at Thornfield and this shows through in her description of the inside of the house, a large fire burning silently on the marble heath, and wax candles shining in bright solitude, druid the exquisite flowers with which the tables were adorned. The crimson curtain hung before the ar" Here is a house, which is warm and pleasant, and this echoes the feelings that are growing in Jane for the house and Mr.. Rochester.

When the staffs at Thornfield get the house ready for visitors and there is a lot of activity and preparation the speed of description increases to match the rushing about. There is enjambment to show long periods of preparation and repetition and listing to stress action, " Three women were gat to help; and such snubbing, such brushing, such washing of paint, and beating of carpets, such taking down and putting up of pictures, such polishing of mirrors and lustre's, such lightning of fires in bedrooms, such airing of sheets and feather beds on heaths, I never behold either before or since."

After she finds out that Mr.. Rochester is already married Jane, who is a woman of morals, leaves Thornfield to make a new life. Although she has no family to upset she will live with Mr.. Rochester without being his wife. She runs away and finds herself at Morton where she becomes a schoolteacher at the village school.

Her first days at Morton are the worse in her life where most sympathy is felt for her. She is hungry and collapses, near to death, at the Rivers house. Finally, she inherits money from an uncle Madeira and shares this fortune with the Rivers who are actually her long lost cousins. Her excitement at inheriting the money and finding cousins is shown in the description of her Christmas preparations at Morton, "My first aim will be to clean down (do you comprehend the full force of the expression?) To clean down Moor House from chamber to cellar; my next to rub it up with bees-wax, oil and an indefinite number of clothes, till it glitters again; my third, to arrange every chair, table, bed, carpet, with mathematical precision, afterwards I shall go rear to ruin you in coals and peat to keep up good fires in every room."

Here there is enjambment and listing to give the feeling of excitement and activity. Jane has finally got a home of her own.

The last setting Jane is at Ferndean. When she was at Morton she wondered what had happened to Mr.. Rochester, and St. John Rivers's proposal, which she turns down, spurs her to enquire about her old master. She learns that he is blind and that his wife his dead. As she approaches his new home at Ferndean the description of the place matches his new situation. The wood around is "thick and dark" and the house walls were "dark and green". writes it was "quite a desolate spat". This place is appropriate for a broken and blind man.

Jane makes Ferndean comfortable for Edward Rochester and later marries him. As she transforms the house, his feelings of the descriptions of Ferndean change.

"I described to him how brilliantiy green they were; how the flowers and hedges looked refreshed; how sparklingly blue was the sky."

Their happiness is shown in this description. This lightness hints at the good news that follows when Mr.. Rochester gets back the sight in one eye.

This novel was written around the time of the early women's rights movement when women were starting to think about equal rights. makes reference to this.

Women are supposed to be very calm generally but women feel just as men feel; they need exercise for their faculties, and a field for their efforts just as their brothers do.' was basically saying women are equal to men in every way. This quote reminds me of a conversation between Viola and Orsino in Shakespeare's 'Twelfth Night' when Viola also talks of women experiencing the same emotion as men.

'Too well what love women to men may owe. In faith, they are as true of heart as we.' In Jane Eyre it's a change in setting but for Viola it means her assuming a completely new identity.

The five settings in Jane Eyre, Gateshead, Lowood, Thornfield, Morton and Ferndean are important to the story. The descriptions of them reveal Jane's feelings at the point that she is living there.

Thornfield's descriptions are positive because she is happy there at first, and Morton's Moor House receives a warm description. Ferndean finally is described with fondness. Gateshead and Lowood are often negatively described because of her unhappiness in those two places.

The pace of description is also important because we know whether she is excited or not. My favourite description is of the horizon at Lowood when Jane bravely decides to make her own way in the world.

This novel shows that some Victorian women were becoming independently minded.

Society's Attitudes to Girls and Education in Charlotte 's Jane Eyre

Q. Discuss the situation of women during the 19th century

Or

Q. Why the success of women was depended purely on men?

Or

Q. "This novel brought about a revolution in existing society conditions." Discuss.

'Jane Eyre', Charlotte 's second completed manuscript, was published in October 1847. Writing was considered a disreputable occupation for women, so wrote Jane Eyre under the pseudonym of Currer Bell in an effort to avoid personal publicity.

In the course of her book, we see how Jane Eyre progresses through life. She begins her story as a penniless orphan forced to live on the charity of her Aunt Reed. Ten-year-old Jane lives at the Gateshead Hall where she is relentlessly abused, ostracized and despised by her benefactors and cousins. She is then send away and suffers the wretchedness in the charity school of Lowood run by the tyrannical Brocklehurst. Later on, Jane advertises and becomes a governess at Thornfield Hall where she meets Mr.. Rochester, her employer, with whom she then falls in love and after many the troubles and disasters, eventually marries 'Jane Eyre' is a spiritual autobiography; it is a person fused into a narrative and speaks to us directly. The novel provides a truthful view of the education and social preconceptions in the nineteenth century England. may have transcribed much of her own life and experiences into the character of Jane. At many points in this book, Jane voices 's then–radical opinions on religion, social class, expectation, gender relations and education.

Nineteenth century society was structured by wealth and social status. The story is placed in such a time when women were seen as second-class citizens, inferior to men and required to be obedient to them. The society's expectations of girls were to make a good marriage, possess social and hostess skills, be pretty and decorative. Boys, however, generally had more opportunities within their class. Wealthy and cultivated family such as the Reeds had more opportunities.

John Reed is provided with the best education available and he goes to a public school. He is expected to have position and authority.

After all, he is going to inherit everything when he grows up. This is illustrated in the very first chapter of the novel when Jane suffers teasing and punishment at his hands. He states, "Now I'll teach you to rummage in my bookshelves, for they are all mine." This phrase reflects that John has already regarded himself as the owner of the house. He also forces Jane to call him "Master Reed". The maids even refer to him as "Master", which shows how high he is in the social standing at Gateshead Hall., however ironically pointed out that the opportunity is wasted and undeserved. John is described as having "dingy and unwholesome skin and a dim and beaded eye". This description reflects his personality – he is a bully and is Jane's chief tormentor. John has neither the respect nor the "affection for his mother and sisters". Despite his cruelty to living thingssuch as "twisted the necks of the pigeons", calling his mother "old girl", "revile her for her dark skin", "bluntly disregarded her wishes" and "tore and spoiled her silk attire", John is much less punished. Mrs. Reed tend to turn a blind eye even though she is well aware of the fact that Jane is being bullied and punished continually – "Mrs. Reed was blind and deaf on the subject".

At Gateshead, no formal education is mentioned for Georgiana and Eliza. Because at that time, girls did not need education. They tend to be motivated by the need to appear composed and beautiful, so later on they could marry men of their own class or above. Portrays Eliza as having a natural intelligence and financially astute.

"She had a turn for traffic, and a marked propensity for saving; shown not only in the vending of eggs and chickens, but also in driving hard bargains with the gardener about flower-roots, seeds, and slips of plants". She would also" have sold the hair off her head if she could have made a handsome profit" and "keeping her accounts in a little book with anxious accuracy", it is John, the boy, who gets all the power, education and opportunities.

As for Georgiana, she is "universally indulged" because of "her beauty, her pink cheeks and golden curls," "which seemed to give delight to all who she looked at her, and to purchase indemnity for every fault." Georgiana is the typical of what was expected nineteenth century girls, she tend to be motivated by the need to appear composed and beautiful, so to make a good marriage. In the book, Jane is depicted as plain and insignificant and revealed that to be a lady wasn't defined through one's character or actions, but by social breeding, physical beauty and musical accomplishment.

Later on, we meet Adele, the little French girl that Jane teaches at Thornfield Hall. Although she has the best education available, her aim in life is still destined to appear beautiful and composed and to be make a good marriage. Through out the entire novel, continually point out that even upper class women had very limited opportunities at those times.

At Gateshead, Jane is considered as a poor relation, a dependant and a burden. In terms of blood, she is the same as the Reeds. Her semi-aristocratic lifestyle is that of upper class, but her poverty puts her in a difficult position. Jane is a kind of second-class citizen. In some way she is below even the servants, who certainly have no obligation to treat her respectfully – "No; you are less than a servant, for you do nothing for your keep"; "if she were a nice, pretty child, one might compassionate her forlornness; but one really cannot care for such a little toad as that." Even worse, John Reed describes Jane as "bad animal". John, like his mother sees Jane as a "dependant" who is not worthy "to live here with gentleman's children". Yet this ambiguous social standing is also one of the reasons that motivate much of the novel's internal tension and conflict. Later on, we meet Mrs. Fairfax, Mr.. Rochester's housekeeper, who is a grown example of what often happened to poor relations. She is a widow and is employed by Mr.. Rochester who treated her well and she has considerable status in the house.

By looking at the advice the maids give to Jane, it is clear that the Reeds expect her to appreciate the house she lives in, be obliged, to show gratitude towards her benefactress, be humble and know that she has limited prospects – "...Missis kindly allows you to be brought up with them. They will have a great deal of money, and you will have none: it is your place to be humble, and to try to make yourself agreeable to them...", "you should try to be useful and pleasant, then perhaps, you would have a home here; but if you become passionate and rude, Missis will send you away."

At Gateshead, it appears that Jane has no education as she often helps Bessie, the nursery servant by doing housework.

During the nineteenth century, many felt that the poor were more susceptible to the "sins of flesh". Religion was often used as a way to suppress the poor, to "subdue" these sins and try to keep the poor in their place. Denying the masses education was another way those in power aimed to keep it. Charlotte uses this novel to attack these opinions and examine different religious views. She included three main religious figures: Mr.. Brocklehurst, Helen Burns, and St.

John Rivers. Each represents a different model of religion. attacks the very austere religious factions like Mr. Brocklehurts and his attitudes to the poor. She includes Brocklehurst to mock him and shows how shocking he is in the hope of making people realise this. also puts forward tolerant views about Helen's belief in forgiveness, which in start contrasts completely different view of Christianity to that of Mr.. Brocklehurst. Later on, Jane encounters the practical and truly charitable St John Rivers who sets up village schools to improve the children's prospects. He sacrifices his emotional deeds for the fulfillment of his moral duties and represents the Christianity of glory, ambitions and self-importance.

When Mr.. Brocklehurst first arrives at Gateshead Hall, we get the impression of a satanic figure who is hardhearted and cold. Clad entirely in black and standing upright, "like a black pillar". He metaphorically injures Jane with his vile utterances, which are a blow at her resolute character. When Brocklehurst questions Jane about hell, her reply is that she "must keep in good health and not die".

This simple answer sums up the wittiness, naivety and the true defiant nature of Jane. It is, however, unbelievably shocking to see that Brocklehurst can create these monstrous images of hell. Jane is only ten years old! Yet, uses humour to poke fun at his damnation.

Jane's early years at Lowood prove to be a period of considerable tribulation as she endures harsh conditions, strict teachers and the tyranny of Mt. Brocklehurst. More over, the harsh conditions she experiences as a student at Lowood show us that, despite Jane's intelligence, talent, and self–assurance, she is merely a burden in the eyes of society, because she is poor.

Lowood Institution was set up for girls that had lost one or both of their parents. In the book, the school is described as a very underprivileged school. depicts the hardships Jane encounters at Lowood to show that the school is not charitable and loving at all - "The porridge is burnt again" and "the water in the pitchers was frozen". also gives detailed descriptions of the Sundays at Lowood. Girls had to walk to Brocklebridge Church with insufficient clothing to protect them from the severe cold, "no boots", and "ungloved hands".

We meet the hypocritical and cruel Brocklehurst again in Chapter 7. He preaches a doctrine of privation, while supporting his own luxuriously wealthy family at the expense of the Lowood. His "Christian teachings" concentrate on sin and obedience rather than love and tolerance. Even though Brocklehurst himself says that humility is a Christian grace, he does not practice it. Instead, he enforces hardness and humility on girls at his school and wishes to strip them of all possible vanity. Girls are undernourished, wearing simple and inadequate clothes, forced to have natural curly hair cut off and spend long days in poor living conditions with harsh regime. Brocklehurst's proscriptions are difficult to follow and it is entirely unchristian, but he insisted on pursuing it. He justify what he does by stating: "I have a Master to serve whose kingdom is not of this world.

My mission is to mortify in these girls the lusts of flesh; to teach them to clothe themselves with shame-facedness and sobriety, not with braided hair and costly apparel; and each of the young persons before us has a string of hair twisted in plaits which vanity itself might have woven..." Yet, ironically at the same time he indulges his clearly proud and conceited wife and children who are "splendidly attired in velvet, silk, and furs" along with "beaver hats", "ostrich plumes", "profusion of light tresses, elabourately curled", "costly velvet shawl, trimmed with ermine" and "false front of French curls". His hypocrisy is accentuated when Miss. Temple informed him that she had been given girls bread and cheese to eat. He insisted to pursue his proscription by saying, "Oh, madam, when you put bread and cheese, instead of burnt porridge, into these children's mouths, you may indeed feed their vile bodies, but you little think how you starve their immortal souls". " wanted to set Brocklehurst up so she could knock him down.

However, Helen and her doctrine of endurance and forgiveness represent a religious position that contrasts with Brocklehurst's. She represents a mode of Christianity that stresses tolerance, acceptance and forgiveness. Helen is described as meek and forbearing and manifests certain strength and intellectual maturity. She told Jane, " Love your enemies; bless them that cursed you; do good to them that hate you and despitefully use you." When Jane asked whether if Mr.. Brocklehusrt is a "good man", she relied "He is a clergyman, and is said to do a great deal of good." This shows Helen's will to believe in other people. She also told Jane "Eternity is a rest – a mighty home, not a terror and an abyss. Besides, with this creed, I can so clearly distinguish between the criminal and his crime; I can sincerely forgive the first while I abhor the last: with this creed revenge never worries my heart, degradation never too deeply disgusts me, injustice never crushes me too low: I live in calm, looking to the end." Helen also believes that everyone would go to heaven and death is merely a peace release and a homecoming – "We all must die one day, and the illness which is removing me is not painful; it is gentle and gradual... By dying young, I shall escape great sufferings." It is clear that approves of Helen's theory of love and forgiveness.

But could these be 's own views? Helen has a great impact on Jane, as it is through her philosophy that Jane is finally able to forgive Mrs. Reeds in Chapter 21 and Mr.. Rochester at the end of this book. 'Jane Eyre' is a severe criticism of the limited educational opportunities open to women, the idea that they "ought to confine themselves to making puddings and knitting stockings, to playing on the piano and embroidering bags." Shows the difference in expectation between the sexes Educational opportunities were usually reserved for boys while girls were often simply trained to be wives. Despite its harsh regimes and poor living conditions, Lowood does give Jane a first class education that was available to girls at the time subjects taught. There were drawing, painting, embroidery and piano lessons, as well as reading, writing, arithmetic, history and geography. Some girls also learnt to speak French, like Jane. This was considered as genteel and educated.

Jane is very accomplished as she is able to grasp all those skills, which ultimately allow her to achieve an independence that was rare for women in those days. She is able to earn a decent wage and be in a respected profession with status as teacher.

At Thornfield Hall, Adele receives the most privilege education that a girl could have. She is Jane's only student, allowing her to pay full attention and spend more time with her. They have an excellent learning environment and equipment, and Adele receives some highly regarded skills, such as painting. "Most of the books were locked up behind glass doors; but there was one bookcase left open containing everything that could be needed in the way of elementary works.

Several volumes of light literature, poetry, biography, travels, a few romances, etc", "In this room, too, there was a cabinet piano, quite new and of superior tone; also an easel for painting and a pair of globes."

As a governess, Jane has certain amount of status, which allows a certain amount of familiarity. She is also respected for being an educated and genteel woman.

In 'Jane Eyre' the clear division of classes and education is shown in the depiction of the higher classes in society being able to afford governess for the education of a child. In this novel, it is obvious that Jane is a figure of ambiguous class standing. She comes from poor background, but her manners, sophistication, and education are those of an aristocrat. Jane remained poor while at Thornfield, but her connections are good. That is what causes her ambiguous state. Yet at Moor House, she enjoys economic independence and freedom and engages in worthwhile and useful work teaching the poor.

St. John's Morton School is an example of a lower class school. It is set up to educate the poor. At that time, the vast majority of the country was illiterate. Education was seen as freeing people up and local factory owners and landowners set up schools for the masses.

They need more educated work forces as industry had developed and more skills were required. However, there was still a sexist preference for boys as their education came first.

When Jane first starts teaching in the village school, she has her own prejudices about educating the poor. She feels "degraded" by teaching those illiterates because of the decline of her social status and asserts that the poor are not capable of being educated. Jane's view of the poor is that of an aristocrat: "Poverty looks grim to grown people; still more so to children: they have not much idea of industrious, working, respectable poverty; they think of the word only as connected with raged clothes, scanty food, fireless grates, rude manners, and debasing vices: poverty for me was synonymous with degradation." Jane is later astonished at finding " estimable characters amongst them – characters desirous for information and disposed for improvement". She is therefore ashamed of what she felt before and starts to take pleasure in teaching those girls whom she use to describe as "heavy-looking" and "gaping rustics". shows the prejudices through Jane, yet at the same time she is telling us that the poor do blossom and they can be educated.

In conclusion, seeks to through the character of Jane. She is advocating the right of girls at whatever level to have a decent education and she shows us that girls can be accomplished, successful and independent if they are well educated.

Jane Eyre: Confronting Repression, Achieving Progression

Q. Does the term Confronting Repression depict male dominance? If yes, then to what extent?

Or

Q. Does Jane Eyre succeed in making her own world ruled by her wishes?

Or

Q. Is Jane Eyre capable of striking balance between two opposite fractions?

Jane Eyre tells the story of a woman progressing on the path of acceptance. Throughout her journey, Jane encounters many obstacles to her intelligence. Male dominance proves to be the biggest obstruction at each stop of Jane's journey: Gateshead Hall, Lowood Institution, Thornfield Manor, Moor House, and Ferndean Manor. As she grows, though, Jane slowly learns how to understand and control repression.

Jane's journey begins at Gateshead Hall. Mrs. Reed, Jane's aunt and guardian, serves as the biased arbitrator of the rivalries that constantly occur between Jane and John Reed. John emerges as the dominant male figure at Gateshead. He insists that Jane concede to him and serve him at all times, threatening her with mental and physical abuse. Mrs. Reed condones John's conduct and sees him as the victim. Jane's rebellion against Mrs. Reed represents a realization that she does not deserve the unjust treatment. Jane refuses to be treated as a subordinate and finally speaks out against her oppressors. Her reactions to Mrs. Reed's hate appear raw and uncensored, and foreshadow possible future responses to restraints. This rebellion also initiates the next phase of her journey.

Lowood Institution represents the next step in Jane's progression. Her obstacle here appears in the form of Mr.. Brocklehurst, the operator of the "respectable" institution. He made his first appearance at Gateshead Hall in order to examine Jane and verify her evil qualities (according to Mrs. Reed). At Lowood, Mr.. Brocklehurst exemplifies the perfect hypocrite. He constantly preached for the denial of "luxury and indulgence" (p.95), though his values conflict with these ideas. His wife and daughters personify the meanings of luxury and indulgence in that "they were splendidly attired in velvet, silk, and furs" (p.97). He extends his hypocrisy in quoting bible passages to support his preachings, though these preachings and passages do not apply to his own life. He says, " I have a master to serve whose kingdom is not of this world: my mission is to mortify in these girls the lusts of the flesh, to teach them to clothe themselves with shamefacedness and sobriety, not with braided hair and costly apparel..." (p.96). Although she must learn to deal with Brocklehurst's complete dominance, Jane changes a lot during her years at Lowood, due mainly to the teachings of Helen Burns and Miss. Temple. Through their instruction, Jane learns how to control her anger over Mr.. Brocklehurst's false accusations and understand her feelings without yielding to a vocal rebellion like the one prompted by Mrs. Reed at Gateshead.

Jane's journey next brings her to Thornfield Manor. Mr.. Rochester becomes the dominant male figure at this juncture. While in residence at Thornfield, Rochester demands undivided attention from the servants, Jane included. He insists on dominance in every aspect of his life, and he needs recognition for his superiority. Jane somehow resolves to accept his control and she concedes to him by calling him "sir," even after beginning their intimate relationship. She even goes so far as to excuse herself for thinking. She says, "I was thinking, sir (you will excuse the idea; it was involuntary), I was thinking of Hercules and Samson with their charmers-" (p.289). Jane's irony suggests displeasure at Rochester's complete dominance of their relationship. Jane's reference to religion also becomes associated with the idea of a dominant (male) sex. For Jane, Rochester embodies the idea of love which has so long been denied to her. She still must continue her pilgrimage when she finds Rochester's physical and material love unacceptable.

Jane's next lesson comes at Moor House. Here, she must answer to St. John, her cousin (though in name only). He portrays the ultimate sacrificer, willing to do anything for others, no matter how undesirable. St John also expects this of Jane, and she must decide whether to answer to his call. By this point in her journey, Jane understands that her search for simpatico can not be realised without real love. She denies St John's marriage proposal by saying, "I have a woman's heart, but not where you are concerned; for you I only have a comrade's constancy; a fellow-soldier's frankness, fidelity, fraternity...nothing more..." (p.433). She knows St John cannot give real love to her and she must continue in her journey.

Ferndean Manor emerges as the final stop in Jane's journey. Once again, Rochester appears as the dominant figure, although his superior air becomes greatly reduced in light of his ailments and complete dependency on those around him. A new man results in this change, and in him, Jane finds her real, spiritual and physical love. She says, "All my heart is yours, sir: it belongs to you; and with you it would remain, were fate to exile the rest of me from your presence forever" (p.469).

Rochester no longer demands a subservient being to boost his ego; he demands an equal partner. He does not try to contain Jane; he sets her free. He says, "Miss Eyre, I repeat it, you can leave me" (p.468). She does not leave him though. In him, Jane finds her simpatico. Rochester embodies the perfect balance between the physical and the spiritual, the natural and graceful, intellectual and physical beauty, and love and servitude. Rather than being ruled, Jane realises her true abilities and she finds her balance.

Jane Eyre makes many stops on her pilgrimage for happiness and equality. Each stop helps her understand and realise qualities in herself and others. With each new experience and trial, she learns how to rationally confront the repression, which leads to her progression. Understanding dominance, though not yielding to it, becomes the key for Jane to achieve her balance.

Miss Temple's Influence on Jane Eyre

Q. In this male oriented world whom does Jane find as her inspiration and how?

Or

Q. Does it prove to be the way towards bashing out male dominance?

Or

Q. What impact does the personality of Miss Temple had on Jane?

Or

Q. How Miss Temple teaches Jane to react in different situations calmly?

"Jane Eyre" is set during the Victorian period, at a time where a women's role in society was restricted and class differences distinct. A job as a governess was one of the only few respectable positions available to the educated but impoverished single women.

Not only is "Jane Eyre" a novel about one woman's journey through life, but Brontë also conveys to the reader the social injustices of the period, such as poverty, lack of universal education and sexual inequality. Jane's plight and her "dependant" status is particularly emphasized at the beginning of the novel.

Miss Temple is the kind and fair-minded superintendent of Lowood School, who plays an important role in the emotional development of Jane Eyre.

Miss Temple is described by Helen as being "good and very clever" and "above the rest, because she knows far more than they do". This description is more significant because it has been said by Helen, and she herself is extremely mature. One of Miss Temple's most outstanding qualities is her ability to command (perhaps unconsciously) respect from everyone around her, "considerable organ of veneration, for I yet retain the sense of admiring awe with which my eyes traced her steps". Even during their first encounter, Jane is "impressed by her voice, look and air".

Throughout Jane's stay at Lowood, Miss Temple frequently demonstrates her human kindness and compassion for people. An Example of this is when after noticing that the burnt porridge was not eaten by anyone, she ordered a lunch of bread and cheese to be served to all, realising their hunger. This incident is also evidence of her courage, of how she is not afraid to stand up to her superior, when she feels that unnecessary suffering has been inflicted on the children. Miss Temple's Christianity contrasts with that of Mr. Brocklehurst, where instead of preaching restrictive and depressing doctrine, which he then proceeds to contradict, she encourages the children by "precept and example.

After the incident involving Mr.. Brocklehurst announcing to the whole school that Jane is a liar, the reader becomes aware of Miss Temple's sense of natural justice, where before accepting what Mr. Brocklehust has said, she inquires from

Jane her version. It is of no coincidence that Bronte choose to coincide Miss Temple's arrival into the schoolroom with the moon's light "streaming in through a window near". Brontë throughout the novel uses weather to set the mood of a character.

Jane's time at Gateshead Hall was one of misery and anguish. She was subjected to domestic tyranny, and abused by her cousin John Reed continually. Jane, from her "very first recollections of existence" had been told that she had better not think herself "on an equality with the Misses Reed and Master Reed" and that it was her "place to be humble". At Gateshead she was made to feel like a "discord" and a person "not worthy of notice". Even the servants treated her with inferiority, because of her "dependant" status, which in Victorian society was viewed without compassion. Her strong desire to love and to be loved was not fulfilled here. Whereas at Lowood Jane was treated with respect and as an equal by Miss Temple, and her desire to be loved and cared for was fulfilled by Miss Temple and Helen Burns.

Jane arrives at Lowood as a passionate little girl, who is deeply resentful of her aunt and cousins, but due to the influence of Helen Burns and Miss Temple's example, Jane learns to control these feelings, and be happy, "I had given in allegiance to duty and order"... "I believed I was content"... "I appeared a disciplined and a subdued character".

Jane admits "to her instruction I owed the best part of my acquirements; her friendship and society and been my continual solace; she had stood me in the stead of mother, governess, and latterly, companion".

Miss Temple's treatment of Helen also has an influence on Jane. Jane has a great deal of admiration for Miss Temple, and in many ways copies her. Miss Temple's treatment of Helen shows Jane how to treat other people, with kindness and respect.

When Miss Temple invites Jane and Helen for tea, Jane listens enraptured to Helen's and Miss Temple's intellectual discussion, while observing a real warmth and affinity between them. It is clear to Jane that both Miss Temple and Helen are both very intelligent and well read, Jane admires these qualities and tries to seek them herself as they lead to an independence of mind, another quality that Jane wishes to acquire. The extent of Miss Temple's influence on Jane can be seen by the way she reacts to Miss Temple's departure, "from the day she left I was no longer the same. With her was gone every settled feeling that made Lowood in some degree a home to me" and without the presence of Miss Temple there to guide her she feels that "the reason to be tranquil was no more".

Miss Temple acts as a strong role model to Jane, and holds the qualities, which Jane aspires to have: kindness, sensitivity to the sufferings of others and resolute in her stance to injustice, "I had imbibed from her something of her nature and much of her habits".

Passion, Dreams, and the Supernatural in Jane Eyre

Q. Is the protagonist's belief in supernatural justified? Or

Q. Does it strike a conflict between the real and paranormal world?

Introspection, half-belief in the supernatural, conflicting emotions, gushing description appear throughout Jane Eyre. Rochester's mention of prescience — both foreshadowing and premonition — come up again and again throughout the work. "I knew... you would do me good in some way... I saw it in your eyes when I first beheld you," Rochester tells Jane. Both he and she believe implicitly the things they read in eyes, in nature, in dreams. Jane has dreams whom she considers unlucky, and sure enough, ill fortune befalls her or her kin. When she is in a garden, which seems "Eden-like" and laden with "honey-dew", the love of her life proposes to her. However, that very night the old horse chestnut tree at the bottom of the garden is struck by lightning and splits in half, hinting at the difficulties that lie in store for the couple.

The turbulent exploration of Jane's emotions so characteristic of the text reveals some of Brontë's most prevalent ideas — that judgment must always "warn passion," and that the sweet "hills of Beulah" are found within oneself.

As Jane grows throughout the book, one of the most important things she learns is to rule her heart with her mind. When a child at Gateshead, she becomes entirely swept up in an emotional tantrum, which proves to be the most painful memory of her childhood. At the pivotal point in the plot when Jane decides to leave Rochester, she puts her love for him second to the knowledge that she cannot ethically remain with him - the "counteracting breeze" once again preventing her from reaching paradise. Only when Rochester has become worthy of her, and judgment and passion move toward the same end, can she marry him and achieve complete happiness.

Charlotte Brontë, like her, traveled to wondrous lands within the confines of her own head. While Jane, engrossed in Bewick's History of British Birds, was mentally traversing "solitary rocks and promontories", her creator might have been calling to mind memories of her own sojourns in imagined lands. By the time, she was a teacher at the Roe Head School, Charlotte and her brother Branwell had been writing stories and poems about an African kingdom called Angria for many years. While she was away at the school, the fate of the inhabitants of the country lay in Branwell's hands, which made her very nervous, as he was portrayal of intrigue and violence. She was unhappy with her situation, loathing the available company and describing herself as "chained to this chair prisoned within these four bare walls," and so her happiest hours were spent in the wild landscapes of her mind. "What I imagined grew morbidly vivid," she says, and indeed her visions of Angria are almost more real to her than what is actually happening around her.

"All this day I have been in a dream, half miserable and half ecstatic: miserable because I could not follow it out uninterruptedly; ecstatic because it showed almost in the vivid light of reality the on goings of the infernal world. (She sometimes referred to Angria as" infernal" or below.") When pupils or fellow teachers interrupt her reveries she is furious, saying once, "But just then a dolt came up with a lesson. I thought I should have vomited."

About 1839 Brontë finally left Angria, saying 'still, I long to quit for a while that burning clime where we have sojourned too long. The mind would cease from excitement and turn now to a cooler region, where the dawn breaks grey and sobre and the coming day, for a time at least, is subdued in clouds all materials from the Norton critical edition of Jane Eyre. Though she did at last consent to leave her imaginary world behind, it played such a large part in her child and early adult hood that there is no doubt her recollection of time spent there affected Jane's experience.

Bertha Mason's Madness in a Contemporary Context

Q. Does the character of Bertha Mason imply racism?

Or

Q. Under what circumstances Bertha was admitted in asylum.

Or

Q. What is the irony in the last scene of Jane's marriage?

Or

Q. What were the conditions of mental asylum in Victorian era?

One of the most controversial — yet essential — plot elements of Charlotte Brontë's widely beloved novel, Jane Eyre, is her depiction of Bertha Mason, Mr.. Rochester's first wife, a once-beautiful Creole woman who is ravaged by mental illness and is hidden away, locked up in a lonely room at Thornfield. Many critics have decried Brontë's delineation of Bertha as both a racist and insensitive portrayal of insanity. Her sensationalistic approach to describing a character suffering from mental illness during the Victorian era, while lending the gothic elements of suspense and intrigue to her cleverly crafted and brilliantly executed novel, nevertheless remains rather unsettling for modern readers, who may often wonder whether her views toward mental illness reflect the prevalent attitudes of her day. An examination of articles contemporary with the initial publication of Jane Eyre in 1847 surprisingly reveals that awareness of mental illness and sensitivity towards the care of suffering patients were remarkably acute, and these issues were being actively discussed in the press, as well as by politicians.

In the March-June, 1845 volume of The Westminster Review of London, an article entitled, "Report of the Metropolitan Commissioners in Lunacy to the Lord Chancellor, Presented to both Houses of Parliament by Command of Her Majesty," appears. This fascinating document — a report from the Metropolitan Commissioners investigating the condition of mental institutions throughout England — provides a detailed overview of various "mental asylums," with statistics regarding the number of "curable" versus "incurable" patients, and reports suggesting that the cases of mental illness reported seemed to be increasing. The report opens with its statement of purpose, briefly detailing its plan to set out a coherent report on British mental institutions. It notes regarding the issue of mental institutions:

An equally striking change is perceptible in the disposition of the public generally on this matter. The time has not long gone by when the mere mention of it was received with aversion and disgust. However, we are glad to say, given place to an interest and attention, which is not merely confined to the enlightened and benevolent portion of the community, but to a great extent, it is shared by the public at large.

Thus, this suggests that attitudes toward mental illness in the Victorian era were already shifting, and the public at large began to recognize the humane necessity of lending attention to the matter of mental institution conditions. The report continues, mentioning that in 1828, Parliament initially appointed a Commission to inspect London mental asylums on account of reports of abuse, and that this inspection resulted in improved conditions and the passing of an act in 1841 that required a Commission from Parliament to inspect every British mental asylum. In contrast to the older asylums, which resemble dreary "prisons or dungeons" and were designed primarily so that its inhabitants could not escape, the more "modern establishments" are designed with the well-being and comfort of the patients as main priorities.

The report argues that "the patients ought to have the benefit of a cheerful look-out on a pleasing prospect" and stresses the fact that older asylums are not suitable for modern-day patients. As these facilities "have been devised more as a means of confinement than as a means of cure, more for the protection of the public than for the treatment of the patient". It is remarkable to observe that the Commissioners who wrote the report are truly concerned about the environment the asylum provides for a patient; they are adamant about ensuring that newly constructed asylums "avoid everything which might give to the patient the impression he is in prison". This seems to contradict markedly with the attitudes expressed towards Bertha and her condition in Jane Eyre. When Bertha is finally revealed on Jane's long-awaited wedding day, she is living sequestered in her hidden apartment, which does not appear to be designed with her comfort in mind:

In a room without a window there burnt a fire, guarded by a high and strong fender, and a lamp suspended from the ceiling by a chain. Grace Poole bent over the fire, apparently cooking something in a saucepan. In the deep shade, at the further end of the room, a figure ran backwards and forwards. What it was, whether beast or human being, one could not, at first sight, tell: it groveled, seemingly, on all fours; it snatched and growled like some strange wild animal: but it was covered with clothing; and a quantity of dark, grizzled hair, wild as a mane, hid its head and face.

Thus, Brontë likens her to a vulgar animal, with wild mannerisms and a disheveled appearance. The descriptions that follow are even less flattering: Brontë uses such epithets as "the clothed hyena," "the maniac," "that purple face," and "the lunatic" to describe Bertha's condition. When she attempts to strangle Rochester, Grace Poole "gave him a cord, and he pinioned them behind her: with more rope, which was at hand, he bound her to a chair"). Quite interestingly, this was not considered acceptable, humane treatment of patients of mental illness, even by Victorian standards. The report in The Westminster Review recalls that when the asylum at West Auckland was examined in 1842, there were discovered the most appalling conditions, where there existed "only one unglazed window" and "one woman was leg-locked by day and chained to her bed at night," as were several of the other male inhabitants.

The article notes: "The Commissioners who first visited the asylum stated their opinion to be that it was entirely unfit for the reception of insane persons". The report also mentions a visit in 1842 to the asylum at Haverford west, where the Commissioners reported that "the asylum was deficient in every comfort, and in almost every convenience: the rooms being small and ill-ventilated". They were appalled by the fact that "the dress of the patients was dirty, ragged, and insufficient," and that "the refractory patients were confined in strong chairs, their arms being also fastened to the chair". This catalogued evidence of abusive treatment in Victorian mental institutions raises two questions for a reader of Jane Eyre. Why is Bertha Mason living sequestered in a house, rather than institutionalized in an asylum, as there were asylums throughout Britain? Since she is living in a room at Thornfield, why is she being exposed to such cruel conditions?

The reader is told only briefly of Bertha's history by Mr.. Rochester. He summarizes her past quite succinctly and without any semblance of sympathy:

Bertha Mason is mad...she came of a mad family; —idiots and maniacs through three generations! Her mother, the Creole, was both a mad woman and a drunkard!-as I found out after I had wed the daughter: for they were silent on family secrets before. Bertha, like a dutiful child, copied her parent in both points...Oh! my experience has been heavenly, if you only knew it! This statement has long been the source of criticism of Jane Eyre as a racist novel, since it is explicitly mentioned that Bertha's mother is "the Creole" and is both an alcoholic and a lunatic — traits which were common stereotypes regarding Creoles. There is no evidence in the novel that Bertha has ever been placed in a formal mental asylum in an attempt to discover a cure for her condition.

This is very unusual to note, as the actual Commissioners' report relates that "the number of insane persons ascertained to exist in England and Wales exceeds 20,000, and there is every reason to believe that this is considerably below the actual amount". Thus, mental illness was a recognized and widespread condition throughout England and Wales. It seems that the number of institutionalized patients was also on the rise; while the Lancaster Asylum had 160 reported patients in 1816, in 1845 it boasted 600 strong (Metropolitan Commissioners. While the poor would face difficulties in finding adequate care at asylums due to financial restrictions, certainly Mr.. Rochester would have no such financial obstacle to surmount in finding appropriate care for his ill wife. Perhaps, however, Brontë envisioned that in the past Bertha might have sought a medical cure, and discovering none, found, as the Commissioners Report remarks, "she should be removed from asylums instituted for the cure of insanity, in order to make room for others whose cases have not yet become hopeless".

However, the statistics in the report suggest that early treatment seemed to prove effective in the Victorian era. The report cites the "General Statement of Insane Persons Confined in Asylums in England and Wales" in 1844; it compares "Private patients" to "Pauper patients." Of 3,790 Private patients, 1,045 were deemed curable, while 2,745 were pronounced incurable. Conversely, of the 7,482 Pauper patients, 1,484 were seen as curable, while 5,998 were viewed as incurable. "From this table," says the authors of the report, "we perceive that the relative proportion of incurable paupers in asylums is double that of the private patients, who have probably had the benefit of early treatment". Furthermore, in the introduction to a letter featured in The Westminster and Foreign Quarterly Review in the October 1847-January 1848 edition, John Conolly, a Fellow of the Royal College of Physicians at London and a physician to the Middlesex Lunatic Asylum at Hanwell, is presented as a leading physician.

The whole of the barbarous system of coercion and restraint...was founded on a fallacy, and that insanity...is simply a state of unsound, physical health — a state of functional disease — in the great majority of cases capable of a cure, under appropriate treatment; capable also, under injudicious treatment, of being rendered permanent and incurable. Although modern readers have the benefit of increased knowledge of mental illness conditions and treatments, it nevertheless is encouraging to realise that even in the Victorian era with its rather antiquated and limited knowledge and views upon mental illness, measures were actively being taken to alleviate the suffering of patients and attempt to implement some sort of beneficial treatment. As the article continues to explain, such victims of ravaging mental illness are incapable of judging their condition with accuracy or realizing the necessity of seeking medical assistance. All of this evidence of increasing understanding and awareness of mental illness in the 1840s then places Mr.. Rochester's character in a rather unfavorable light. He allows Bertha, whose family has a history of mental illness, to be locked up like a prisoner in a cheerless, windowless room, wearing dirty and ragged clothing and subject to the abuse of Grace Poole, who binds her to a chair to subdue her. There is no evidence any real attempts have been made in the past to address her situation by medical professionals and try to lessen the suffering she inevitably experiences.

Ultimately, investigation into the condition of mental institutions at the time of the publication of Jane Eyre reveals that poor, abusive conditions and overcrowding were prevalent in Victorian era mental asylums. There also existed a surprising level of awareness on the plight of the mentally ill and a widespread desire to improve the conditions of asylums. The treatments they offered to those who were incapable of functioning in regular society due to mental illness. In both selected articles, the issue of mental illness is handled with an impressive degree of respect, sensitivity, and understanding. As the Commissioners Report authors declare, "We sympathize with the lower animals and protect them from cruelty, whilst we suffer every species of barbarity to be heaped with impunity on our afflicted brethren".

They hope to that improved conditions and understanding will "suffice to provide the means of comfort, freedom, and happiness to the many afflicted and worse than slave-bound of our fellow countrymen". This evidence leads one to question with much greater scrutiny Mr.. Rochester's character, for his treatment of Bertha Mason is unpardonable. More importantly, however, is the criticism one might direct towards Charlotte Brontë herself for her sensationalistic, highly stereotypical, and unsympathetic portrayal of a woman who has been removed from her home country, has suffered mental illness, is kept like a caged animal in deplorable conditions without medical treatment, and ultimately is compelled to end her tragic life by suicide.

'She bit me... like a tigress': Charlotte 's construction of the Other in Jane Eyre

Q. Explain the dichotomy in Jane's character
Or
Q. "The other side of Jane is fierce and full of power" Explain

The circulation of power at the domestic level allows the coloniser to monitor the bodies and actions of others in myriad ways. This is nowhere more evident than in Charlotte Brontë's Jane Eyre. Brontë dismissed socio-political agendas in a letter she wrote to her publisher in October 1852, telling him, 'I cannot write books handling the topics of the day, it is no use trying. Nonetheless, despite her disavowal of the social significance of her novel, Jane Eyre negotiates with the colonial dynamic in myriad ways.

The Abolition of Slavery Act was finally passed on the 23 August 1833 and the issue was definitely part of the national consciousness when Brontë began writing her novel. Rochester's reference to slave trade: 'bargaining for so many tons of flesh and an assortment of black eyes' foregrounds the centrality of the debate to the Victorian conscious. However, Brontë goes a step further than Austen, by appropriating the metaphor of slavery to underline the nature of the patriarchal gaze and articulate resistance. 'He smiled; and I thought his smile was such as a sultan might, in a blissful and fond moment bestow on a slave his gems had enriched: I crushed his hand... and thrust it back to him.'

The novel, published between the Reform Bill of 1832 and mid-century prosperity, traces the induction of Jane, a 'poor', 'obscure', 'plain' governess into the leisure class. Jane's marginality, like Fanny's in Mansfield Park, is articulated in spatial terms since the very beginning — she confines herself to the small room adjoining the drawing-room and draws the red curtain about her, to shrine 'in double retirement'. However Jane moves from a position of liminality to occupy centre-stage by using the rhetoric of abolition in post-emancipation Britain. Brontë's interventionist method appropriates the metaphor of slavery to espouse a dual critique to serve this end: of the subjugation of women within the domestic space and the subjugation of the racial other in the colonies. But the implicit critique of British domination gradually metamorphoses into a validation of the imperial project. Jane's 'rebellious feminism' is premised on ethnocentric descriptions of Bertha and the Caribbean. *Jane Eyre* highlights shared oppression, drawing attention to British exploitation but the novel's figurative use of the racial other betrays this agenda and disturbs any neat categorization.

Jamaica is constructed as the spatial other while signs of bestiality and grotesquery are constantly displaced onto body of the Creole subject. Bertha's body becomes the repository of the social space, an attestation of the political and economic exploitation involved in Imperialism. The topic of racial otherness are evident in the descriptions of Bertha, who is described as 'dised', 'purple', 'swelled', 'blackened'. Interestingly Bertha, the racial Other is also morally 'stained' by intemperance, infidelity, impurity, profanity, madness and bestiality form a cluster of referents by which Brontë denotes the person of Bertha. Brontë reinforces typologies of the untrustworthy, sensuous native, which demonise the historically muted subaltern woman. An examination of the authorial gaze exposes the mechanics of constitution of the Oriental habitus by the Occidental subject.

However this is complicated by the fact that Bertha's presence upsets the stable domesticity of the Victorian country-house. Thornfield Hall proves to be a 'contact zone' which paves way for the co-habitation of the coloniser and the colonised subject. The spatial dynamics of this 'contact zone' deserves fuller attention — Bertha's presence allows the author to introduce desire within the parameters of the bourgeois domestic novel. Clearly, it is only in a dialectical relationship that the other that the Self can define its own subject position — the Other impinges on the subject, creating disturbance and fracturing the stability it seeks. But this is deemed possible only via the introduction of the trope of the gothic and the segregation of desire within the space of the attic, the room where Bertha is imprisoned. Moreover this unsettlement is followed by the obliteration of the other i.e. Bertha, in Jane Eyre. This entails the reconfiguration of the potentially hetero topic space of the attic within Oriental paradigms.

Furthermore despite Jane's insistence that she would not be 'hurried away in a Suttee' and the British Abolition of widow sacrifice in 1829, Bertha's death, vaguely reminiscent of the act of Sati, allies the Oriental to older norms and pagan rituals. This conformity is ideologically loaded as the novel seems to validate self-immolation of the Oriental subject. It is in this tension, between disturbance and subsequent obliteration that Jane Eyre needs to be situated. Jane and Rochester cannot be united until and unless Bertha sets Thornfield Hall, a signifier of misbegotten colonial wealth and her own person on fire.

The free will of the Oriental female subject is effaced in order to affirm the will of the English subject. A stark contrast is established between the two women: '... 'that is my wife' said he. 'Such is the sole conjugal embrace I am ever to know... and this is what I wished to have' 'compare this clear eyes with the red balls yonder-this face with that mask-this form with that bulk''.

The demonisation of Bertha Mason underscores the dual act of containment of the political and sexual other and the naturalisation of the virtuous as normative. The novel ultimately relies on a valorisation of the bourgeois norms of domesticity: the rhetoric of selfhood, love and conjugality is used to reaffirm and circulate colonial stereotypes. In fact, it is the ideology of imperialism that aids Brontë in her vindication of the socially marginalized woman.

To avoid simplistic conclusions, one must remember that an author's dependence of pre-existing representations to incite pre-conscious apprehension amongst the reading public cannot be underestimated. For instance, the change brought about in Sir Thomas Bertram owing to the weather in the colonies — 'he had grown thinner and had the burnt, fagged, worn look of fatigue and a hot climate' as opposed to Fanny's ruddy and blushing self is replicated by Brontë in her depiction of the Jamaica and India. Stereotypes about colonial territories/ peoples, or what I have called the oriental habitus, then become part of the genre Brontë inherits.

This is immensely visible in her reproduction of colonialist historiographies, grounded upon what Gautam Chakravarty calls the 'syntagmata of caste, religion, language and geography'), in order to counter-pose the chaos of Thornfield Hall with the order of Evangelicalism. Missionary efforts during the nineteenth century, premised on the axiomatic supremacy of the white Christian race, were institutionalised to target whole communities and peoples. St. John's doctrines are based on the evangelical vision, and are predicated on the assumption that heathenism resided outside the individual and was characteristic of entire communities.

His ideology seems to replicate the assumptions of colonialist treatises like Charles Grant's Observations on the state of society among the Asiatic subjects of Great Britain (1792) and James Mills's History of India (1826) which offered polemical accounts of Indian manners and morals. The insistence on an evangelical system of mission education conducted in the English language was partly a belief in political reform along Christian lines. The suggestion seems to be that the diffusion of Christianity, and consequent moral improvements will construct a particularly appropriate form of colonial subjectivity. This is mirrored in Brontë's characterisation of India as 'the realm of ignorance... war... superstition'), the Rivers's insistence on Jane being 'much too pretty, as well as too good to be grilled alive in Calcutta' and Jane's reiteration of the same idea 'Alas! If I go to India, I go to premature death'.

Historically the period saw the formation of numerous organisations, which reflect the evangelical spirit: The Baptist

Missionary Society, The Church Missionary Society, London Missionary Society and The Bible Society. The Christian mission furthered the process of empire building by creating a hegemonic cultural practice that offered middle-class evangelical men and other marginalised citizens a means of identifying with the English state — the empowerment of the marginalised worked as a covert stratagem to quell resistance within the body politic. Brontë seems to draw attention to this aspect by illumining the dark underside of the St. John's character, coldness and an inability to love. Brontë goes to great lengths to illustrate that 'he did not appear to enjoy that mental serenity, that inward content, which should be the reward of every Christian'.

However, the daughter of an Anglican minister and a conventional Christian, Brontë seems to approve of the 'world redeeming work of the missionary'. It is for this reason perhaps, that, Jane's closing thoughts revolve, not around herself, but St. John's missionary activities in India.

The novel culminates with Jane's inheritance of her uncle's money, an offshoot of British earnings in Madeira, which seems to validate capitalism and international trade. Then again, the rhetoric of emancipation, used to describe Jane's personal struggle throughout the novel, climaxes with her retirement to the periphery of the country estate. Brontë's vision is fraught with an ambiguity and is clearly not absolutist as some postcolonial critics would have one believe. This points to the conflictual economy of colonial discourse and it is from such gaps, slippages and 'paradoxical half-openings of discourse' that authorial interventions, which have the potential of generating dissent, may emerge.

However Brontë's novel remains an incomplete gesture circumscribed by the spatio-cultural architectonics of colonial ideology. On the one hand, Jane Eyre makes a case for desire by showing that conformation to domestic ideology entails a relegation of sexuality to other spaces, whilst on the other, it relates Bertha's disruptive presence to the disintegration of the domestic space. The novel acknowledges Otherness, only to disavow it and critiques Evangelicalism, only to reinforce it.

Masculinity in Charlotte Brontë's Jane Eyre

Q. Depict the masculine element in Jane Eyre
Or
Q. What is the impact of first meeting with Rochester on Jane?
Or
Q. Is male dominance other side of flashing masculinity?

Though many texts often attempt to define femininity, few do the same for masculinity. Looking at the way Victorian women depict contrasts with the way men see themselves. Jane Eyre and Aurora Leigh both clearly represent men as both deficient in morality and dependent on women to be their spiritual and moral guides. Carlyle offers quite a different view, one in which women are not even mentioned. Instead, Carlyle sees a true man as a sincere and spiritual person who functions as guide for the rest of the world — much like the roles of women in contemporary novels by women.

In Brontë's Jane Eyre, we first see the interaction between Jane and Rochester in a completely different setting than the house that they both come to inhabit. Jane first encounters her soon-to-be-master; he has fallen off his horse in the middle of the woods and is completely helpless. She comes to his assistance with no idea who he is. Even in their very first encounter, Jane appears in a position to help the fallen Rochester, foreshadowing the form their relationship will come to take: Rochester as fallen and helpless, and Jane as his capable savior. From this moment on she is figured as helping him back on his moral horse, guiding him to the correct path from which he has wandered in so many ways.

When she describes their first encounter, his gruffness, she tells us, drew her to him for help. If he had been "handsome" or "heroic", she would have passed him by without assistance.

Had he been a handsome, heroic-looking young gentleman, I should not have dared to stand thus questioning him against his will, and offering my services unasked. I had a theoretical reverence and homage for beauty, elegance, gallantry, fascination; but had I met those qualities incarnate in masculine shape, I should have known instinctively that they neither had nor could have sympathy with anything in me, and should have shunned them as one would fire, lightning, or anything else that is bright but antipathetic.

If even this stranger had smiled and been good-humoured to me when I addressed him; if he had put off my offer of assistance gaily and with thanks, I should have gone on my way and not felt any vocation to renew inquiries: but the frown, the roughness of the traveller, set me at my ease.

Here, Brontë depicts the masculine not as something heroic or beautiful, but as gruff, mysterious, and ill tempered. Men are not supposed to possess "beauty, elegance, gallantry, fascination"; they are meant to be mean, rough about the edges, a challenge to unravel. To be beautiful, elegant, and a male is to be "antipathetic", to cause dismay, not t be masculine. Brontë does not value heroism in a man; instead she wishes him to be rough around the edges, misshapen and ready to be reformed. Men are not beautiful and righteous; it is the women who must be so, as counterpart to the men.

Rochester finds in Jane a willing ear ready to hear about all of his past and present miseries; he tells her, "it is not your forte to tell of yourself, but to listen while others talk of themselves" (p. 116). Jane is a patient, if somber, listener and falls into the role of Rochester's moral conscience, listening quietly to every gripe and responding with advice as to the path he should take to become morally upright. Rochester, who appears to have no innate moral guidance of his own, must look to the closest woman nearby, Jane, to discover the correct way to solve his problems. Brontë portrays Jane as the religious, moral, persuasive force that keeps erring Rochester on the righteous path from which he seems so willing to stray.

"You would say, I should have been superior to circumstances; so I should — so I should; but you see I was not. When fate wronged me, I had not the wisdom to remain cool: I turned desperate; then I degenerated... I wish I had stood firm — God knows I do!... I have a right to get pleasure out of life: and I will get it, cost what it may."

"Then you will degenerate still more, sir."

"... How do you know?... You have no right to preach to

me, you neophyte, that have not passed the porch of life, and are absolutely unacquainted with its mysteries."

"... Only one thing I know: you said you were not as good as you should like to be, and that you regretted your own imperfection; — one thing I can comprehend: you intimated that to have a sullied memory was a perpetual bane. It seems to me, that if you tried hard, you would in time find it possible to become what you yourself would approve; and that if from this day you began with resolution to correct your thoughts and actions, you would in a few years have laid up a new and stainless store of recollections, to which you might revert with pleasure."

"... You seem to doubt me; I don't doubt myself: I know what my aim is, what my motives are; and at this moment I pass a law, unalterable as that of the Medes and Persians, that both are right."

"They cannot be, sir, if they require a new statue to legalise them."

"They are, Miss Eyre, though they absolutely require a new statute; unheard-of combinations of circumstances demand unheard-of rules."

"... You are human and fallible." "I am; so are you — what then?"

"The human and fallible should not arrogate a power with which the divine and perfect alone can be safely entrusted... May it be right then,' I said, as I rose, deeming it useless to continue." Rochester seems unable to follow the correct path on his own, leading himself hither and thither, unable to see clearly. Telling him what to do is an easy task for Jane; she has no problem cutting directly through his stories and showing him where he has erred and how he should go about fixing himself. In this passage Rochester sees where he has gone wrong in his past, but he is unable to see that he has the power to change his ways. Only Jane can show him where he needs to reform his life, and she reminds him that he is "human and fallible" and therefore cannot go about doing anything he wishes and claiming it to be right. Jane possesses all the correct answers to the questions that daily assault Rochester;

for him, "to live... is to stand on a crater-crust which may crack and spew fire any day" (p. 184), but Jane can steady it by her clear perception and strict advice. Rochester is at every turn tempted into doing the wrong thing. Jane stands next to him as a barrier against temptation, a stoic, righteous wall against which he can lean when in the tempest of the enticements of the world. She is confident that everything she does is just: "I know my Maker sanctions what I do. For the world's judgment — I wash my hands thereof. For man's opinion — I defy it" (p. 218). Jane possesses no moral doubt, whereas that is all that Rochester seems to possess. But she does assert: "I am not an angel... and I will not be one till I die: I will be myself" (p. 221), and later on, "I had rather be a thing than an angel" (p. 223). She refuses to deem herself divine; she is only a follower of the divine, a disciple, and a guide.

Though Brontë allows Jane to view all of Rochester's faults in plain light, she still perceives something good in him, perceiving a kernel of his true nature hidden behind his mask of gruff persona. She adheres to the belief that he is just a victim of fate and circumstance and that underneath his rough appearance and crooked morality he is naturally a good person.

> I believed that his moodiness, his harshness, and his former faults of morality (I say former, for now he seemed corrected of them) had their source in some cruel cross of fate. I believed he was naturally a man of better tendencies, higher principles, and purer tastes than such as circumstances had developed, education instilled, or destiny encouraged. I thought there were excellent materials in him; though for the present they hung together somewhat spoiled and tangled. [p. 125]

She sees a man with a naturally good soul corrupted by the world, and therefore she finds that she must take the responsibility to correct him. She views human nature as fundamentally good; it is "circumstances", "education", and "destiny" that are to be blamed. Men are basically good; it is the job of a morally just woman, such as herself, to guide such a wandering lamb back onto the right path.

Rochester recognizes the changes that Jane is bringing about in him. He responds to her encouragement to become a better person, believes that she is guiding him to a better existence, and, in his gratitude, wishes to marry her. He attempts to describe to her what she does for him by asking her to place herself in his position.

In this stranger are much of the good and bright qualities which you have sought for twenty years, and never before encountered; and they are all fresh, healthy, without soil and without taint. Such society revives, regenerates: you feel better days come back — higher wishes, purer feelings; you desire to recommence your life, and to spend what remains to you of days in a way more worthy of an immortal being. [p. 186]

For him, Jane represents all that is good in the world, all that he searched for. She is free of the taint of the world that has so blighted his naturally good character; she is immune to the soiling of her soul. She rises above the baseness of the world as a beacon of his salvation.

The novel ends with Jane returning to the blinded, disfigured, and penniless Rochester. His house has been burned, and he blinded, symbolizing the cleansing of his past and his character. She returns to him, her heart full of pity, and taunts him about her return. "'It is time some one undertook to rehumanise you,' said I, parting his thick and long uncut locks; 'for I see you are being metamorphosed into a lion, or something of that sort'" (p. 371). Though she is commenting on his appearance, it is Jane's job to "rehumanise" Rochester, to remake him into a moral human being from the ashes that he has come to be. He is finally cleansed by the fire and his blinding, but has also become completely helpless and is left completely at the mercy of Jane. This vision of a man is that of one who must be reborn from his corruption, but once this is done, must rely entirely on a woman for his salvation.

The tension between Reason and Passion in Jane Eyre

Q. How the internal and external worlds contradict each other?
Or

Q. "Jane marrying Rochester is an act of foolishness hiding reality" Explain

Or

Q. At what point u feel the passion of Jane for men completely burns out.

In Jane Eyre, Charlotte Brontë uses various characters to embody aspects of reason and passion, thereby establishing a tension between the two. In fact, it could be argued that these various characters are really aspects of her central character, Jane, and in turn, that Jane is a fictionalised version of Brontë herself. From this, it could be argued that the tension between these two aspects really takes place only within her own head. Brontë is able to enact this tension through her characters and thus show dramatically the journey of a woman striving for balance within her nature.

A novel creates its own internal world through the language that it uses, and this fictional world may be quite independent from the real physical world in which we live. Writing in the style of an autobiography, Brontë distinguishes Jane Eyre, who quite clearly from the purely fictional worlds of Angria and Glasstown, locates her work within the world of Victorian England. But although Brontë's world is undoubtedly based on nineteenth-century society, it should be remembered that the world conjured in Jane Eyre is not reality: it is but a world constructed by Brontë in which to tell a story.

A novel based only on the mores and customs of Victorian society would surely hold limited appeal today, except as a historical document, yet Jane Eyre retains power and force even in a post-modern world, as shown by its continued popularity and the many TV and film versions it has inspired. Perhaps Jane Eyre retains such power and relevance because Charlotte fabricated the book from the cloth of her own psyche, her own passionate nature, and so, although our culture has changed drastically since the book was written, the insights into human nature, which Brontë gave us, remain.

Taking this view makes the characters in Jane Eyre seem denizens of Charlotte's own psyche. Some of them, such as the passionate Bertha and the cold St John, personify aspects of her character, her emotional and logical natures. Others, such as Brocklehurst and John Reed, which seem more two dimensional, could be viewed more as scenery, foils against which the main characters define themselves. Jane herself is Charlotte's most highly resolved character. Over the course of the book readers come to know every aspect of her intimately as she moves through Brontë's world. Readers also come to know her through her reflections, as she embodies aspects of the other characters. Charlotte seems to know Jane intimately, so intimately that it seems likely that Jane is Charlotte's avatar within her fictional world. If Brontë is Jane, it follows that the other characters, which came from Brontë might also be aspects of Jane. Through these aspects, we see a development of tension within Jane between emotional and logical natures, and this tension is played out in the events of the book.

Taking this argument further, if the book is seen as a reflection of Brontë's own psyche, the source of the various supernatural events described within the book must be Brontë herself. Thus she not only plays the main character in her story but also the supporting cast and the spiritual force which intervenes on Jane's behalf at crucial moments throughout. In this light Jane's meeting with her cousins, which many critics have seen as intolerably far-fetched suddenly makes sense. There are no coincidences in this book. Jane is kept from harm by the ever-present pen of her creator, just as Charlotte herself presumably felt protected and guided by her own protestant faith. Jane meets her cousins because Charlotte felt it was time for her to do so. No other explanation is required.

Passion and reason, their opposition and eventual reconciliation, serve as constant themes throughout the book. From Jane's first explosion of emotion when she rebels against John Reed, Jane is powerfully passionate. Just as Bertha's passion destroys Thornfield, Jane's passion, which destroys her ties to Gateshead, leaves the way clear for her progression to the next chapter of her life at Lowood. However, as Bertha's passion eventually proves fatal, it becomes clear that Jane must gain control over her passion or be destroyed.

We see the dangers of nature and passion untempered by reason in the scene in which Charlotte almost marries Rochester. Jane cannot 'see God for his creature' of whom she has 'made an idol.' If the God of the novel is Charlotte, and Jane is Charlotte's creature, we can see that in losing sight of God through overwhelming passion for Mr. Rochester, Jane runs the risk of loosing herself, of losing sight of Charlotte who she embodies. In this case, passion nearly gains a victory over reason. Jane nearly looses her own personality in her overwhelming love. Only Brontë's intercession through the medium of the supernatural preserves her character from passionate dissolution in the arms of Rochester.

The opposite is true when Jane is tempted to marry St John. Jane longs 'to rush down the torrent of his St John's will into the gulf of his existence, and there to loose my own' Again Jane almost looses herself, however, this time reason is nearly the victor. Jane's passionate nature is nearly entrapped by St John's icy reason and self-control. Once again, Charlotte intercedes on her characters behalf, this time with a disembodied voice which directs her to return to Rochester, and saves her passionate nature from destruction. St John's death in India could be said to show the danger that Charlotte saw in icy reason without emotion. Conversely, Bertha's death in a conflagration of her own making shows the danger of the unthinking passion which Jane feels for Rochester. Thus, these two deaths could be said to represent the more subtle death of individuality, in which Jane risks loosing herself and her separate identity.

It is interesting to note that Bertha is portrayed as being ugly, 'a vampire', a 'clothed hyena' whilst St John is uncommonly handsome. This fits with Brontë's use of fire and ice imagery to symbolise reason and passion. Ice may be hewn into any form, where it will remain, fixed and perfect as long as it stays frozen. Fire on the other hand can be hard to control. It cannot be moulded into exact shapes, it is constantly changing, and if unchecked will consume the ground on which it burns, leaving black cinders and ash, just as Bertha is blackened and swollen. This use of imagery gives us an interesting paradox, since much of the book seems to concern Jane's attempt to reconcile her passionate and reasonable natures. When ice and fire are combined the result is warm slush, hardly a suitable metaphor for a desirable state of being. One or the other, perhaps both must be destroyed. For how then can there be a reconciliation between the two?

Throughout the book Charlotte provides Jane with a number of mentors, each of whom provides her with a piece of the puzzle. The first is Brocklehurst. His Calvinistic philosophy teaches the mortification of the flesh as the way to obtain balance. By crushing Jane's physical body, he hopes to burn excess passion out of her, leaving a balance in which reason may be the ultimate victor. However, this method, like all other false or incomplete doctrines presented in Jane Eyre ultimately ends in death. Typhoid comes to Lowood and Brontë punishes Brocklehurst with shame and scandal. Interestingly, Brocklehurst's philosophy is re-enacted for Rochester when his pride and unreasoning passion is burnt out of him in the fire at Thornfield. Rochester flesh is mortified as he looses an eye and a hand. Through this somewhat drastic method, Rochester, who becomes a more suitable match for Jane, perhaps somehow attains a balance of his own.

Helen Burns seems to offer Jane another method by which tension may be resolved. She shows Jane that she can release her negative emotions, and make them less destructive through forgiveness, and that, by loving her enemies her hatred and anger may fade. We see this philosophy in action when Jane visits her dying aunt and is able to forgive her. She receives a just reward for this kindly act, the knowledge of an uncle living in the East Indies. However, Helens selfless acceptance of all the crimes perpetrated against her does nothing to change those crimes, or to deter their repetition. Had Helen been at Gateshead rather than Jane she would never have escaped. Helen's beliefs prove to be only an incomplete part of a whole, and so, she too dies.

At the end of many trials Charlotte permits Jane to return at last to her lover. It is a wiser Jane, and also perhaps a wiser Charlotte who welcomes this happy event. At this point it seems that the tension between reason and passion should have been resolved. However, this is not the case. There is no sense of any realistic resolution of tension between Jane's reasoning and passionate natures. Perhaps Jane could have attained logical emotion, or emotional logic, or to extend the Brontë's fire and ice metaphor, some sort of interplay between the two like sunlight glinting on the sea or torches focussed through a crystal lens. Instead, Jane and Rochester live in 'perfect concord', their happiness is complete.

They feel no passion or intrigue, only a warm sentimentality that seems wholly out of place in a book which has traversed such a vast ranges of emotion. Instead of fire and ice, Charlotte gives us warm slush. Perhaps she never resolved the tension between reason and passion for herself, and so was unable to write convincingly about it. Maybe, because of this she simply tacked on the happiest ending she could contrive, or maybe she wrote what she hoped to gain for herself, without understanding how she could get it. On an account of one woman's journey of spiritual growth, whether Jane's or Charlottes, Jane Eyre succeeds admirably. However, in the arrival it fails. Perhaps this is because at the time she wrote the book, Charlotte herself had not found happiness with a partner. The weakest element of the book remains its climax that is profoundly unsatisfying regardless of reasons.

Jane Eyre may be seen in a postmodernist light as an expression of Charlotte Brontë's own character. The players she peoples her world with seem to be aspects of herself, and Jane seems to represent her totality. Throughout the book a tension is established between the forces of reason, championed by St John, and those of passion, headed by Bertha. This tension exists within Jane's head, and also presumably within Charlotte's, but Brontë uses the medium of the novel to play out this conflict among all her characters, and so brings it out into the light. Eventually the champions, Bertha and St John are killed off, symbolising the danger Brontë saw in taking either of these paths to the exclusion of the other, and also symbolising the less obvious death that Jane risks, that of loss of self, either by surrendering to Rochester, or to St John.

The purveyors of incomplete solutions to this conflict are also killed. Brocklehurst, dies symbolically when he is removed from his position as headmaster of Lowood, Helen Burns dies of consumption. At the end of the story, the tension which Brontë has built up between reason and passion is not satisfactorily resolved, which weakens the ending somewhat, however Jane Eyre succeeds because it is taken directly from a young woman's psyche. It speaks to us today because it takes its inspirations from an internal reality that has remained constant.

Dreams in Jane Eyre

Q. At what point does the dreams and reality of life clash
Or
Q. Where does this day dreaming lead Jane in her life's journey?

Jane Eyre contains a number of significant dreams and daydreams. Despite her distaste for fantasies and inefficiency, the eponymous narrator, Jane, is a frequent daydreamer. Edward Rochester, Jane's employer at Thornfield, recounts observing her pace around in a day-dream. When the voice of a servant, Mrs. Fairfax, awakens Jane, Rochester imagines her thinking "My fine visions are all very well, but I must not forget they are absolutely unreal," and finding a task to complete to ensure she does not slip back into daydreaming.

This suppression of daydreams reflects the trend of Jane learning to suppress her passions over the course of the novel. After a turbulent childhood, Jane fulfills a Victorian ideal of womanhood, and grows more graceful and composed as she completes her education. Despite her placid exterior, Jane still maintains a wild and active dream life According to Maurianne Adams, Jane even pays "inordinate attention to the details of her dream life". Jane's dreams thus reveal the raw emotions she attempts to mask in order to be an ideal Victorian lady.

When Jane becomes a governess at Thornfield, Rochester takes interest in three watercolour imaginative landscapes she painted while at Lowood school. They reveal her great awareness for dreams. Jane describes the drawings as visions of her "spiritual eye" and notes, "The subjects had indeed risen vividly on my mind". Rochester declares, "I daresay you did exist in a kind of artist's dreamland while you blend and arranged these".

The first painting shows a ship's mast a bare hand, and a bracelet rising out of a turbulent green sea. The second painting is of a wind-rustled hill below a night sky in which a cosmic female form is visible. The third is a monumental bleak human head rising out of the ocean, supported by hands and resting on an iceberg. Adams argues that the pictures represent the scope of Jane's unconscious life. In the first two, the mast, arm, and the hill are Jane's consciousness, while the submerged ship and body and the faint cosmic woman are her consciousness. The third image "depicts the ice-bound landscape of Jane's despair". Jane's dream art may thus reveal the extent of her suppressed, passionate, and unconscious.

Besides providing glimpses into the unconscious, dreams in Jane Eyre can also serve as "presentiments," or warnings of future events. As Homans notes, Charlotte Brontë often uses the gothic form of literalizing, or making some aspect of the dreams come true.

A dream in Jane Eyre can serve as a general symbol. Jane believes the superstition of her old governess Bessie, that "to dream of children was a sure sign of trouble, either to one's self or one's kin". Indeed, the day after Bessie dreamt of a child, Bessie found out her sister was dead.

Dreams can also serve as complex representations for events in Jane's life. In volume two, chapter six, Jane herself begins having dreams about children. Gilbert and Gubar argue that these dreams correspond to the increasing apprehension Jane feels towards a romance with Rochester. After taking an idyllic walk around Thornfield with Rochester, Jane has an initial series of child dreams. "... during the past week scarcely a night had gone over my couch that had not brought with it a dream of an infant: which I sometimes hushed in my arms, sometimes dandled on my knee, sometimes watched playing with daisies on a lawn; or again, dabbling its hands in running water. It was a wailing child this night, and a laughing one the next: now it nestled close to me, and now it ran from me".

In accordance with Bessie's beliefs, Jane's visions bring her trouble. Jane wakes up from one of her dreams to the murderous cry of Bertha Mason, Rochester's mad wife whom he keeps locked in the attic of Thornfield. The day after that, Jane finds out that her cousin John has died and her Aunt Reed lies on her deathbed.

After Jane and Rochester become engaged, Jane has another pair of child dreams. During the first, Jane experiences "a strange, regretful consciousness of some barrier" dividing Rochester and her. She dreams that she carries a bawling child on an unknown road, and Rochester walks ahead of her. She tries to catch up to him, but her entreaties are muffled and her steps slowed, and Rochester walks farther and farther away.

In the second dream, Jane images the destruction of Thornfield. She wanders around the ruined estate, clutching the child because she "might not lay it down anywhere, however tired were my arms however much its weight impeded my progress". As she struggles to climb a wall to get a better view of Rochester, the child clings to her neck, nearly strangling her. When she reaches the summit of the wall, she glimpses Rochester as a vanishing speck. The wall crumbles and she and they baby fall away as she wakes.

These dreams may reflect a fear that Jane muffles from herself and others, namely that marrying Rochester will alter her identity. Homans suggests that the child of the dreams may represent Jane's love for Rochester, or "Mrs. Rochester," the new identity Jane will assume after marriage. Alternately, the dreams may represent Jane's orphan childhood, an alter ego that Jane cannot free herself of, even with marriage to Rochester. In any case, the dreams give marriage-anxious Jane an uneasy "intimation of what it would be like to become other than herself".

Again in accordance with Bessie's prophecy, the dreams of children bring trouble. Jane wakes from the second dream to discover Bertha Mason tearing her wedding dress. Shortly thereafter, Richard Mason will break up Jane and Rochester's attempted marriage with the news that Rochester is still legally married to Bertha.

The pair of dreams is also eventually literalized. The barrier separating Jane and Rochester in her dream represents Rochester's preexisting marriage to Bertha Mason, a force that stands between Jane's union with him. Rochester riding away from Jane in her dream forewarns of his imminent separation from Jane. The dream of the destruction of Thornfield comes true when Bertha Mason burns down the estate. In volume three, when Jane returns to Thornfield and finds it "a blackened ruin," she remarks that part of Thornfield looks "as I had once seen it in a dream".

Jane has another symbolic dream the night she decides to leave Rochester and Thornfield. In this dream, she has returned to the red room of Gateshead. As she looks up at the ceiling, it turns into clouds. A human form reminiscent of the cosmic woman in Jane's imaginative watercolour painting appears. Jane recounts,

She broke forth as never moon yet burst from cloud: a hand first penetrated the sable folds and waved them away; then, not a moon, but a white human form shone in the azure, inclining a glorious brow earthward. It gazed and gazed on me. It spoke, to my spirit: immeasurably distant was the tone, yet so near, it whispered in my heart — "My daughter, flee temptation!".

Again, Jane's emotions are reflected in her dream. Its decreased foreboding corresponds with Jane's release from marital apprehension as she decides to leave Thornfield. Again, the dream provides foreshadowing. The rising woman prefigures the spirit that later re-unites Jane and Rochester by inexplicably transmitting their messages, "Jane! Jane! Jane!" "I am coming: wait for me!" to each other over dozens of miles.

Jane's dreams can also directly depict her emotions. In Chapter 7 of volume 2, Jane hears that Rochester will marry Blanche Ingram, and she dreams of Blanche "closing the gates of Thornfield against me and pointing me out another road" while Rochester smiles sardonically. This dream reveals Jane's unhappiness at the prospect of Mr. Rochester marrying Blanche. In chapter 5 of volume 3, after her separation from Rochester, Jane recounts her recurring dreams "dreams many coloured, agitated, full of the ideal, the stirring, the stormy &mesh; dreams where, amidst unusual scenes, charged with adventure, with agitating risk and romantic chance, I still again and again met Mr.. Rochester always at some exciting crisis; and then the sense of being in his arms, hearing his voice, meeting his eye, touching his hand and cheek, loving him, being loved by him &mesh; the hope of passing a lifetime at his side, would be renewed, with all its first force and fire".

These dreams reveal the love Jane maintains for Rochester, and prefigure her return and subsequent marriage to him.

While Jane has a vibrant dream life, she is usually able to differentiate distinctly between waking life and dreaming, even in ambiguous situations. Twice, Rochester and his servant Mrs. Fairfax unsuccessfully attempt to convince Jane that her sightings of Bertha Mason are dreams. One night, shortly before Jane discovers Rochester's room is ablaze, she hears a "demonic laugh" emanate from her keyhole. Mrs. Fairfax tells Jane that the laugh she perceived was not real by saying "you must have been dreaming". Jane remains unconvinced and replies heatedly, "I was not dreaming" Another night, Jane wakes to find Bertha tearing her wedding dress. Rochester assures her that her vision was "half dream, half reality," claiming that the woman Jane saw was Grace Poole and that her state "between sleeping and waking" caused her to envision the Grace in a hideous form. Jane outwardly accepts this reasoning, but reflects, "satisfied I was not." Clearly, Jane can distinguish well between dream and reality.

Jane also emphasizes the distinction between dream and reality when she and Rochester first become engaged. Rochester becomes giddy at the prospect of marriage, and he speaks of his love for Jane in exuberant terms. "You are a beauty, in my eyes; and a beauty just after the desire of my heart, — delicate and aerial". Jane quickly refutes him on the grounds that his statements belong in the dream world, not the world of reality. She rejects the idealized future he imagines for them, calling his musings "a fairy tale &mesh; a day-dream". She brushes off his compliments of her beauty, saying "You are dreaming, sir &mesh; or you are sneering"

Dreamlike states intrude upon Jane's waking life only on momentous occasions. When a gypsy fortune-teller who later proves to be Rochester in disguise demonstrates uncanny knowledge about her life, Jane loses her skepticism for the supernatural and falls into "a kind of dream". After the gypsy woman analyses Jane's physiognomy in a "rave of delirium," Jane wonders, "Where was I? Did I wake or sleep? Had I been dreaming? Did I dream still?" In another instance of dream confusion, the day after Rochester asks Jane to marry him, Jane wonders "if it were a dream". For Jane, confusing dream and wake requires an event of great magnitude.

Dreams in Jane Eyre thus serve several complex functions. They forewarn Jane of trouble or good fortune, and reveal Jane's passionate inner self to the reader. They can serve as general symbols, interpretive representations, or direct reflections of Jane's emotions. Despite their prevalence, Jane tries to separate her dreams from her waking life, and in her novel, Brontë maintains sturdy barriers between England and "dreamland."

Jane Eyre and the Love mad Woman

Q. Does the love of Jane take her at the journey of becoming insane?
Or
Q. Does the insanity of Jane and Bertha share some similarity?

I was experiencing an ordeal: a hand of fiery iron grasped my vitals. Terrible moment: full of struggle blackness, burning! No human being that ever lived could wish to be loved better then I was loved; and him who thus loved me I absolutely worshipped: and I must renounce love and idol.

Jane Eyre's inner struggle over leaving an already married Rochester is the epitome of the new "love mad" woman in nineteenth-century literature. Jane Eyre is the story of a love mad woman who has two parts to her personality (herself and Bertha Mason) to accommodate this madness. Charlotte takes the already used character of the love mad woman and uses her to be an outlet for the confinement that comes from being in a male-dominated society. Jane has to control this madness, whereas the other part of her personality, her counterpart, Bertha Mason, is able to express her rage at being caged up. As what it means to be insane was changing during time, changed insanity in literature so that it is made not to be a weakness but rather a form of rebellion. Jane ultimately is able to overcome her love madness through sheer force of her will.

As a proponent of the love mad woman Charlotte can be looked at closely and be seen as almost love mad herself did not have the love of her mother, who died at an early age. However, she had her sisters, brother and father, Charlotte seemed to lacking love. Through her "affair" with Monsieur, Charlotte seems to be able to fit the definition of the love mad woman. While away at school, Charlotte developed an attachment to one of her teachers whose sources vary as whether or not this lead to an attachment. As an already married man, Charlotte's attachment to was immoral. When decided to ignore Charlotte, Charlotte saw this as desertion and this was seen in many of her writings.

Through her "tryst" with, Charlotte could certainly identify with the emotions of a love mad woman. She was rejected by her "lover" and can be seen as almost mad because of the emotions that she projects into her writings due to this "affair." Charlotte also was well read on the psychology of the time. She attended medical lectures and would have discussed such with her father Patrick. Charlotte eventually settled for her father's curate, Mr. Nicholls, as her husband, though initially she did not love him.

Through the events of Charlotte's life it is easy to see parts of her in the characters of Jane Eyre and Bertha Mason. Charlotte uses Bertha as a rebellious outlet for not only Jane but for herself as well. The feminist critics Sandra Gilbert and Susan Gubar clearly summarize this phenomenon when they state "By projecting their rebellious impulses not into their s but into mad or monstrous women, female authors dramatize their own self-division.". In other words Charlotte has Bertha as a sort of scapegoat that she can express her true rebellious feelings without demeaning herself or her. Charlotte makes

Jane different from Bertha in the end because Jane uses her will to overcome her madness and ultimately gets the happy ending that neither Bertha nor Charlotte herself, it seems, were able to obtain.

Jane begins her fall into being a rebellious love mad woman in the Reed household. She has an almost complete lack of love. She has the abandonment of both her parents through their deaths and then the desertion through death also of her Uncle Reed, who seems to be the only member of the Reed family who could have been sympathetic to her plight. Jane already may be looked at as mad because of her inability to control her passion, her rage. When she flies at John like a "mad cat", she is led to her imprisonment in the red room. This is parallel to the real-life treatment of women who became hysterical and then were treated through confinement. The fact that Jane is described in animal terms such as mad cat is very important. She is seen as bestial in her inability to control her emotions. Those who are insane are considered to be weak-willed, like animals that only do things for their own pleasure. She must therefore be punished for these feelings.

Jane's confinement in the red room is just the beginning of her journey as a love mad woman. Evidence of Jane's temporary madness can be seen in her thoughts during her imprisonment in the room. She thinks "unjust!—unjust!... instigated some strange expedient to achieve escape from insupportable oppression.... What a consternation of soul was mine that dreary afternoon! How all my brain was in tumult, and all my heart in insurrection! Yet in what darkness, what dense ignorance, was the mental battle fought!".

Jane has a consternation of soul, she is in tumult, in insurrection from the insupportable oppression. These words—"consternation, tumult and insurrection"—all denote a kind of madness in Jane. Jane as a woman should be controlling these emotions, not being driven to an almost hysterical by them. Here is using this temporary madness to give Jane an outlet for her anger at being oppressed. She has this mental battle in order to free herself from the society into which she is confined, not only the red room of course, but her position in the Reed family, her position in society as a female who wants to show her anger and is without a device to do so except for anger. This is one of the few examples where Jane allows herself to have this mental tumult whereas later on in the book Bertha Mason is used for this purpose.

The fact that Jane will have a double who will be able to act out Jane's mental tumult is foreshadowed in the passage when she is looking into the looking glass. As she gazes at herself in the mirror Jane says:

I had to cross before the looking glass; my fascinated glance involuntary explored the depth it revealed. All looked colder and darker in the visionary hollow than in reality: and the strange little figure there gazing at me, with a white face and arms specking the gloom, and glittering eyes of fear moving where all else was still, had the effect of a real spirit.

Jane describes herself as a strange little figure, she is unable to recognize herself in her mounting madness. She is fascinated by what is in the glass because it is colder and darker then reality. This can be seen as her true inner feelings. Her feelings of rebelliousness and passion that may be seen as cold and dark and ugly because they are not meant to be viewed by the world that Jane lives in. Jane has a white face and the glittering eyes of a spirit. This correlates with the fact that later on Jane compares Bertha to a monster.

This is a connection to the fact that at some points of the book Bertha and Jane as seen as supernatural, monstrous beings. Jane obviously sees some of this supernatural being in herself though she chooses not to recognize it. Jane chooses to give into her madness, as a child she does not have the will to overcome it. Jane says, "My heart beat thick my head grew hot... I was oppressed, suffocated: endurance broke down". These physical symptoms show her mental anguish. Jane chooses to give into madness to fight the suffocating oppression. After being removed from the room Jane is able to regain her senses and her anger/passion that creates her madness is only seen once more at the Reed house hold when she rages at her aunt before she goes off to Lowood. The red room serves as a microcosm for Jane's world of oppression.

Not only does the room literally oppress her, but so does her life in the Reed household which could stand as itself a microcosm to the oppression of the patriarchal Victorian society.

Though Jane is still confined at Lowood she doesn't demonstrate the passionate madness that came from her confinement in the Reed household. Jane still talks of rebellion but she herself is very quiet. She goes about her business of being a good student and later on a good teacher. She still lacks the love of a family, so the love madness is bound to come back at her. Eventually she decides she needs a change and a slight insanity comes from that. Once again this insanity can be seen in her thoughts: "I desired liberty; for liberty I gasped; for liberty I uttered a prayer... 'Then,' I cried, half desperate, 'Grant me at least a new servitude!'" Jane gasped and uttered, much like in the red room where she felt suffocated. She is gasping as if she can't breathe, like a type of claustrophobia where she can breathe in confinement. Jane is half desperate with the passion of needing to be unconfined. Her passion is on the border of the insanity seen in the red room.

Finally Jane comes to Thornfield where her insanity is allotted to her double, Bertha Mason. The existence of this "psychological double" is talked about in The Mad Woman in the Attic by Susan Gubar and Sandra Gilbert. Though Helen Small, who researched the love mad woman, does not believe that such a double exists in the book, her description of the love mad woman is a clear combination of Bertha and Jane. By combining some of the views of these feminists critics a more clear understanding of Jane Eyre can be seen. From the very beginning of her stay at Thornfield, Jane and Bertha are parallel. When Jane goes for a nighttime walk on the roof her contemplations are almost echoed by Bertha's laughter.

"A tale my imagination created, and narrated continuously; quickened with all of incident, life fire, feeling that I desired and had not in my actual existence". Jane quickens with feeling; she is once again gasping as she was in the red room for freedom to do what she is unable to do, for rebellion. Jane goes on to say, "Women are supposed to be very calm generally: but women feel just as men feel". This is of course the exact kind of language that would have gotten her committed in a Victorian society That women can feel as men do is insane; the passion Jane feels inside would have been considered mad. Jane uses words like "restraint, stagnation, suffering" to describe the plight of women in general. Though Jane herself does not fall into hysterics here, Bertha's laughter is a reminder of the madness that is caused by this constraint. Bertha's laughter is the call for rebellion that Jane doesn't allow herself to completely follow through with.

Even Rochester recognizes Jane's imprisonment. In one of his discussions with her he says, " I see... a bird through the close-set bars of a cage: a vivid, restless, resolute captive is there; were it but free, it would soar cloud high". Jane is caged in close-set bars of society, but what is ironic is that Rochester is a part of this society that does not let the vivid, restless, and passionate Janebird out.

As the story progresses Bertha continues to act as an outline for the emotion that Jane does not allow herself to express. After finding out after Rochester's immoral past, Jane says that she still respects him. That night Bertha, Jane's double, tries to set fire to Rochester. This is an insane reaction to the emotion that Jane must be repressing about her true feeling towards Rochester's actions. During this scene Jane gets a glimpse of Bertha and describes her as "goblin like" and the "devil." This is interesting since it is later discovered that Bertha's love madness comes from the fact that she has a moral madness. Victorians of course saw immoral, passionate women as monsters and that is how Jane sees Bertha.

It is also slightly reminiscent of the fact that Jane had once saw herself as a supernatural being in the mirror in the red room. After Rochester fools Jane in the guise of a gypsy Bertha once again is about to lash out for Jane Bertha attacks Mason that night and is described in terms such as "a tigress," and Mason compares her to a vampire, saying "she sucked the blood; she said she'd drain my heart". Bertha is once again reduced to Medusa-like terms. She is the immoral woman who has become a monster. The name "tigress" is much like Jane being called a "mad cat" at the beginning of the book. Bertha is acting out in the bestial way that Jane used to allow herself to act out in. Bertha, like a tigress to a mad cat, is a larger version of Jane's bestial nature.

While Jane seems to no longer have the problem of love madness when she is engaged to Rochester, this is just a façade. Jane's love madness occurs from her inability to be who she wants to be in society, to express all her emotions out loud. Jane still needs Bertha to act as her double in this matter. Jane cannot recognize herself as Rochester tries to dress her up. When she looks at the fancy veil she knows that it is just another kind of confinement. Rochester is trying to get Jane to conform so that she looks and acts like the Victorian ideal of a woman. As Jane Rochester she will still have to be a person she is not meant to be. The fact that Jane's love madness is not gone is also seen in her dreams. In them she is carrying a child, which can be seen as her double self that she still needs to carry with her. Bertha is able to rip up Jane's veil, and in effect she is ripping up the illusion of Jane Rochester.

When Jane is finally confronted by Bertha it would seem as though they are polar opposites. Bertha is described as "a big woman: she showed virile force in the contest", whereas Jane is described as "this young girl who stands so grave and quiet". These differences only complete the picture of Jane and Bertha as one. Bertha is strong and big and able to overcome Rochester, while Jane is small and incapable of doing that. Bertha is able to shout and fight and show her anger at confinement, while Jane is quietly resolved to deal with it. Jane comes close to the insanity she experienced in the red room once again when she decides she must leave Rochester. Staying as Rochester's mistress would make her along the lines of Bertha. Jane believes if she stays with Rochester she will fall into a moral madness:

> I was experiencing an ordeal: a hand of fiery iron grasped my vitals. Terrible moment: full of struggle blackness, burning! No human being that ever lived could wish to be loved better then I was loved; and him who thus loved me I absolutely worshipped: and I must renounce love and idol.

The hand of fiery iron is that same suffocation Jane experiences in her confinement. The language of fiery blackness and burning makes Jane's mental state seem almost like hell. She once again becomes the love mad woman by her choice in order not to become the moral mad woman as Bertha did.

Jane's stay with her cousins at Moor house just shows her force of will. Jane once again goes back to the confinement of the monotony of life that she felt at Lowood. She lives in her love mad state for lack of Rochester but she does not believe that she does not deserve love because otherwise she would have married St. John. The fact that she does not marry St. John is proof that Jane is the "new" love mad woman. Though she feels the desertion of her over (through his immorality), she does not let complete madness overcome her. Jane continues her independent, rebellious thoughts and is able to stand up to the patriarch cal society she lives in though her ability to remain without a man in her life.

Jane is finally purged of her love mad state with the purging of Bertha through her suicide. In her dreams, Jane dreams herself of dropping the child she had to carry. Jane is essentially dropping the madness that she had to carry. With one last act Bertha is able to do something Jane could not, she destroys Thornfield, which is a symbol of confinement for both women. With Bertha out of the way and Jane independent due to her inheritance, she is finally able to find true love. She finds Rochester in his mutilated state and confirms her status when she tells Rochester "no, sir; I am an independent woman now". With this statement Jane affirms that she is in control of her will and it is her decision to be with him. With Bertha dead, Jane's love for Rochester can no longer be seen as madness for Jane is now in control of the love. Jane, by being independent, is not controlled by a patriarchal society and the love mad woman has served her purpose of breaking the binds of which she was confined under.

Jane Eyre is definitely an example of the new love mad woman. is able to use her and Bertha as a voice to express her feelings toward the society that she lived in. Jane Eyre was able to overcome the love mad repression of a male-dominated society. This is what was able to do: she took the old character of the love mad woman, who can be seen as the prototype for the weak, dependent female, and made her to be an object of rebellion. She used this madness to show that women have feelings worth showing, and that if they do show their true emotions, they too can have the happy ending.

The Fated Modernist Heroine: Female Protagonists in Jane Eyre and Wide Sargasso Sea

Q. Is Charlotte Bronte's novel an inspiration of Wide Sargasso Sea?

Or

Q. What are the similar attributes in the female protagonists of both the novels?

Jean Rhys's Wide Sargasso Sea is a modernist revision of Charlotte Brontë's Jane Eyre. The female protagonists of both novels share many traits of character and circumstance, most notable of which being a marriage to Mr. Rochester. Jane can assert notions of female individuality and self-respect because she operates in a society based on Christian virtues of justice and fairness. The modernist revision by Rhys, however, defines the world as a rotting paradise, literally a place where the values of Jane's world fail to exist. Antoinette Cosway, the fated of Wide Sargasso Sea, is culturally divided between worlds of hating races. This racial tension not only undermines any feelings of security she might possess but fatally marks Antoinette as a character unable to survive in an immoral universe. Good and evil become indistinguishable as races mix; misfortune becomes obvious as a paradise based on merciless slavery attempts to right itself.

The blacks of Jamaica have been emancipated, yet justice exists nowhere for the female hero. Whereas Jane Eyre details a woman's relentless struggle for emotional and spiritual satisfaction, Wide Sargasso Sea depicts a woman unable to find security because of the burdens of her society. An incompatible marriage, a familial history of madness — these are simply struggles that Antoinette attempts to endure. But the proverbial garden has already fallen, and as a woman she is banished to a world of pain and frustration where she has no control.

Antoinette's problems are deeply rooted in colonialism. The violence of both her family's and country's pasts have hindered her ability to live a full, happy life. Antoinette becomes obsessed with security and protection, looking for comfort with the victims of slavery. Rhys's postcolonial lens characterizes Antoinette as existing between the harshly divided worlds of blacks and whites, between formers slaves and former slave owners. As a Creole woman, Antoinette's relationship to the black population combines hatred and pity, wants of acceptance and desires for separation. During such an ebb and flow of emotions Antoinette first forms a relationship with, a black girl of approximately the same age. After blacks set fire to Coulibri, the family escapes from ther burning mansion, and Antoinette runs toward. She is unable to hate the blacks despite their violent reactions to her presence: "As I ran I thought, I will live with and I will be like her. Not to leave Coulibri. Not to go. Not"Antoinette identifies with a different racial group, at the same time that she flees from the result of its violent actions. She cannot fully come to terms with her own guilt and its resulting isolation.

Antoinette's life becomes a continuous struggle to find a place where she may be happy and peaceful. She exists in a society in which actions have no redemptive value. Antoinette's notion that she could in fact live and thrive among a different race deteriorates after her interaction with. literally shatters the idea when she throws a rock that pierces Antoinette's face, causing her to bleed: "When I was close I saw the jagged stone in her hand but did not see her throw it. I did not feel it either, only something wet, running down my face. I looked at her and I saw her face crumple up as she began to cry. We stared at each other, blood on my face, tears on hers. It was if I saw myself. Like in a looking glass". This act confirms that Antoinette is not wanted by the black population; she must remain separate and isolated from them, despite her intense desire to gain safety and security among them. Her reference to a looking glass is at once absurd and at the same time crucial to understanding the roots of her fate. Her connection to a crying symbolizes her connection to both pain and suffering. Antoinette's face bleeds, demonstrating a physical pain. Yet, she internalizes 's tears and makes them her own as she realises that she can no longer be comfortable with an identity that straddles such opposing worlds. This rift is later a major source of her complete emotional breakdown.

Although both Jane Eyre and Wide Sargasso Sea concern issues of justice and social fairness, these novels operate in entirely different settings. The settings created by both authors clearly connect to their beliefs whether or not good and evil are separate entities and whether or not the universe is an inherently fair place. Jamaica, the setting of much of Wide Sargasso Sea, is a lost Eden — full of social injustice and cultural tension. Despite her estrangement from much of her home's population, Antoinette has an affinity for this land. She is engrossed by its exoticism and wildness, yet at the same time she understands that its forbidding future is both harsh and bleak. It is almost as if the lush wildness of her home has become too ripe and is beginning to rot: "Our garden was large and beautiful as that garden in the Bible — the tree of life grew here. But it had grown wild.

The paths were overgrown and a smell of dead flowers mixed with that fresh living smell." The Biblical reference to the lost paradise continues: "Orchids flourished out of reach or for some reason not to be touched. One was snaky looking, another like an octopus with long thin brown tentacles bare of leaves hanging from a twisted root" (Rhys p. 19). Almost all that had previously existed in a peaceful harmony had become a changing, dying place. Rhys does not doubt the proverbial garden's existence, but she sees its demise as a result of a society built on human suffering. Those still living in this dying place are therefore banished to a life of uncertain moral footing and unclear values.

Antoinette and Rochester's marriage, and its eventual unraveling, exemplifies the immoral world view of Rhys. Antoinette thrives during the early part of her honeymoon; physical pleasure is only matched with her thrill of isolated happiness. Yet Rochester fails to offer the protection for which his new bride yearns, remaining emotionally and morally unformed. Antoinette offers herself to Rochester in every possible way, but he refuses to give any of himself. He is a cold Englishman, incapable of aiding his Creole bride to find any semblance of safety in his arms. "'You are safe,' I'd say. She'd like that — to be told 'you are safe.' Or I'd touch her face gently and touch tears. Tears — nothing! Words — less than nothing. I did not love her. I was thirsty for her, but that is not love. I felt very little tenderness for her, she was a stranger to me, a stranger who did no think or feel as I did," (Rhys, p. 93). Rochester finds Antoinette's otherness greatly incompatible with his personal feelings, although he intellectually comprehends her desires. He is aware, yet unable to act accordingly. Unlike the Rochester who appears in Brontë's novel, Rhys's character does not grow morally or spiritually.

Rhys's Rochester believes that life in Jamaica may exist with different rules and requirements than those of Victorian English society. Rochester does not grant legitimacy to his marriage, his wife, or the land he temporarily occupies. Like Rhys, Rochester sees no moral hierarchy to dictate his actions. The sensuality apparent during their honeymoon therefore reflects not only isolated episodes of sexual fulfillment but also a foreboding of the eventual unraveling of his marriage. He is initially intoxicated by her erotic sensuality, and comments, "one afternoon the sight of a dress which she'd left lying on her bedroom floor made me breathless and savage with desire," (Rhys, p. 93). He awakes, almost hung-over from love making, drunk with physical passion and emotional stagnation. He can put aside true consideration of his actions because he exists in a world that is not real to him — thus his use of the word "savage" to reflect feelings rooted not in his emotions but rather in his physical environment. He continually uses lunar images when describing his bride, for in reality he considers her a priority only in the hiding darkness of night. Antoinette has no chance of being a moral compass or emotional outlet for Rochester because he does not grant her any consideration during daytime hours.

Once the letter arrives from Daniel Cosway, which symbolizes the intrusion of the outside world, Antoinette cannot even occupy her husband's interests at bedtime. Once Rochester believes that his actions are being judged outside Granbois, he must consider everything with a distinctly upright edge. Acting with neither emotion nor love, Rochester avoids any morally ambiguous situation because he lacks the tools to make an informed decision regarding his actions. Apart from a corrupt colonial government, there is no overall force to distinguish good from evil. Neither legal nor spiritual laws apply to these lands, and Rochester does not bring with him any sense of right and wrong.

Rochester's reaction to the natural world of the Caribbean not only directly correlates to his feelings for his wife but also explains his inability to offer Antoinette any security. Rochester cannot rationally enjoy the natural beauty he sees and feels. Continually wishing to dominate, he is instantly at odds with tangible feelings in a way that he cannot define: "It was a beautiful place — wild, untouched, above all untouched, with an alien, disturbing secret loveliness.

And it kept its secret. I'd find myself thinking, "what I see is nothing — I want what it hides — that is not nothing" (Rhys, p. 87). Rochester is unable to simply enjoy the natural splendor of the islands because it threatens his strict, controlling character. Because he is not morally developed enough to appreciate the ambiguities of his surroundings, he comes to despise them: "I hated the mountains and the hills, the rivers and the rain. I hated the sunsets of whatever, I hated its beauty and its magic and the secret I would never know. I hated its indifference and the cruelty which was part of its loveliness." He continues relating the natural world to his wife, "Above all I hated her. For she belonged to the magic and the loveliness. She had left me thirsty and all my life would be thirst and longing for what I had lost before I found it" (Rhys, p. 172). Rochester looks to answer the undefined universe, to solve problems with answers he has yet to discover the questions for. Struggling to define this world is a fruitless pursuit because it is inherently incomprehensible and illogical.

The world of Wide Sargasso Sea is not the just and moral realm of Jane Eyre of which Brontë's Rochester is an obvious product. It is instead an incomprehensible sphere lacking absolute truths.

Daniel Cosway's letter to Mr.. Rochester traps Antoinette, cementing her fate as a feminine without the power to determine her own happiness. Rochester's reaction to it reveals his true feelings for Antoinette. It also reveals that he no longer perceives her as exotically alluring but savage and rude. It is of course an outside correspondence that changes Rochester's opinions of his bride. Again, Antoinette's cultural divide makes Rochester's classification that much easier to apply. She can longer able to align herself with the black population but remains tainted by any past association. Her world, unlike Jane Eyre's, holds no possibility for redemption. After running away from Thornfield in the middle of the night, Jane nearly perishes as she seeks shelter.

Turned away into cold, harsh rain, Jane prepares herself for death. St. John Rivers saves her just in time: "'All men must die, said a voice quite close at hand; 'but all are not condemned to meet a lingering and premature doom, such as yours would be if you perished here of want" (Brontë, p. 286). Jane's character exists in a world of continual hope, derived in part from her own spirituality and the Christian kindness of others. The world of Wide Sargasso Sea is tainted by colonialism and the slave trade. It is therefore impossible for Antoinette to improve her situation in a world where upward movement based on moral goodness does not exist.

The female s of both Jane Eyre and Wide Sargasso Sea rely upon various forms of spirituality during troubling times in their respective relationships with Mr.. Rochester. Whereas morality and spirituality unite in Jane Eyre, they do not in Rhys's novel. Jane is told to "flee temptation!" and a begging Rochester by the visage of her mother in a dream (Brontë, p. 272). She obliges and escapes into the night. Her faith allows Jane to persevere through harsh conditions she arrives at a minister's door. Wide Sargasso Sea entirely inverts such a notion of spirituality. Antoinette does look for guidance to the mother-figure of Christophine, but she wants to evoke temptation, not flee it. She turns to obeah, or black magic, to entice her husband, pleading, "Christophine, if he, my husband, could come to me one night. Once more I would make him love me" (Rhys, p. 113). She longs to return to those nights that characterized the beginning of her honeymoon, to those times when she could make Rochester drunk with pleasure. While Jane, moral and upright as ever, must fend off Rochester enticements, Antoinette uses so-called primitive means to allure her husband. These differing actions exist because the two characters exist in fundamentally different imagined worlds.

A meaningful, mutually fulfilling marriage between Antoinette and Rochester is not possible because they exist in world where temporary paradise was created by a gross social injustice. The setting Rhys creates is not capable of allowing a successful marriage between persons differing so greatly in their emotional needs. Brontë's imagined world is virtuous, clearly demonstrated by the way in which Rochester proposes to Jane. It is surely not an arranged marriage for profit as in Wide Sargasso Sea. It is an alliance of two people who need each other for emotional and spiritual satisfaction. Rochester's proposal to Jane is explicitly linked to a worship service: "He put me off his knee, rose and reverently lifting his hat from his brow, and bending his sightless eyes to the earth, he stood in mute devotion. Only the last words of the worship were audible" (Brontë, p. 382). Rochester's disability represents a moral resurrection; although physically blind, he can finally see his love for Jane clearly. Guided by a higher being, Rochester remedies his previously abhorrent behaviour: "'I thank my Maker that in the midst of judgment He has remembered mercy. I humbly entreat my Redeemer to give me strength to lead henceforth a purer life than I have done hitherto'" (Brontë, p. 382). Jane's happy ending, "Reader, I married him," is possible because of the spiritual and social forces Brontë creates in her imagined setting.

In contrast, Antoinette and Rochester's marriage in Jamaica, rather then representing the positive end result of a moral journey, is the beginning of the end for Antoinette. The marriage not only drives her mad but literally and figuratively separates her from her beloved homeland. She dies in England and comes to hate the lost paradise of the islands before her departure. Her failed relationship reveals the utter lack of redemption available to her. Robbed of her name, her spirit, and her money, Antoinette crumbles upon understanding that hope no longer exists in any capacity:

If my father, my real father was alive you wouldn't come back here in a hurry after he'd finished with you. If he was alive. Do you know what you've done to me? It's not the girl, not the girl. But I loved this place and you have made it into a place I hate. I used to think that if everything else went out of my life I would still have this, and now you have spoilt it. It's just somewhere else where I have been unhappy, and all the other things are nothing to what has happened here. I hate it now like I hate you and before I die I will show you how much I hate you.

The temporary paradise of Antoinette's childhood, to which she obviously refers in the mention of her father, was based upon human suffering. Antoinette, who has no hope in her present or past life, is forced to turn into herself. With Antoinette's insanity Rhys argues that justice is not available to any member of any race. Although the slave trade has officially ended, its consequences remain irreversible.

Greed is mentioned frequently in Wide Sargasso Sea, to explain both Rochester's motives for marrying Antoinette Cosway and the present chaos resulting from the slave trade. The paradise that Antoinette long searched for in her childhood and tried to possess during her honeymoon was constructed upon a great social injustice. Her marriage to Rochester was based on similarly wicked foundation, thus connecting her personal problems to the greater political dilemmas of her homeland. Antoinette, acting as the mad woman in the attic at Thornfield, states: "Then I heard a clock ticking and it was made of gold. Gold is the idol they worship" (Rhys, p. 188). The religious aspect so noticeable in Jane Eyre is not possible in Rhys's novel because of a spirituality directed to earthly possession and wealth.

Later Christophine criticizes Rochester's reasons for marrying Antoinette: "Everybody know that you marry her for her money and you take it all. And then you want to break her up, because you jealous of her. She is more better than you, she have better blood in her and she don't care for money — it's nothing for her" (Rhys, p. 152). The greed has overwhelmed most of the characters, and Antoinette's life has been ruined in the process. Those interested in financial gain exemplify a wicked world where actions do not have direct consequences. True Christian justice does not exist in this modern novel because no character can right the wrongs of his or her past. Rhys's characters have less possibility for salvation than Brontë's Victorian ones, simply because their world is not fair or ordered.

If Wide Sargasso Sea begins after the fall of Eden, Jane Eyre ends with its re-creation. These novels work towards different directions — Wide Sargasso Sea details the demise of the in an unjust world whereas Jane Eyre depicts a protagonist able to find fulfillment in the presence of a spiritual justice. In following the progression of Jane's character, the reader cannot help but notice her gratitude to a benevolent world order. Her happy ending is clearly a result of a world where salvation is possible: "I hold myself supremely blest — blest beyond what language can express; because I am my husband's life as fully as he is mine. No woman was very nearer to her mate than I am; ever more absolutely bone of his bone and flesh of his flesh" (Brontë, p. 384). Not only does Jane's statement about her marriage to Rochester represent supreme happiness from her point of view, but it also makes a very important Biblical reference. She relates herself to Eve, created from the "bone" of Adam. By using the image of these characters from Genesis, Brontë emphasizes that she believes good and evil are fundamentally separate. By the end of her novel she has in fact reversed the Biblical tale, bringing Adam and Eve back to their enchanted paradise.

Jean Rhys's novel ends with the implied death of its; the woman surrenders after learning that not even human laws can bring order to her chaotic universe. Despite her trouble thoughts, Antoinette believes that she can legally change her position. Her step-brother, Richard Mason, comes to visit her at Thornfield and reveals that he is unable to legally intervene in her marital problems. Not even government intervention and human law can right the wrongs suffered by Antoinette; it is of course far too late for any type of spiritual remedy. Grace Poole describes Antoinette's desperate attempts to save herself from bitter unhappiness: "I was in the room but I didn't hear all he said except 'I cannot interfere legally between yourself and your husband'. It was when he said 'legally' that you flew at him and when he twisted the knife out of your hand you bit him" (Rhys, p. 184). With this last recourse abandoned, Antoinette finally takes action into her own hands, harming her brother and eventually trying to kill her husband. Her eventual death signifies that not even a woman's personal strength and determination are enough to correct a malevolent, patriarchal world order.

Although Rhys makes use of the exoticism and "otherness" of the Caribbean, she asserts that the unfairness suffered by Antoinette is not simply limited to the West Indies. Antoinette loses her life in England, in this "cold cardboard house where I walk at night" (Rhys, p. 181). Rhys's England is not like Brontë's, justice finds so meaning here. She mentions England in a worldly context, bringing to mind its far-reaching influences. As a postcolonial author, Rhys challengesthe notion of England as a bastion of justice and fairness: "England, rosy pink in the geography book map, but on the page opposite the words are closely crowded, heavy looking. Exports coal, iron, wool" (Rhys, p. 111). Antoinette, who fears a vast cultural change, also knows that Europe might hold problems of its own. Besides foreshadowing of her imminent demise in that foreign land, Antoinette's characterization of the place represents a voice from the colony. In examining the land of the colonizers, she firmly attests that it is to blame in part for the fall of a poorly constructed paradise. More than simply the slave owners have benefited from its riches, Rhys explains. There is notdefinite characteristic or place that frees a person from culpability in her imagined world.

The fire Antoinette creates at the close of Wide Sargasso Sea brings about the end of her struggle for happiness and security. Her fire clearly echoes the one set at Coulibri by the former slaves. In both instances the repressed act upon their oppressors, and we see a direct alignment with a group for which Antoinette could never completely belong. The end of Rhys's narrative demonstrates once and for all that redemption is not possible for the of her novel. The destruction of Coulibri by the emancipated blacks represented their desire to gain vengeance for the injustices they suffered; this act was their revolt against the oppressive forces of colonialism. Antoinette burns down Thornfield to battle the patriarchal forces that have kept her married to a man whom she despises.

The fire does not, however, bring about a happy ending for Antoinette — in fact Rochester is permitted to marry his true love. This unfairness is central to Wide Sargasso Sea's literary purpose: remedies fail to exist because of larger, structural imbalance. Coulibri's destruction gave only a momentary satisfaction to the former slaves forced to live still among postcolonial oppression, and the end of Thornfield simply meant the death of Antoinette Cosway and the marriage of Jane Eyre and Mr.. Rochester. The modernist 's life is a sacrifice to a world too corrupt to even notice.

The subversive structure of Wide Sargasso Sea's narrative not only reveals Rhys imagined worldview, but also demonstrates a fundamental difference in style from Jane Eyre. Brontë's work offers only Jane's perspective on the events that occur chronologically. Such a structure already has inherent order, an order that does not exist in any aspect of Wide Sargasso Sea. Rhys's novel has much displacement. The narrative moves forward at different paces, and certain flashbacks are described in various manners. More importantly, more than simply one character is granted an internal monologue in this novel. This barrage of voices appears to create a more chaotic setting, making it easier for Rhys to use a whose spirit is never able to find a comfortable and secure place. The increase in characters that are granted an internal voice only serves to create a more readily available sense of isolation: more characters speak through their thoughts because there is no other character suitable to relay their inner most emotions. Each statement offered points to the moral relativity of Wide Sargasso Sea. Without one direct narrator it is impossible to have one set of rules impartially applied to all.

Jean Rhys's attempt to reexamine a Victorian masterpiece is inherently political. One must read Wide Sargasso Sea with the analytic lenses of feminism, post colonialism, and modernism. From its narrative structure to the voices of its characters, this novel is clearly not a work of Victorian literature, despite its setting in that period. Antoinette Cosway, also known by Brontë's readers as Bertha Mason, is a female character unable ever to find security or happiness. The fallen paradise that surrounded her life in the Caribbean was never in fact a heaven-like place.

This fact plagues her internal demons as she desperately attempts to escape her fate as a tragic. Antoinette Cosway is divided between two cultures, and not simply between the black and white populations of Jamaica. She is caught between existing in a Victorian time characterized by a modern writer. Her allegiance to Victorian ideals explains why she fights so hard to keep her relationship with her husband and her isolated life at Granbois intact. It is, however, her modern characterization by Rhys that causes her to fail. She cannot survive an imagined world where justice is lost and actions are not redemptive. Jane Eyre's individuality and strong perseverance are only possible because she still exits in a just world. Chaos appears when that world begins to examine itself, free its slaves, and question the horrors of its past. It is in this chaos that Antoinette Cosway is burned alive.

Treating Bertha

Q. Discuss the treatment of lunatic people in Victorian age. Was it justified?

Or

Q. Does the condition of Bertha drive any sympathy from the readers towards her?

Or

Q. Does this treatment imply racism prevalent in that age?

The accepted treatment in the Victorian period for the wealthy who were insane was keeping them locked away in their homes. Bertha "had of course been shut up" upon being declared mad by a doctor reflects Victorian humanitarianism when she criticizes Rochester's treatment of Bertha. Elaine Showalter in *The Female Malady* states, "during the first half of the nineteenth century... the idea that... lunatic patients could be handled without resource to physical restraint won wide acceptance in England" (31). This type of treatment for the insane was named moral management. Moral management includes therapy, non-restraint, regular visits by a doctor, and a suitable "moral" environment to cure patients of their insanity. And yet, when he is unable to control Bertha, Rochester ties her up. Jane admonishes him, stating "'you are inexorable for that unfortunate lady.... It is cruel—she cannot help being mad"' (297; 27).

This reflects the Victorian disapproval of physically restraining the insane. They believed that therapy was a better, more humane treatment for mental illness than locking people away. Victorian psychiatry held that "violence of manic patients was in large part caused by the harsh way they were treated. Treating the patient like a rational person, they suggested, was the best way to cultivate the sense of self-esteem that would lead to self-control" (Showalter 31). The physical restraint that Rochester used would have been seen as outdated and non-productive by modern Victorian science.

By locking Bertha up, Rochester would not be seen as cruel, but merely outdated. The Madhouse Act (1828) and the Lunatics Act (1845) allowed for a more humane treatment of the mentally ill, providing a clean, safe environment to cure insanity. But the social stigma of having a mad wife is too great for Rochester. It would be unwise for Rochester to beat or use excessive force on Bertha, for he would be unable to recover any favorable opinion from the reader. When Bertha attacks him, Rochester "could have settled her with a well-planted blow; but he would not strike: he would only wrestle" (290; 26).

Conversely, allows a dig at moral management through the visit of Mason. Mason is attacked and severely wounded by Bertha. Rochester admonishes him saying, '"I warned you... I said—be your guard"' (213; 20) to which Mason answers, '"I thought I could have done some good"' (214; 20). Mason's treatment of Bertha reflects the moral management way of treating the insane—no restraint coupled with therapy. Neither the restraint of Rochester nor the moral management of Mason are successful with the ill fated Bertha. This ambiguity suggests two things: is suggesting either Bertha is beyond any type of help or treatment or she believes that neither moral management nor restraint are effectual. This ambiguity is reflected in Jane herself. On one hand she sympathizes with Bertha, defending her to Rochester. On the other hand she contributes to dehumanizing her as an animal and fearing her. Jane has sympathy for the insane but her feelings are not used to help.

Diagnosing Bertha

Q. "The insanity of Bertha is used as an effective plot driving device". Explain

Or

Q. Does Rochester find himself guilty for the condition of Bertha?

Or

Q. Up to what extent is Jane responsible for this insanity of Bertha?

By contemporary Victorian standards, of which Rochester and Jane are representatives, Bertha Rochester is insane. This fact is irrefutable due to the irrational, dangerous, and depraved behaviour she exhibits in the text as well as placing her within the Victorian definition of "insane." The causes of her madness though are questionable. Rochester would have us believe that her insanity was inherent in her family and it was her moral depravity, which caused her madness to surface.

Yet suggests that perhaps she did not become insane on her own—that the imposition of Victorian ideals of female behaviour, and her confinement by Rochester is the true instigator of her mental illness. By examining Jane's own experiences in her childhood we see how presents confinement and exile as a possible cause for an agitated mental state which madness can be inferred. Most convincingly, while Rochester may represent the common opinions on madness, we, the reader, are never given clear evidence of true mental illness before her confinement—only a refusal to conform to Victorian standards for women.

The figure of the "madwoman in the attic" is a popular device in Victorian literature. Bertha Rochester in *Jane Eyre* is the stereotypical representation of this character type. As a plot device she is effective: she adds mystery and a stunning story twist; she is the instigator of several thrilling events, including several murderous attempts; and finally, she is the cause of Rochester's disfigurement and poverty which allows him to be dependent on and equal to Jane. The reader is not given much direct information about the symptoms of Bertha's mental disorder though. Our only facts come from Jane, Rochester, and a nameless host at the inn from whom Jane learns of Bertha's death and Rochester's disfigurement.

We witness Bertha's destructive and violent tendencies—burning Rochester's bed and, ultimately, Thornfield; destroying Jane's veil; attacking Mason; and "haunting" the house with her mysterious laugh. These acts are not the cause of her illness but merely symptoms. To try to diagnose Bertha's illness in modern terms would be nearly impossible; we can must use Victorian psychiatric terminology to understand her diagnosis and her treatment.

Victorian psychiatry held that the beginnings of insanity was hereditary and was passed on through mothers (Showalter 67). As a true representative of his era, this is the first criterion, which Rochester uses in his diagnosis of Bertha's insanity. He states that his honeymoon with Bertha ended when he learned that his mother-in-law was "'mad, and shut up in a lunatic asylum"' (308; 27). As Showalter states, "'s account echoes the beliefs of Victorian psychiatry about the transmission of madness: since the reproductive system was the source of mental illness in women, women were the prime carriers of madness" (67).

Women were seen as especially susceptible to madness which is linked to their menstrual cycle. Doctors believed that either "an abnormal quantity or quality of the blood, according to this theory, could affect the brain" (56). It should be noted that Bertha's violent escapades are on nights when the moon is "blood-red" (227; 25) or "broad and red" (302; 27) while at other times she is quiet and calm. Her reproductive cycle, and her femininity is also seen to be a contribution to her insanity.

Rochester admits that there was nothing wrong with Bertha, per se, when he married her, telling Jane, "this was no lie. I found her a fine woman, in the style of Blanche Ingram; tall, dark, majestic... All the men in her circle seemed to admire her and envy me"' (307; 27). But he continues to describe Bertha's condition in the vaguest of terms as "corse and trite," woman who exhibits "outbreaks of... violent and unreasonable temper" (308; 27). These symptoms are, without question, purely subjective. What is "trite" to one may be very important to another. Bertha is diagnosed as insane by Rochester because he is imposing Victorian ideals about how wives should behave. They should be quiet, subservient, meek, and complementary to their husbands; from Rochester's description of her, it can be assumed that she was not the typical English wife.

Victorian psychiatry held that madness could stem from moral causes; be it jealousy, grief, alcoholism, or over stimulated sexuality. Rochester states that "her excesses had prematurely developed the germs of insanity" (309; 27). It was the excess of anything that Victorians abhorred. It cannot be refuted that when the reader encounters Bertha she is in fact insane—she is violent, incoherent, and animalistic. But does not fully accept Rochester's reason for her madness, even though it fits with contemporary Victorian psychology. By drawing comparisons between Jane and Bertha we see that the real root of Bertha's madness is Rochester himself, and thus, Victorian ideas of morality.

Rochester admits that after learning about Bertha's family medical history (an insane mother and an idiot brother) he starts to treat her differently:

> These were vile discoveries; but, except for the treachery of concealment, I should have made them no subject of reproach to my wife. Even when I found her nature totally alien to mine; her tastes obnoxious to me; her caste of mind common, low, narrow, and singularly incapable of being led to anything higher, expanded to anything larger... even then I restrained myself... I repressed the deep antipathy I felt. (308; 27)

This description of Bertha's faults are extremely vague and in no way describe mental illness in our modern definition. If Rochester had taken time to know Bertha Mason before marrying her he might have discovered her failings, instead he, in "the blindness of youth" (307; 27) rushed into marriage. It merely sounds as if they are incompatible as husband and wife. Rochester never gives specifics about her initial spiral into madness, instead, he states, "I will not trouble you with abominable details" (308; 27) and reveals only that "her character ripened... only cruelty could check them" (308; 27). Herein is where the true cause of Bertha's madness lies.

It could be assumed, without any specific text evidence, that Bertha was in love with Rochester but he aggressively spurns her love, friendship, or companionship as is shown by his total revulsion of her character as quoted earlier (308; 27). She becomes more and more aggressive in her desire for Rochester which Victorians in turn interpret as "intemperate and unchaste" (309; 27). Rochester brings doctors to see Bertha and "since the medical men had pronounced her mad, she had of course been shut up" (310; 27).

This chain of events fit perfectly with the Victorian definition of moral insanity. Her sexual desires and excesses break Victorian taboos, and only those who are insane would violate these laws. Factually, a doctor would have been brought in to declare insanity and an acceptable treatment for upper class "lunatics" was to shut them up in an attic or ship them to the continent. It is only behind locked doors that Bertha becomes the animalistic lunatic who violently attacks and destroys. This confinement is a direct parallel of Jane's confinement at Gateshead.

After one of Jane's childhood arguments with John Reed, she is punished by being locked in the red-room. While there, she becomes afraid. Jane describes the mental process she experienced in confinement: "shaken as my nerves were by agitation... My heart beat thick, my head grew hot; a sound filled my ears, which I deemed the rushing of wings... I was oppressed, suffocated: endurance broke down" (19; 2). These feelings cause Jane to scream and call out. When help arrives, Mrs. Reed abhors her actions which she describes as "violence" (20; 2). The parallels between Jane's and Bertha's confinements are confirmed when Mrs. Reed, on her death bed, describes Jane as "incomprehensible" (233; 21), remembers that "she talked to me once like something mad" (233; 21).

Both Jane and Bertha are guilty of not conforming to the traditional roles they are expected to fill in society. Puberty was an especially trying time for Victorian girls due to their "growing awareness of this social dependence and constraint, the realization of her immobility and disadvantage as compared with her brothers, and other boys, may well have precipitated an emotional crisis" (Showalter 57). Jane's childhood experience in the red room is a metaphorical example of this confinement which she tries to rebel against.

Jane does not fit Mrs. Reed's qualifications as a perfect daughter, and Bertha does not fit into Rochester's definition of an ideal wife. Both Mrs. Reed and Rochester hold preconceived notions of guilt over Jane and Bertha, respectively, which taint their judgement of madness or sanity. Madness is easier to assign than hatred because connotes the existence of a relationship; madness merely renders the insane subhuman. Often animal imagery is used to describe Jane in her youth and Bertha such as "clothed hyena," "wild beast," and "demon" (26, 27). Jane understands the misunderstandings that can lead to a diagnosis of madness because of her experiences at Gateshead and so she sympathizes with Bertha stating that Rochester is "inexorable for that unfortunate lady: you speak of her with hate, with vindictive antipathy. It is cruel, she cannot help being mad" (301; 27). is making a statement here about female insanity.

She is speaking against the common practice of locking a woman up, isolated and confined. Both Jane and Bertha are forced with confinement, but Jane is able to succeed and be defined as "sane" because she is able to adapt to the system. Whether Bertha was ever truly mad is never known because Rochester locks her up and thus contributes to her madness. Rochester's behaviour is socially acceptable by the Victorians and yet Jane criticizes him because she can see that perhaps her moral foibles were correctable as were hers. Yet, because Jane is also part of the Victorian belief system of morals she cannot help but agree and contribute to hiding Bertha in the attic through her silence and inaction.

From the Attic to the Asylum

Q. Why Bertha was shifted from her house at Thornfield to a proper asylum?

Or

Q. Was insanity considered as an act of embarrassment for the Victorian society? Explain.

Bertha Rochester is considered insane both by Rochester and by the common opinion of the day. She is kept locked on the third floor of Thornfield instead of being placed in an asylum for therapy. While Bertha's treatment would not necessarily have been regarded as terribly cruel, it would not be considered as the best or most modern approa Jane Eyre was written after the Madhouse Act (1828) and Lunatics Act (1845), which provided for a safer, more controlled environment in which to keep the insane. The implementation of moral management in the asylums made them more modern, humane, and medically sound.

Yet, the action in the novel takes place before these two acts and so the contemporary audience may have considered Rochester keeping Bertha locked in the house as outdated. But still, keeping the insane at home would have been an alternative to the embarrassment of public committal to an asylum. Elaine Showalter summarizes in her study The Female Malady: Women, Madness and English Culture, 1830-1980, in the chapter titled "Domesticating Insanity" (26-27) how class played a part in keeping the insane at home or committing them to an asylum: Class remained a strong determinant of the individual's psychiatric career. The rich could avoid the stigma of certification by keeping mad relatives at home, or by seeking private care. Among the wealthier classes, bizarre behaviour could be described as nervousness or eccentricity until the patient became unmanageable, suicidal, or violent. For a steep price, the rich lunatic might be put to lodge with a doctor who specialized in the discreet care of a few eccentric "guests"; sent to one of the large private asylums that catered to the rich, such as Laverstock House or Ticehurst; or shipped off to be hidden away in a Continental maison de sante.

The middle classes regarded the public asylums as a disgrace, the "Bluebeard's cupboard" of the neighborhood, "an evil to be staved off as long as possible." When institutionalization became unavoidable, they sought out the cheaper private asylums, or the registered hospitals such as Bethlem and St. Luke's, where most patients paid a small fee. But insanity was an expensive disease, especially when it struck down the family breadwinner, and thus middle-class patients too were often forced to seek public assistance.

For the poor, however, the public asylum was a welcome alternative to the workhouse or the home care.... So, while the asylum was considered to be a system of national pride and modern advancement for the Victorians, insanity was still considered embarrassing. Rochester's confinement of Bertha then would have been within the bounds of acceptability.

Woman as Demon

Q. "The other evil side of women is also depicted in novel" Discuss

Women in Victorian literature were considered to have "the other side" or more in direct terms, as somehow demonized. This is certainly true in *Jane Eyre*. Bertha Mason, Rochester's mad wife, is the epitome of the demon in the attic. By virtue of being the first wife she is in continually compared to Jane. Although there are parallels in plot and language between the two women, they are completely different people.

In addition, also depicts other women throughout the novel as something to be feared. Whereas earlier in English literature, men were typically depicted as monsters, in the nineteenth century women came to be seen as threatening creatures. They entrap men through their sexuality and then reveal their true demon-like natures.

Just as Jane is the angel in the house, Bertha represents her opposite—the demon in the house. Jane is a sobre, sturdy Englishwoman of scrupulous morals. Bertha Mason, even before she goes mad, is depicted as an excitable foreigner of unacceptable values descended from a family of lunatics and idiots. She is shown as the exotic temptress whom Rochester cannot resist. He tells Jane:

She flattered me, and lavishly displayed for my pleasure her charms and accomplishments. All the men in her circle seemed to admire her and envy me. I was dazzled, stimulated my senses were excited; and being ignorant, raw, and inexperienced, I thought I loved her (332; 27)

Bertha's behaviour is diametrically opposed to Jane's. Jane does not flatter Rochester or over-stimulate his senses. is presenting readers with an ideal relationship as Jane and Rochester's marriage is not based on flirtation or lust alone. Bertha Mason is depicted as an Eve-like temptress devoid of any sense of morality. Rochester, lamenting his marriage to Jane, explodes "With less sin I might have—but let me remember to whom I am speaking" (333; 27). Even though Rochester leaves the final word out, the meaning is obvious. He might have made Bertha his mistress. By this exclamation, he is asserting his physical lust for her and his belief that he could have made her his lover, hence, his assertion that she possesses few morals. He is also making a major distinction between Bertha and Jane, in that he will not even finish speaking of these sordid affairs with Jane.

In addition to being represented as the seductress, Bertha is now shown in all her animal nature. Whereas before her madness, she lived solely for her animal appetites, now she has been reduced to the animal physical state as well. This reduction to bestiality is shown on various occasions when she is referred to as "a wolfish thing," "a dog," and "a tigress" (335; 27, 238; 20, 241; 20). But it is her comparison to a "clothed hyena" that is alluded to most often (321; 26). Helen Small, in her study *Love's Madness*, notes, "The animal's perceived sexual ambivalence and its association with female revenge continued through to the nineteenth century" (159). Bertha's sexuality and desire for her revenge are something to be greatly feared by men.

Female madness itself seems to be associated with the demonic. Bertha goes from sexual seducer to something bestial because of her lack of morals. The idea of moral insanity was growing in the nineteenth century. J. C. Prichard, physician to the Bristol Royal Infirmary and St. Peter's Hospital in Bristol, defined moral insanity as "a morbid perversion of the natural feelings, affections, inclinations, temper, habits, and moral dispositions, without any notable lesion of the intellect or knowing and reasoning faculties" (Small 163-64). Thus, one sees Bertha herself at fault for her condition. It is because of her lack of will and dissolute lifestyle that she is judged by society as mad. Rochester explains to Jane when he realised his wife's true nature. He states:

Her character ripened and developed with frightful rapidity; her vices sprang up fast and rank...Bertha Mason, the true daughter of an infamous mother, dragged me through all the hideous and degrading agonies which must attend a man bound to a wife at once intemperate and unchaste. (333-34; 27)

Bertha is exposed as being sexually promiscuous. The language Rochester uses to describe her is frightening; it is as if a real demon is being born in front of the reader's eyes. Rochester finally realises Bertha's demonic nature. He also tells the wedding party that she is an alcoholic: "Her mother, the Creole, was both a madwoman and a drunkard!... Bertha, like a dutiful child, copied her parent in both points" (320; 26). She is depicted as being excessive in both vices. These are the true signs of a woman with a weak will.

Charlotte viewed this type of insanity as hideous. This is shown in a letter she wrote to a reader of *Jane Eyre*, W.S. Williams:

> There is a phase of insanity, which may be called moral madness, in which all that is good or even human seems to disappear from the mind a fiend-like nature replaces it. The sole aim of the being thus possessed is to exasperate, to molest, to destroy, and preternatural ingenuity and energy are often expressed to that dreadful end. The aspect in such cases, assimilates with the disposition; all seems demonized. (qtd. in Small 165)

Thus, Bertha's previous lifestyle combines with her tendency for madness to make her illness a form of moral madness. Through her degeneration resulting from her lack of a solid moral system, she becomes the vision of woman as demon.

Although Bertha and Jane are clearly contrasting characters, it is important to note similarities in their positions and the plots that engage them at Thornfield Hall. Bertha is literally trapped in the mansion and Jane feels figuratively trapped. Jane paces the attic floor when she felt extremely restless and closed in: "Then my sole relief was to walk along the corridor of the third story, backwards and forwards, safe in the silence and solitude of the spot, and allow my mind's eye to dwell on whatever bright visions rose before it" (141; 12). This is reminiscent of Bertha's continual pacing and running about in her attic cell. It is important to note also that the two women are really only separated at this moment by one wall.

Another similarity between the two characters lies in the language Rochester uses to describe them. He often associates the women with the supernatural. Bertha has a "goblin appearance" (336; 27) and he often refers to Jane as a "malicious elf" or a "sorceress" (150; 13, 180; 15). Jane, however, soon turns into Rochester's angel while Bertha always remains the demon that must be imprisoned in the attic.

Some critics have suggested that Bertha represents Jane's double—that in fact, they are not opposite characters. They believe Jane and Bertha are mirror images, with Bertha representing Jane's repressed self. They contend that Bertha is the embodiment of Jane's frustration at being perceived as virtually powerless. Gilbert and Gubar contend "Bertha, in other words, is Jane's truest and darkest double: she is the angry aspect of the orphan child, the ferocious secret self Jane has been trying to repress ever since her days at Gateshead" (360).

This view of Bertha as Jane's double is a strained interpretation of the text, as many other critics have contended: "In seeing parallels between Bertha and Jane, and in turning Jane into the mirror image of Bertha critics ignore obvious differences between the small poor sobre chaste Jane and her large loose-living predecessor". They are extremely different characters, as Rochester asserts when he compares the two women. When Jane and Bertha first come directly face to face, he notes "'That is my wife...And this is what I wished to have... this young girl, who stands so grave and quiet at the mouth of hell, looking collectively at the gambols of a demon'" (322; 26). Rochester, who so often has called Jane his angel, firmly shows the difference between her and his "demon-wife." Small believes that is emphatically stating Jane and Bertha are opposite characters: "The taste, current in earlier romantic fiction, for symbolic alliances between a sympathetic female lead and a mad 'other woman' is invoked only to be firmly repudiated" (167). Thus, many critics do not agree with Gilbert and Gubar's radical interpretation of the novel.

There are two other characters presented in the novel as sexual (or potential) temptresses. These characters are also contrasted with Jane as the "exotic other," frivolous and flirtatious. Rochester has a problem, in that he continually looks toward superficiality to make him happy until he meets Jane, his "angel," who saves him. He can not see beyond hypocrisy, deceit, or physical lust. This is how Bertha entraps him into marriage and, his French mistress, gets him to "keep" her. Rochester can never see without thinking of her mocking him with her lover. He had thought of her as his idol to be worshipped, as his description of to Jane shows: so I sat down in her budoir, happy to breathe the air consecrated so lately by her presence. No—I exaggerate; I never thought there was any consecrating virtue about her; it was rather a sort of pastille perfume she had left, a scent of musk and amber, than an odour of sanctity. (172; 15)

He had wanted to adore, but she was not in the manner of a Mary—she was an Eve, the untrustworthy seducer. She is only associated with sexuality, hence the odor of musk and amber. These are physical, lusty scents. is also shown to have no moral system in that she abandons her six-year old daughter to the "slime and mud of Paris" (176; 15). She is depicted as a demon and an unnatural woman.

Adele, although such a young child, is at first presented in a negative light. She attempts to practice her mother's arts; she begs for presents, pouts when she does not get her way, and loves to be the center of attention. "She longs for fashionable gowns rather than for love or freedom, and the way her mother did, sings and dances for her supper as if she were a clockwork temptress" (Gilbert and Gubar 350). Adele believes at first that these arts will get her what she desires; however, she needs to learn to rely on herself and her own appropriate moral system. She is in danger of becoming a full-grown demonic seducer. It is only when she becomes Anglicized and loses her French faults that she is able to shed the demon stigma. Jane tells the reader, "As she grew up, a sound English education corrected in a great measure her French defects; and when she left school, I found in her a pleasing companion—docile, good-tempered, and well-principled" (475; 38). Thus, it is only through Jane's help and a proper English school that Adele ceases to be the exotic seducer.

Many women in nineteenth century literature were depicted as demonized or something to be greatly feared either because of their sexuality or their resulting madness. Often times, these women were stereotyped as the "exotic other," such as Adele and Varens. This is also true of Bertha Mason, Rochester's Creole wife, who has become a prisoner in the attic because of her madness. Bertha is often compared with Jane because of similar plot twists, but they are clearly intended as opposite characters. Because of Bertha's lax moral system she becomes prey to her own excesses. She suffers from moral madness which results from her lack of morality, and she is now depicted in all her brutish, vicious nature.

Woman as Angel

Q. How in this novel a woman is depicted as an angel?

Jane Eyre, at first, challenges the widespread Victorian concept of woman as the angel of the house or the domestic goddess. However, upon closer inspection the novel upholds this belief, which is demonstrated by the who conforms to this role by the end of the novel. Jane presents a problem in the beginning of the novel because she cannot fit into this narrow model. The woman as angel is a middle-class belief and Jane is by birth of this class, but she does not possess the monetary means to assume her place in it. She is rebellious and temperamental in her youth and is financially dependent on others throughout most of the novel. It is only through her continuing education from other women, like Miss Temple and the Rivers sisters, and eventual financial independence that she comes to embody the middle-class ideal of a domestic angel.

Prior to the Victorian era, in the English literary tradition, writers like Milton and Shakespeare depicted angels as heroic male characters. Throughout *Paradise Lost* and Shakespeare's major plays, angels were shown as having a definite purpose, which usually involved performing some heavenly errand like delivering a message from God. In the nineteenth century, however, this began to change. Nina Auerbach, in *Woman and the Demon,* notes that "Victorian England... cast angels as irrefutably female and by definition domestic, rather than as the striding martial and potentially bisexual males they had been". Through this widespread ideal of the period and such literary works as Coventry Patmore's "Angel in the House"—the 1854 poetic rendering of married love—came the notion of woman as a domestic goddess. The domestic goddess was to provide a comfortable sanctuary for her husband after his long day of work. As a result, the woman transformed into the guiding light of the family sphere.

Jane, however, is not yet the angelic middle-class wife. She is financially dependent on her employment by Mr.. Rochester. Although her birth status is middle-class, she does not possess the monetary requirements to technically be of that class. In the first half of the novel, she is not on a comparable social footing with Rochester. This is the barrier she must overcome to fully assume the role of angel of the house. Even if Jane is not conscious that she is not yet an angel, Mr.. Rochester certainly seems to be. During her life at Thornfield Hall, Rochester continually likens Jane to many non-angelic things. In their first formal encounter, he accuses her of causing his horse to fall. Rochester says to her, "'When you came on me in Hay Lane last night, I thought unaccountably of fairy tales, and had half a mind to demand whether you had bewitched my horse: I am not sure yet'". He, at first, cannot see her for the angel she will become, for this can only happen after she becomes financially independent.

This freedom is brought about during Jane's stay with the two other angel figures in the novel, Diana and Mary Rivers. These women turn out to be Jane's long lost relatives. It is their brother whom discovers the family connection and Jane's subsequent inheritance. It is significant that it is these good angels who take Jane in just as she is on the verge of death. Even their names are allegorical in that they "recall the Great Mother in her dual aspects of Diana the huntress and Mary the virgin mother". Even though the middle-class angelic role is a Christian ideal, it should be noted that Diana is a pagan goddess. However, Diana is associated with chastity and virtue. These women are instrumental in Jane's education of prudence and the pleasures of domesticity.

Jane explains that she idolizes them and attempts to emulate their behaviour: "I liked to read what they liked to read: what they enjoyed, delighted me; what they approved I reverenced. They loved their sequestered home" Although the Rivers sisters are not married, their brother serves as the domestic equal of a husband, and together they form a household. Through them, Jane is provided with a well-rounded version of angels of the house with which to model herself after.

Eventually, she gains enough inheritance to make herself a gentlewoman. Therefor, she goes to Rochester on an equal social level. Jane exhibits a middle-class mentality that is consistent with the domestic goddess when she decides to take care of Adele at the end of the novel. Jane decides to remove Adele from the boarding school in order to educate her at home: "I meant to become her governess once more, but I soon found this impracticable; my time and cares were now required by another—my husband needed them all". Jane becomes the guiding light and support of her family. She now takes care of Rochester's needs and truly becomes his angel. She no longer works in the care of others; instead, all her time and efforts are spent on her husband, which is the middle-class role of the angel in the house.

Jane began her education in rationality thereby taming her rebellious spirit with Miss Temple at Lowood School. Jane's teacher's name is especially significant because she represents all the angelic piety and peace of mind Jane would like to possess. In the novel, Miss Temple is described "As if invented by Coventry Patmore or by Mrs. Sarah Ellis, that indefatigable writer of conduct books for Victorian girls; she dispenses food to the hungry, visits the sick, encourages the worthy, and averts her glance from the unworthy". She is the ideal mother, the guiding inspirational light of her family (in this case, a family of girls). Jane also learns from Miss Temple that a woman eventually needs a husband in order to fulfill the role of the angel in the house. For instance, Jane states, "destiny, in the shape of the Rev. Mr. Nesmith, came between me and Miss Temple. Miss Temple's marriage is significant because this is what ends her relationship with Jane.

The angel in the house not only acts in the domestic sphere, but she functions in the spiritual as well. She becomes elevated almost to the level of an icon, like a Mary figure to worship. Due the fact that religion cannot necessarily be counted on to support people in times of need, many transferred these religious feelings onto other objects. Many men chose to direct this worship onto women: "The outworn love and agony of Christ on the Cross are translated into the vividly contemporary love and agony of the Angel in the House". Thus, in one sense, the woman became the man's ideal to love and worship.

This form of love is the kind Rochester develops for Jane, and she fulfills it by symbolically redeeming him twice in the novel. The first time occurs when she agrees to marry him. Rochester declares, "'Ten years since, I flew through Europe half-mad: with disgust, hate, and rage as my companions; now I shall visit it healed and cleansed, with a very angel as my comforter'". The second time she saves him, at the end of the novel, is when he has learned the error of his ways and proclaims his new closeness with God. At this point, he is and learns, through Jane, not to tempt the ways of God. Bigamy is a grave sin in the Anglican Church, and it is seen as deceit before the very altar of God. By the end of the novel, when Jane begins to see herself in the role of the savior, she can fully assume her role as angel: In Rochester's conversion and salvation, Jane recognizes herself as the humble instrument of divine providence. Thus the solitary, yearning for freedom and action ends by playing the role prescribed for women in family and society, that of moral Guide and Angel of the Home.

It is not until Jane has completed her education through becoming more rational, domestic, financially independent, and able to see herself in the role of savior, that she can truly become the middle-class angel figure.

Although the Victorian concept of the angel was de-sexualized, it is important to note that Jane is not a prude merely because she subscribes to the angel mythology of the day. Even though she is a chaste English woman, she is also a human being with wants and desires. It would be a contradiction in ideology for her to be frigid because a woman is the mother figure of the household and is designed to produce heirs. understands this and acknowledges the attraction and duty a woman should have towards the man she wishes to be her husband. One critic of the novel, Tom Winnifrith, notes:

Hostile criticism of *Jane Eyre* and her own conventional church upbringing would seem to have led to feel that a woman's sexual needs could not and should not be openly expressed. Yet she acknowledged the presence of these needs and despised the conventions in which they were masked, while recognizing the need for a moral framework to control them.

is not disapproving of sexual attraction between Jane and Rochester, but she realises that it must be tempered. This is why she does not let Jane become Rochester's mistress. It is not until he can legitimately marry her that any sort of sexual union is achieved. When Jane understands his plans to whisk her off to the south of France, she emphatically declares, "'I do love you... more than ever: but I must not show or indulge the feeling; and this is the last time I must express it'. Due to the fact that Jane has a strong moral background, she would rather abandon her love than become Rochester's mistress.

The Victorian concept of the woman as the angel of the house was a middle-class ideal. Jane presents a problem with this role because she is middle-class, but she does not have the monetary status to fully be of the class. It is not until she becomes educated in the virtues of patience, domesticity, rationale and becomes financially independent, thereby gaining her place in the middle-class, that she assumes her role as a domestic angel. Through the models of Miss Temple and the two Rivers sisters, she slowly emerges as the angel by the end of the novel.

Poking the Eye of the Beholder: Triumph of the Plain in *Jane Eyre*

Q. "A woman is the one who has an enchanting natural beauty" Explain

Convinced that the beautiful her sisters portrayed in their novels were a disservice to their readers, Charlotte deliberately set out to create the anti- that became Jane Eyre.

She once told her sisters that they were morally wrong - in making their s beautiful as a matter of course. They replied that it was impossible to make a interesting on any other terms. Her answer was "I will prove to you that you are wrong; I will show you a as plain and small as myself, who shall be as interesting as any of yours." could well be considered a proto-feminist. She was clearly rebelling against Victorian literary conventions, which typically reflect, says Reed, "certain fears, anxieties and desires of Victorian men". That was successful in revolutionizing the Victorian is evident in the term "post-Jane " which indicates a departure from the "sweet and submissive s" found elsewhere in the literature of the period. In *Jane Eyre*, firmly rejects Victorian ideals of beauty (most notably the "ne plus ultra" female and the classical Greek male) in favor of a spiritually and intellectually superior, if plain,.

Why was Jane's plainness so extraordinary? In an era when the elabourate and the ornate were considered most attractive (in everything from architecture and furniture to hairstyles), Jane, with her "Quakerish" black frocks and hair "combed behind her ears" is refreshing in her simplicity. In "plain Jane" (her name itself is suggestive of a new type of, according to Gilbert and Gubar), offers a character whose interior self actually surpasses the exterior in beauty. With a typical Victorian obsession for physical appearance, Jane gives many descriptions of herself, as well as others' responses to her appearance. Jane recalls with painful awareness the deficiencies of her physical appearance even in the earliest chapters of her autobiography. If her state of "dependence" causes her only vague grief, her plainness is a constant reminder of her "outsider" status at Gateshead. She is "the strange little figure there... with a white face and arms specking the gloom...". Even at an early age, Jane recognizes the power held by the beautiful.

At Gateshead, the selfish Georgiana is not just tolerated but adored, simply because she is pretty: "Georgiana, who had a spoiled temper, a very acrid spite, a captious and insolent carriage, was universally indulged. Her beauty, her pink cheeks, and golden curls, seemed to give delight to all who looked at her, and to purchase indemnity for every fault". Young Jane recognizes that even now her situation is tied to her physical appearance: "I know that had I been a... handsome child—though equally dependent and friendless—Mrs. Reed would have endured my presence more complacently". It also seems she is not alone in this estimation; her only friend at Gateshead, Bessie, agrees: "at any rate, a beauty like Miss Georgiana would be more moving in the same condition". The heavy importance placed on female beauty is nicely summed up by Miss Abbot, a servant at Gateshead. For all the Victorians' emphasis on money and class, Jane's supposed lack of attractiveness is more damning to her socially than her financial straits: "[I]f she were a nice, pretty child, one might compassionate her forlornness; but one really cannot care for such a little toad as that".

Perceptive child as she is, Jane has the ability to see through the disguises that appearance can present. She recognizes that one's actions are far more important than one's physical appearance. Bessie, when she treats Jane with kindness, seems radiantly beautiful to Jane: "When thus gentle, Bessie seemed to me the best, prettiest, kindest being in the world". Helen Burns, perhaps the purest, most angelic character in the whole novel, is characterized by "A beauty neither of fine nor long eyelash, nor penciled brow, but of meaning, of movement, of radiance" seems to propose the following moral: conventional beauty is at best shallow, at worst morally bankrupt, while plainness is unfailingly virtuous and good.

Jane's situation doesn't improve at Lowood, where she learns of the hypocritical standards society applies to both the poor and the plain. Mr.. Brocklehurst takes fear of beautiful (lower class) woman to the extreme: "'Miss Temple, Miss Temple, what—what is that girl with curled hair? Red hair, ma'am, curled—curled all over?'". Julia Severn's hair horrifies him to such an extent he is reduced to stuttering. Such is the Victorian fear of female sexuality. Rea asserts that "His arousal at the sight of Julia's red curls is unconsciously sexual, and he discharges this sexual rage against Julia by focusing his inner rage on the other girls' hair". The text seems to agree with this assertion: "'All these top-knots must be cut off... my mission is to mortify these girls the lusts of the flesh" Naturally unpretentious, Jane conforms easily and naturally to what Joanne E. Rea calls the "deliberately ascetic" **physical** appearance of the her fellow inmates, but she doesn't fail to notice that Mr.. Brocklehurst applies quite a different set of rules to his own daughters, who are elabourately coiffed and richly dressed: "they were splendidly attired in velvet, silk, and furs... from under the brim of this graceful headdress fell a profusion of light tresses, elabourately curled". Beauty in the poor, it seems, it threatening because it implies only sexuality. In the privileged, however, beauty (even in the most flagrant display of the ladies Brocklehurst) is respected and admired because of the necessity to attract a suitable husband. Appropriately, the practical and realistic Jane is not transformed, swan-like, into a great beauty, upon reaching maturity. As an adult, she is by now somewhat resigned to her plainness, although she still aspires to the early Victorian ideal:

I ever wished to look as well as I could, and to please as much as my want of beauty would permit. I sometimes regretted that I was not handsomer: I sometimes wished to have rosy cheeks, a straight nose, and a small cherry mouth: I desired to be tall, stately, and finely developed in figure; I felt it a misfortune that I was so little, so pale, and had features so irregular and marked.

Jane's imaginary ideal arrives at Thornfield in the character and figure of Blanche Ingram. Blanche personifies the "ne plus ultra" female form that was so desirable in the first half of the nineteenth century. Not coincidentally, she is everything Jane is not. While Jane is quite short, Blanche and her sister are "straight and tall as poplars". Federico describes the sharp contrast between Blanche and Jane: "Blanche displays all the features of the ne plus ultra: her 'Grecian neck and bust' are in the classical vogue...and Jane is positively dwarfed beside the 'Tall, fine, sloping shoulders, and long graceful neck'. Jane is wearing, as usual, her drab, Quakerish black; Blanche is "attired in spotless white". In short, Blanche is "the very type of majesty"

Despite her majestic carriage, Blanche is not (like Queen Victoria herself) a benevolent queen. Reed characterizes her as a type called the "Man-destroying woman; frequently and quite naturally presented as handsome, but their beauty has a peculiar quality... although they usually exhibit astounding beauty, it is really abrupt masculinity that characterizes these conventional types". But despite her outward charms, Blanche is not "good natured," in fact it is revealed later that she is positively shallow, even greedy. The moment she hears a rumor that Rochester is not worth as much as she had thought, she immediately drops him. Her beauty, though, is legendary, and Jane compares herself to Blanche, sight unseen, with mixed results. Jane, as usual, portrays herself as "Governess, disconnected, poor, and plain". She endows Blanche with "the loveliest face you can imagine... the Grecian neck and bust... and the delicate hand" Compared with her, physically speaking," concludes Jane, "I am nothing". Yet the ever-perceptive Jane considers Blanche beneath her jealousy, because she recognizes that Blanche's appearance conceals an inner emptiness. She is one-dimensional and lacking in goodness, or as the French proverb says, "Beauty without virtue is a flower without perfume." Jane describes Blanche's faults mercilessly: "She was very showy, but she was not genuine; she had a fine

person, many brilliant attainments, but her mind was poor, her heart barren by nature; nothing bloomed spontaneously on that soil; no unforced natural fruit delighted by its freshness. She was not good; she was not original: she used to repeat sounding phrases from books: she never offered, nor had, an opinion of her own. She advocated a high tone of sentiment, but she did not know the sensations of sympathy and pity; tenderness and truth were not in her" (. "She was not good," says Jane, and indeed, Blanche doesn't even have the goodwill to be kind to a child:

"Too often she betrayed this, by the undue vent she gave to a spiteful antipathy she had conceived against little Adele, pushing her away with some contumelious epithet... sometimes ordering her from the room, and always treating her with coldness and acrimony". Blanche has a powerful personality to match her height, which is reinforced, according to Reed, by her role in the charades game played at Thornfield: "The identification with the Old Testament Israelitish princesses hints also at other commanding females such as Judith and Jael". But it must be remembered that the biblical Rebecca was barren. This makes her an even more appropriate role for Blanche, whose coldness renders her "barren" in the sense that she is incapable of love. Blanche and Rochester share some characteristics, such as their dark complexion and "large and dark eyes" but they are not compatible as a couple because Rochester is not withhout a soul.

It is also important that Jane describes Blanche as "not original." Victorian women, according to Reed, were not supposed to have independent thoughts, as that might undermine their utter dependence upon their husbands. "An aggressive, liberated woman, seeking ideals of her own and the freedom that would enable her to pursue those ideals" was considered flawed., in making the unoriginal Blanche so thoroughly unlikable, is clearly reacting against this attitude. The inner beauty that seems to advocate a break from both the physical and intellectual standards to which Victorian women were held.

Like Blanche Ingram, Bertha Rochester competes and contrasts with Jane. physically. Though Jane knows her only as a mad, frightening beast of a woman, was considered quite a beauty in her youth. In the classical form, Bertha is tall: "She was a big woman, in stature almost equalling her husband". She has other similarities to Blanche: she was a legendary beauty, and dark-complected: "Miss Mason was the boast of Spanish Town for her beauty: and this was no lie. I found her a fine woman, in the style of Blanche Ingram: tall, dark, and majestic". Bertha Mason's "majestic"—this term linking her directly to Blanche Ingram—exterior conceals something much more hideous than Blanche's coldness: her latent insanity. Bertha's beauty blinded the young, naive Rochester in a way that Blanche's does not.

He is fooled first by Bertha's attractive appearance, then by the beautiful French dancer, who uses him coldly and mercilessly. By the time he meets Jane, he has learned the "beauty is so often false" lesson that seeks to teach her readers. The ease and speed with which Bertha disintegrates into corpulent, diseased monster from lovely maiden is astonishing and terrifying:. "Her character ripened and developed with frightful rapidity; her vices sprang up fast and rank". It's no wonder Rochester is drawn to his small, plain, simple governess.

Of course Rochester himself is no great beauty. Much as she loves him, Jane is not blind to his physical defects. "Do you think me handsome?" Rochester has the audacity to ask when they are formally introduced, and Jane just as bluntly answers "No" before she can stop herself. Even later, when she gazes at him in love, she sees a rather ugly man: "My master's less, olive face, square, massive brow, broad and jetty eyebrows, deep eyes, strong features, firm grim mouth... were not beautiful, according to rule". If Rochester does not conform to what Jane knows as the "rule" of beauty, he does resemble a popular Victorian type called the Byronic hero. According to Lefkovitz, "Rochester has all the appeal of a Byronic hero; he is wild, dark, rootless, troubled and brooding... Rochester sports the same kind of brutal beauty that was coming into popularity in the early decades of the century".

As a man, and more importantly, as a wealthy man, he is not so adversely affected by his looks. He would be sought out by families like the Masons and the Ingrams based on his wealth alone, regardless of his looks. makes him unattractive primarily to promote his relationship with Jane. Like Jane, his "beauty" is born of his sufferings and of his basic goodness.

Lefkovitz says, "Moreover, because Rochester loves Jane in spite of her plainness and social status, and because he rejects the lovely, but unlovable, Miss Ingram, the reader comes to admire the rough edges of his beauty". Rochester's visage may lack "benevolence," but he does show some sign of inner goodness:

he takes responsibility for Adele, who constantly reminds him of experiences in France he would rather forget. Additionally, his slightly savage looks insure his redemption in the readers' eyes, because we are supposed to be learning 's lesson: "The polish which money puts on beauty conceals either the mad beastliness of a Bertha or the worldly greediness of a Miss Ingram". The constant importance of Jane's plainness is evidenced in Rochester's rather unromantic marriage proposal. "You—poor and obscure, and small and plain as you are—I entreat you to accept me as a husband". She accepts, of course, and Rochester seems to enter his second period of blindness, this time to Jane's desire for simplicity. He wants the world to think her as beautiful as he does, which is both impossible and unnecessary, according to the insulted Jane:

"No, no sir! Think of other subjects, and speak of other things, and in another strain. Don't address me as if I were a beauty; I am your plain Quakerish governess."

"You are a beauty in my eyes; and a beauty just after the desire of my heart—delicate and aerial. I will make the world acknowledge you a beauty too... I will attire my Jane in satin and lace, and she shall have roses in her hair; and I will cover the head I love best with a priceless veil."

To attire Jane in this manner would violate not only Jane's personality but also severely weaken the whole argument of the novel, which places itself firmly against the "arbitrary politics of female beauty". Lefkovitz thinks the reader will agree with Jane's assessment of this situation: "Jane's beauty is the beauty of plainness, plain good sense and plain good looks, and by now, the reader is sufficiently won over that we believe Jane to be better off without the expensive ornaments".

Rochester's maiming and this time, literal blindness are widely read as the ultimate symbol of the unimportance of physical beauty. Federico says, "Rochester's blindness may epitomize the transcendence of mind and spirit over body and beauty, since he no longer has the power of the gaze". If there was any residual doubt regarding the compatibility of Jane and Rochester, it is completely removed when he is blinded. His deformities allow them to attain an almost neoplatonic relationship, based on something far greater than outward beauty. Even before Jane actually arrives at Ferndean, they communicate, literally, on a spiritual level: "'I could have deemed that in some wild, lone scene, I and Jane were meeting. In spirit, I believe, we must have met'". Thus their relationship is reduced to its essence, and Rochester finally comes to a true understanding and appreciation of Jane's plain nature: "'Never mind find clothes and jewels, now: all that is not worth a fillip'".

Further, not only is Rochester now truly dependent upon Jane's most important trait—her kindness—she never again has to worry about him being distracted by the superficial beauty of the flashy Blanche Ingrams of the world. Rochester's physical opposite, and also his chief competitor for Jane's hand, is found in the figure of the classically handsome St. John Rivers. He is an unusually Grecian figure, as Jane marvels:

Had he been a statue instead of a man, he could not have been easier... tall, slender; his face riveted the eye; it was like a Greek face, very pure in outline: quite a straight, classic nose; quite an Athenian mouth and chin. It is seldom, indeed, an English face comes so near the antique models as did his... His eyes were large and blue, with brown lashes; his high forehead, less as ivory, was partially streaked over by careless locks of hair. Like the similarly classically formed Blanche Ingram, St. John's character is somehow deficient. He is a parson, yet he is hardly personable, according to Jane: "He... scarcely impressed one with the idea of a gentle, a yielding, an impressible, or even of a placid nature.

Quiescent as he now sat, there was something about his nostril, his mouth, his brow... which indicated elements within either restless, or hard, or eager"). There is an impenetrable coldness about him, and though Lefkovitz calls him "excessively spiritual", he is distanced and unhappy; Jane even goes so far as to question his sincerity as a Christian. "Zealous in his ministerial labours, blameless in his life and habits, he yet did not appear to enjoy that mental serenity, the inward content, which should be the reward of every sincere Christian and practical philanthropist" As with Blanche Ingram, we have the feeling this sculpted, perfect exterior is hiding an icy cold soul. Jane is not elevated by his religious sermons; on the contrary, she is depressed and saddened. Though now convinced he a sincere Christian, she also knows that he "Had not yet found the peace of God which passeth all understanding"

Jane eventually finds that St. John's character flaw is an over-developed desire to deny himself happiness. Greek sculpture is supposed to represent a balance between the physical, intellectual and spiritual, but St. John clearly fails to strike that balance. Though not incapable of love (he is passionately in love with the beautiful, if vain, Rosamond Oliver) he is incapable of allowing himself to succumb to anything that might cause him (heavenly) joy. As Jane puts it, "That heart is already laid on a sacred altar: the fire is arranged around it. It will soon be a sacrifice consumed". It might seem strange of Jane to fault St. John for refusing to marry Miss Oliver, who is similar to Blanche Ingram in her striking beauty".

Anything more exquisite than her appearance, in her purple habit with her Amazon'e cap of black velvet placed gracefully above the long curls that kissed her cheek and floated to her shoulders, can scarcely be imagined". Though she notes that Rosamond is "not profoundly interesting or thoroughly impressive", she seems to favor the match: "'You ought to marry her'" is her blunt advice to St. John. Yet this recommendation is not completely inconsistent with 's rejection of traditional beauty, because of certain mitigating circumstances: first, that Rosamond Oliver is a shallow and childlike minor character, not a; and second, that St. John truly loves her. Jane disapproves of Rochester and Blanche's supposed match because (aside from her personal feelings) she recognizes the absence of love in the relationship.

Furthermore, as a classical figure, St. John is desperately in need of balance in his life. Since his own beauty means nothing to him, perhaps the lovely to look at Rosamond (and she is just that) could be an external source of harmony for him. Perhaps on some level Jane recognizes this, and because she does care for St. John, tries to encourage what she believes will bring him happiness. But, St. John proposes to our instead, not because he loves her, but because the unpretentious Jane fits in perfectly with his plan to "[lay] his genius out to wither, and his strength to waste, under a tropical sun". He immediately identifies Jane as physically undesirable: "Ill or well, she would always be plain. The grace and harmony of beauty are quite wanting in those features". She is, however, "Formed for labour, not for love" as he tells her in a marriage proposal even more tactless than Rochester's). Her plainness, in his mind, makes her the perfect partner for his missionary work, which he described in rather unhumanitarian terms: "My foundation laid on earth for a mansion in heaven...". Jane at once recognizes the unsuitability of this match because "He is handsome and she is plain". Or as Jane explains to Diana, "We should never suit". Jane, for all her Quakerish appearance, is as passionate as an adult as she was in the days of the red-room, and a marriage to a self-described "cold, hard man" would only mean unhappiness for her.

Jane and Rochester's suitability lies in their shared unconventional looks. Jane is a "plain beauty" and Rochester is the similarly oxymoronic "noble savage". "Beauty is of little consequence," Jane tells Rochester, and although this is certainly untrue in the outside world, it is certainly true of their relationship. Their mutual unattractiveness to the outside world overcomes the disparity in their ages and class. Rochester recognizes this common ground early in their relationship:

"...you are not pretty any more than I am handsome...". Jane radiates with happiness at the end of the novel, and as Lefkovitz concludes, "Jane and Rochester acquire beauty. Their appearances are not so much altered as we are made to reassess our criteria for appreciating beauty". The ending of the novel is all the more satisfying because Jane and Rochester achieve a mature and lasting love: "Mature love...requires the ability to see beyond the appearance to the reality, and the acceptance of that reality in all its aspects". Their relationship will almost assuredly be a long one, because it is not based on appearances that will eventually "fade." "Most true is that 'beauty is in the eye of the gazer,'" Jane notes, and this is the moral of her tale, though she manages its telling with more sophistication than this platitude might suggest. is successful in making an "interesting" plain, even more so because Jane is interesting because of her lack of beauty, not despite it. Lest we forget, the reader is reminded just once more that it is plain Jane that triumphs. An old servant remarks after the wedding: "If she ben't one of the handsomest, she's noan faal and varry good-natured; and i' his een she's fair beautiful, ony body may see that:

Pride Among the Men and Women of Jane Eyre

Q. "Pride is the most floating element of Jane Eyre's characters" Explain

Pride can be defined as showing distaste for or otherwise looking down upon a person or thing. In the periods leading up to the Victorian Age, pride was looked down upon by authors. It was considered a deadly sin by many. Restoration authors like Alexander Pope in his "Essay on Criticism" and "Essay on Man" despised pride in authors. In his "Essay on Man," Pope states "In pride [...] our error lies". Pride was a trait to be weary of for the Restoration authors. The Victorian authors did not follow so far after those of the Restoration. These thoughts of pride and of a vengeful God were seen in Victorian Era literature.

How did pride find its way into the character traits of the gentleman? Did the Victorian's and Charlotte in particular believe it necessary for the gentleman to have some level of pride? How much was enough? Were those with excessive pride in Victorian literature, and again more specifically, punished in some way? It can be said that each of the main male characters in the novel has some if not many of the characteristics that define a Victorian gentleman. Therefore, these characters can be used as a study to see how pride affected the characters in the novel. In Charlotte 's Jane Eyre, the old belief that severe punishment was the result of pride is revisited in the main male characters, Mr.. Rochester and St. John Rivers.

It can be assumed from looking at Rochester's character and his actions that he is a gentleman full of pride. He locks his demented wife in a cage on the top floor of Thornfield believing that no one will know that she is up there except for her caretaker Grace Poole. This is evidenced by his plans to marry Jane although he already has a wife. Even in the church with Jane he denies it to the last. When an official document is produced to show his marriage, Rochester replies it "may prove [he] may have been married, but it does not prove that the woman mentioned therein as my wife is still living". He plans to carry out this charade even after he marries Jane and would have if not for Mr.. Mason delivering the news. Rochester is accustomed to having people listen to him when he gives an order. By his own admission he is normally the most powerful person in the room.

He explains this to Jane, "Excuse my tone of command; I am used to say 'Do this,' and it is done: I cannot alter my customary habits for one new inmate". When he and Jane agree to marry, Jane objects to being made an idol: "I ask only this: don't send for the jewels, and don't crown me with roses". Rochester continues to give her more clothes and jewelry then she wants. He does not listen or respect her wishes. He is more important than she is, and it is his pride that causes him to think so. And he wishes her to be his equal. He tries to place her on the same level as he: "I will make the world acknowledge you a beauty, too" He wants to show her off to the world but not until he changes her appearance. If he was seen with a governess, his social standing would be in ill repute. His pride causes him to try to change Jane's appearance.

Rochester is punished for these actions. First, his plot to keep Bertha concealed is found out. Dick Mason bounds in on Jane and Rochester's wedding ceremony to tell the world of Rochester's prior marriage. This leads to Jane, his love, leaving Thornfield. While Jane is away Rochester agonizes over his lost love. Also while Jane is away, Thornfield burns, and Rochester is crippled and blinded. All of these results are punishments for his actions earlier in the novel. When Jane returns to him at Ferndean, he seems to have a change of heart. He is overjoyed at her arrival. He greets Jane by calling her his "living darling" Though, it is not stated, is not obsessed with money or deception. After Rochester's punishment, the burning of Thornfield and his crippling, Rochester gains a high moral status that makes him more of a gentleman than he ever has been. Through this suffering he is serving his punishment for being a man full of pride. When he is finally "fixed" of his prideful ways, he is rewarded for this with a son and the regeneration of his sight in one eye.

St. John Rivers is another character in the novel who is a prideful individual. St. John's pride comes from his occupation and his family standing. He is the priest of Morton, a position that commands much respect. Men of the clergy were often looked upon with much respect from their congregations. He is respected by the townspeople and is shown a great amount of admiration. He is also the only surviving male member in his family. He is the head of the household. He cares for his sisters as well as their old housekeeper. When Jane arrived at his lodging, although he takes her in and feeds her, he is constantly suspicious of her because she is a stranger. At the moment St. John allows her into the house, he explains to Hannah that "this is a peculiar case – I must at least examine into it

St. John's pride comes most into play after he asks Jane to marry and be a missionary with him. He wants to take control of Jane's life: "A missionary's wife you must — shall be. You shall be mine: I claim you". Her refusal sends him into a state of defence that makes him spiteful. He feels that he cannot go to India with Jane as a friend. He states quite adamantly that "it will not do. He treats her coldly and ignores her. He pulls his sisters closer during this time and pushes Jane further away. The night after Jane rejects his proposal; St. John "kissed his sisters, [but] he thought proper to forget even to shake hands with me; but left the room in silence"

St. John shows his pride when he goes to India without Jane. His calling is to serve God, and he will not miss his opportunity. Because St. John is full of pride he suffers a downfall similar to Rochester's. Although St. John does not seem to miss any of the things that are taken away from him as a punishment, he loses things that might make him happy. He does not ever have a relationship with Rosamond Oliver, whom he finds attractive. He also goes off to be a missionary where according to Jane he will eventually die. Because he takes such pride in his work, it is his work that will eventually kill him. Jane explains his fate: "St. John is unmarried: he never will marry now. Himself has hitherto sufficed to the toil; and the toil draws near its close,[...] I know that a stranger's hand will write to me next, to say that the good and faithful servant has been called at length into the joy of his Lord"

Throughout the Victorian novel, as with its predecessors in the Romantic and Restoration ages, the undesirable virtue of pride is depicted in its characters. In addition, like the writings of the past, those with pride are depicted as usually good people but have a great downfall as a result of their pride. This is true in 's Jane Eyre. The gentlemen in the novel are afflicted with great doses of pride that haunt their characters toward the end of the novel. Although as in the case of Rochester, those who repent for their sins of pride are rewarded for their change of heart. Pride, as depicted in the novel, has a role in the fate of the male characters of the novel.

In Charlotte 's Jane Eyre, her characters, Edward Rochester, St. John Rivers, and Brocklehurst are good examples of typical gentlemen in Victorian literature. All of these gentlemen are also drawn together with another characteristic, pride. With these high levels of pride, the characters are punished in compliance with historical tradition of English writing.

Misconceptions, Chastity and Deviance in Victorian-Era Sexuality in *Jane Eyre*

Q. What were the myths prevalent to the concept of sex in the Victorian Era?

Or

Q. "Sex was considered unethical in relationship before marriage" Explain

Or

Q. How this pleasurable act is attached to the act of whores?

Sexuality in Victorian England is perhaps marked mostly by our conception that sex was disallowed or very strongly discouraged outside of the charge of procreation and outside of marriage entirely. Sex became first pathologized – and subsequently medicalized and "psychiatrized" – in the nineteenth century, as Jane Usher in *Women's Madness: Misogyny or Mental Illness* points out, so this view of the Victorians is far from groundless. For at least this reason, Victorians seem to have thought quite a lot about sex, creating theories, rules and reasons that were often very incongruent with regard to the way sex began to be understood in times following. In such a patriarchal society as was nineteenth-century England, female sexuality became most scrutinized, and often many mistaken beliefs were formed.

Victorian England being a highly religious society, a great deal of scrutiny was placed upon women who were unchaste before and outside out marriage, and the literature of the time reflects this. The character of Céline, Rochester's French mistress and the mother of Jane's illegitimate little pupil in Charlotte Brontë's 1848 novel, *Jane Eyre,* exemplifies this tension. Additionally, when we examine the relationship between Rochester and Céline—a French opera-dancer, a *Parisienne*—we understand how it resembles an exchange (Céline's looks for Rochester's money) not unlike prostitution, which was an underlying current in Victorian society deviant from the "norm" or ideal.

Everything from a woman's sex drive and "appetite" to the "seat" of her sexual pleasure was pored over, and a vast number of these were misconceptions – at the very least slight twists of the truth if not entirely misguided altogether. Michael Mason in *The Making Victorian Sexuality,* his landmark book on the topic, points out that during the nineteenth century, the belief existed that women's sexuality with regard to the menstrual cycle mirrored that of animals. We know that women neither are most fertile nor do they have the most heightened sexual appetite during this time, which is an apparent departure from other mammals.

The female orgasm was another widely and severely misunderstood aspect of women's sexuality. Though, as Mason points out, surely everyone at the time understood that the orgasm was linked to the stimulation of women's external genitalia, Victorians were still very misguided in their understanding of this concept. He notes that Victorians were greatly deluded about the cause of female orgasm: "It could be believed that women experienced orgasm in response to the menstrual flow, or in mere conversation with a lover, or just from a touching of the cervix, or in defecation".

This fallacy led only to further blunders surrounding the mythical female orgasm; notably, it became linked with conception. The belief was held at the time that orgasm was necessary for a woman to conceive a child, termed reproductive orgasm. Further, it was understood that "...it is the sheer pleasurable intensity of the woman's orgasm which is functionally reproductive," i.e., the degree of a woman's fertility was believed to be directly related to the "degree" of pleasure she experienced.

The linkage of female orgasm to conception proliferated the larger linkage of female sexuality with child-rearing in general. Mason points out that in addition to the belief that reproductive orgasm was a requirement, Victorians thought that "the main site of a woman's sexuality is her womb and its appendages" and also that orgasm was the cause of ovulation. The linkage in this way may seem to have been to the benefit of women by not only allowing but seemingly promoting their sexual enjoyment, something that a contemporary understanding of Victorians would have assumed nonexistent at the time. It, however, prove to be problematic for Victorian women when we consider the implication for the converse of sex for procreation. Sex outside of procreation was discouraged and disallowed; if pleasure were to be present with conception, it can be assumed that female pleasure and orgasm during non-procreative sex was also discouraged somewhat if not altogether. In short, if a woman did not wish to have another child, sexual pleasure and orgasm were also to be excluded from her experience.

The notion of chastity, the abstinence from unlawful sexual intercourse or entirely, is overwhelmingly associated the Victorian period. Though chastity—at least outside of marriage, especially for women—may have been an aim or an idealized value of the Victorians, we can assume by mere common sense about what we know of human sexual nature that, though a goal, it was surely not often a reality. In addition to simple assumption, we know this by Victorian misunderstandings of sex that actually discouraged chastity, but this of course added much ambivalence about the topic. Mason points out that medical doctors believed that "...enforced chastity...could cause hysteria, of course, but also cancer and syphilis, and generally shorten a woman's life". In a further medicalization of female sexuality, doctors thought chastity especially after marriage was "dangerous" because, as Mason words it, "...semen was supposed to have a healthy action on a wife's organs". Therefore, Victorian women—as it is fair to assume—were far from chaste.

As is the case today, men and women had a good deal of sex outside of marriage despite the overt social pressures discouraging it. This shows up distinctly in *Jane Eyre* when Rochester recounts the story of what happened with his mistress Céline and how he came to have custody of her illegitimate daughter, Adèle. Though he does not state this outright, Céline was his mistress for whom he had a "grand passion" because she, being a French opera-dancer, was surely a strikingly beautiful and entertaining woman. She was beautiful with want for money, while the wealthy Rochester "thought himself her idol; ugly as he was"; at the time, they were a perfect match for both parties. Rochester's looks were certainly not an issue, especially because he was wealthy. Roy Porter and Lesley Hall in *The Facts of Life,* their account of sexual knowledge in Britain during the last four centuries, describe how easily a relationship between these two sorts of people could take place: "Men found no difficulty in getting sexual partners. Actresses and dancers were assumed to be sexually easygoing, and many females obviously felt better off as kept women than as servants or as wives".

An illicit affair between the two ensued (illicit for Victorian times because they were not married, but not too illicit when we consider her occupation and that it took place in the much "freer" country of France) deeply entrenched in money, and we see that Céline indeed was a "kept woman." Rochester notes that he showered her with gifts, acknowledging the physical disparity between the two: "'... I was so flattered by this preference of the Gallic sylph for her British gnome, that I installed her in an hotel; gave her a complete establishment of servants, a carriage, cashmeres, diamonds, dentelles, etc.'". During this speech we are nearly able to forget the novel's Victorian setting, as Rochester is so surprisingly open with the sheltered, "plain" Jane about the scenario.

Even while speaking of Céline's unchaste behaviour with a man other than him, Rochester still lingers upon her physical appearance. Years after the heartbreak, she is still his graceful, highly sexualized Parisienne: "'I knew her instantly by her little foot, seen peeping from the skirt of her dress, as she skipped from the carriage-step'". Céline's presence in the novel is striking, as she provides a stark contrast to the other women—namely, Jane and Blanche (both aptly named)—who both conform quite well to the Victorian convention of a chaste, modest woman. Céline, on the other hand, lines up more congruently with the notion of a prostitute, another area on the painting of women's sexuality at the time. Prostitution was very existent in the Victorian period, as Fraser Harrison states in *The Dark Angel:* "Prostitutes and prostitution were an unavoidable feature of Victorian life, and they occupied a far more prominent and obtrusive position in the public mind than they do today".

Though Céline may not match up to the sense we may normally think of with regard to a prostitute living in a brothel or walking the street, if we consider the way in which Rochester describes their relationship as a sort of exchange, we realise how much their pairing did resemble a both a physical and financial association. While recounting the episode to Jane in this scene, Rochester also states very plainly the basis of his feelings about Céline, remarking, "...I never thought there was any consecrating virtue about her: it was rather a sort of pastille perfume she had left; a scent of musk and amber, than an odour of sanctity"). Céline, the strikingly attractive Parisienne is far from the ideal Victorian woman—especially the markedly more modest English version, which consequently posits her as a highly sexualized being – one who receives lavish gifts from lovers, conducts her affairs and conceives a child outside of marriage. Bearing a child outside of wedlock, Porter and Hall note, was often commonplace. In addition to possessing the stigma of a prostitute in *Jane Eyre,* Céline also left Adèle with Rochester "...and ran away to Italy with a musician, or singer". Rochester takes custody of Adéle even though he did not acknowledge as her as his child and "...[saw] no proofs of such grim paternity written in her countenance". This also was not entirely a rare situation at the time, as "few men were ashamed of owning their bastards".

Judging by the amount and type of scrutiny of female sexuality, it is apparent that Victorians thought and conjectured quite a bit about sex. Consequently, we can assume that beyond thinking about it, they were far-from chaste, whether male or female, young or old, married or unmarried, even though some attitudes medicalized and pathologized female sexuality. Sexual relationships mirroring prostitution and outright prostitution were not uncommon as we see illustrated in *Jane Eyre.* Bastard children like Adéle and fleeing mothers like Céline constituted a sizable part of Victorian society, the result of relationships and an obvious avoidance of the ambivalent ideal of chastity outside of marriage.

The Materialization of Victorian Female Sexuality in *Jane Eyre*

Q. "The female sexuality considered to be of some material gain to people" Explain
Or

Q. Is this the reason why male exerts their dominance over society? Give your views.

Those living in Victorian England are believed to have been chaste and frigid regarding sexuality, often repressing their thoughts, desires and actions. Charlotte Brontë's 1848 novel, *Jane Eyre,* reveals that repressed Victorian sexuality manifested itself in many ways. In the novel, Mr.. Brocklehurst is a metaphoric example of the realization of male power and patriarchy upon female sexuality. Rochester's insane wife, Bertha, can be read as the materialization of overt and excessive female "passion" in the form of madness. Additionally in the novel, the virginal and aptly named Jane and Blanche constitutes a sort of counterpoint to Bertha (and the harlot Céline), embodying more closely the Victorian ideal of female modesty and chastity.

In *Jane Eyre,* the headmaster of Lowood, Mr.. Brocklehurst, absolutely epitomizes patriarchy. Beyond this, his maleness is sexualized by means of descriptive terms, beginning with Jane's first description of him as the realization of penis as person: "a black pillar...standing erect on the rug," his head "placed above the shaft by way of capital". Again, during his second appearance in the novel when he visits Lowood, Jane illustrates him as phallic, noting the return of "the same black column". The climax of Mr.. Brocklehurst's sexual superiority occurs when he orders that the hair of the Lowood students be cut. Though he intends to "mortify in these girls the lusts of the flesh," his order can be read in sexual terms. Because the expression of Victorian sexuality often took covert forms such as in hairstyle, the decree by the near-literal embodiment of both penis and power in man is a direct means of controlling women's sexuality at the time. By having Mr.. Brocklehurst order the cutting of the girls' hair, Brontë suggests metaphorically the desire of many men – possibly pointing to this wish of patriarchal society in the larger sense – to sever women's connection with and control of their own sexualities at the time.

In the nineteenth century, women's madness and their sexuality were often linked with the causation going in both directions: madness as a result of unbridled sexuality, increased sexuality or deviance as a result of female insanity. Jane Ussher notes in *Women's Madness: Misogyny or Mental Illness?,* "A central component associating madness with femininity and with the female body was the continued association between female sexuality and deviancy, construed as madness". In *Jane Eyre,* Bertha, Rochester's mad wife he keeps locked away upstairs, is characterized by Rochester in sexual terms, pointing no doubt to her insanity as linked to her sexuality. When recounting to Jane the story of his marriage to Bertha and her subsequent fall to madness, Rochester describes his wife as "intemperate and unchaste" and a "professed harlot". Whether Bertha's latent insanity was an impetus for her sexual deviance or a result of it is unclear, but Rochester clearly links the two.

By locking Bertha on the third floor essentially in a cell, like a criminal or an animal, Rochester metaphorically draws the line of female sexual deviance and relegates Bertha to the side of the convicted. This notion can be opened up to a more general sense that men and patriarchy, just like Mr.. Brocklehurst, seek during the Victorian period to control female sexuality by creating norms and "punishing" (in some cases banishing) women who do not conform to the norms. Ussher notes this results in Bertha's exact plight: "Thus the rigid image of 'woman' or 'femininity' could be used to punish, to convict, to control – women out of control were clearly sexual and dangerous, and mad". Barbara Hill Rigney opens this statement up a bit beyond just sexuality, stating, "Bertha's sexuality, her capacity for passion, apparently presented Rochester with real difficulties". As injury or death to characters can often be read as indirect punishment for "wrongs" previously committed in a story, at the end of the novel Brontë has Rochester maimed and blinded in a fire, which can be understood as a lashing out against the patriarchal system for pathologizing the realization of female sexuality.

In the novel, Blanche Ingram—as her name suggests—serves as a stark contrast to the dark, out-of-control Bertha. When Jane first sees her, she expresses that "...Blanche was moulded like a Dian," white (virginal) and glowing like the moon. She further describes the modest, model Victorian woman Blanche as "the very type of majesty," which is the absolute opposite of Rochester's lowly, animal wife locked away upstairs. Though he does not end up with Blanche, her presence in the novel is important to provide a balance between the women in the novel with regard to sexuality. Blanche, though depicted as both an extremely attractive and respectful, virginal woman, is unable to compete with the literally "plain," inexperienced puritan, Jane.

Rochester's discarding of the gold-digging Blanche in exchange for Jane, the epitome of Victorian modesty and chastity, suggests a gradual progression for his character away from the harlot and the wanton (Céline and Bertha) eventually towards less sexually deviant embodiments of sexuality at the time. This further suggests the former type of representation of female sexuality taking precedence over the one more divergent from the Victorian ideal, and perhaps this on the part of Brontë, hoping to show favor for the norm.

By exposing Mr.. Brocklehurst as a near-literal embodiment of the male sex organ and as a metaphor for the dominant male patriarchal paradigm at the time, and by revealing Rochester's treatment of Bertha as yet another materialization of men controlling women's sexuality, we begin to unpack the repressed sexuality of the Victorians. Additionally, Rochester's eventual marriage to Jane after discarding a string of women far less modest and virginal than she points to a preference for Jane's type over the others. In this way, questions and frustrations about the expression of female sexuality and its consequences are brought to the surface in *Jane Eyre*. By looking at sexuality lying on a more veiled or covert level – the level more akin to repression – we are able to better understand the system under which sexuality operated in nineteenth-century England.

The Fallen Social Class: Portrayals of Prostitution in *Jane Eyre*

Q. Why the society of whores is still looked down upon?
Or
Q. Explain the term "The love of Finery" in the novel.

Christie Zablocki paints many parallels between the characters in the novel and the trade of prostitution. One of the main characters that attribute to poverty is the character of Jane. Jane's poverty is intrinsically important to the plot of the novel because uses Jane's poverty to allow the reader to picture Jane as a virtuous woman, such as when Jane flees from Thornfield to escape the entrapment of Rochester. The reader is urged to feel sympathy for Jane as she adheres to her strict, virtuous moral codes and does not allow herself to succumb to temptation. Jane exhibits her desperate situation when she has fled from Thornfield and is struggling to sustain herself. Jane states, "Once more I took off my handkerchief-once more I thought of the cakes of bread in the little shop.

Oh, but for a crust! For but one mouthful to allay the pang of famine!". The language used in the passage shows that Jane is in a state of desperation and she still does not resort to prostitution, even though in many respects she does not have another choice. Jane is at a point in her life where she must do something to sustain her life, but Jane never even contemplates prostitution as an option to enable her to obtain money or food. In Victorian society Jane's poverty and subsequent life would have rendered her a prime candidate for taking up the trade of prostitution. The description given by Vicinus of the woman most vulnerable to fall victim to the trade of prostitution is similar to Jane's life. Jane is a domestic servant in her roles as a governess at Lowood and Thornfield and she has no familial ties.

One of the dominant distinctions of a Victorian prostitute was her dress or "love of finery." When the love of finery is introduced veers off the course of identifying Jane with the likeness of a prostitute. The Victorian prostitute is associated with the love of fine dresses, like that of the upper-class society. The prostitute's dress denoted her as a disgraceful and immoral character because she wore the type of dress that was not associated with her class. Valverde states, "...What was or was not finery depended upon the socioeconomic status of the wearer".

The love of finery is relentlessly associated with the Victorian prostitute, but Jane portrays an image of plainness in the attire that she wears. Jane portrays this image when Rochester takes her to Millcote to buy her some dresses. Jane says,

The hour spent at Millcote was a somewhat harassing one to me. Mr.. Rochester obliged me to go to a certain silk warehouse: there I was ordered to choose half a dozen dresses. I hated the business, I begged to defer it: no - it should be gone through with now. By dint of entreaties expressed in energetic whispers, I reduced the half-dozen to two: these, however, he vowed he would select himself. With anxiety I watched his eye rove over the gray stores: he fixed on a rich silk of the most brilliant amethyst dye, and a superb pink satin. I told him in a new series of whispers, that he might as well buy me a gold gown and a silver bonnet at once: I should certainly never venture to wear his choice. With infinite difficulty, for he was as stubborn as a stone, I persuaded him to make an exchange in favour of a sobre black and a pearl-gray silk. Jane does not display a "love of finery." Jane portrays a woman that is simplistic and plain in the way that she dresses. So in this aspect Jane does not resemble the portrait of the prostitute.

The love of finery is more significantly related to the character of who is portrayed as a sexual predator in the novel. lives a luxurious lifestyle. is described to the reader when Rochester flashes back to his encounter of the betrayal of taking up with another man while Rochester pays for all of the luxuries of her life. Rochester states, "The couple were thus revealed to me clearly: both removed their cloaks, and there was 'the Varens' shining in satin and jewels, - my gifts of course...". Rochester portrays as a figure that is extravagant in what she wears. She does not seem to give away any of the luxuries that Rochester provides for her. lives happily with all of the luxuries that are provided for her by Rochester, whereas Jane is content to walk to town rather than have a carriage provided. Jane denies many of the other luxuries that Rochester wants to give her, such as the dresses and jewelry that he wants to buy her.

Bertha is also a character that is portrayed as a sexual heathen. Rochester states, "Bertha Mason, - the true daughter of an infamous mother, - dragged me through all the hideous and degrading agonies which must attend a man bound to a wife at once intemperate and unchaste" (27; 302). Bertha is portrayed as a prostitute figure in the way that she acts rather than the way that she dresses. Amanda Anderson states, "Most of Victorian studies acknowledge the fluidity of the term 'fallen woman', its application to a range of feminine identities: prostitutes, unmarried women who engage in sexual relations with men, victims of seduction, adulteresses, as well as variously delinquent lower class women" (Anderson 2). Bertha falls into the category of "unmarried women who engage in sexual relations with men" (Anderson 2). Not only does Rochester state that Bertha is unchaste but he also insinuates that there were sexual relations between the two before they were married. When Rochester is talking about the mistake that he made when he married Bertha he says, "With less sin I might have -..." (27; 301). Rochester insinuates that if he had not committed the sin of sex before marriage he would not have been tied to marrying Bertha.

Portrays Blanche as a prostitute when she describes her as a character that is dressed in a revealing way for the time period that she lives in. In the instance when Rochester and his guests are playing charades, Blanches attire is described in detail. Jane described Blanche as "...attired in oriental fashion: a crimson scarf tied sash-like round the waist; an embroidered handkerchief knotted about her temples; her beautifully-moulded arms bare..." (18; 186). The description of Blanches bare arms portrays Blanche in a sexual manner. Blanche is not only described in a sexual manner, but she is also portrayed as a prostitute in her actions toward Rochester.

Blanche is trying to solicit the affections of Rochester to gain a husband who will be able to support her and the prostitutes are trying to attain the affections of the men so that they can make extra money to support themselves and perhaps their families. The Ingram family is described as needing to marry their daughters to a man that has his own fortune because their they do not have any fortune of their own. The connection between Blanche and Rochester seems ideal because Rochester will then gain the connections of the Ingram name while Blanche will gain a husband that has enough money to sustain her upper-class lifestyle.

uses stereotypes that specifically refer to prostitution when she talks about Bertha,, and Blanche as living unchaste

leads the reader to understand that is using prostitution as a mode to destroy the stereotypes of the social classes of the time period.

The Rake Figure

Q. Describe the element of Rake in concern with Rochester.

Edward Rochester, the male protagonist of Charlotte 's *Jane Eyre* embodies a number of different roles of masculinity. One of the least recognized but very influential roles played by Rochester is the rake. The idea of the "rake" is commonly related to the Restoration period in England; yet this figure does not completely disappear during the eighteenth and nineteenth centuries. Historical figures such as John Wilmot the second Earl of Rochester are described as leading rakish lifestyles. Literature and Art also played an important role in defining the rake.

The rake character is primarily defined by his sexual nature. A rake was concerned about his status among other men. He spent most of his time in search of sexual liaisons or relating tales of past sexual escapades. Harold Weber in *The Restoration Rake-Hero* explains that "most rakes possess little identity outside of the love game, their lives responding largely to the rhythms of courtship and seduction, pursuit and conquest, foreplay and release". However, as Weber further points out "the rake is too complex and enigmatic a figure to be reduced to a sexual machine: his love of disguise, need for freedom, and fondness for play all establish the complexity of the rakish personality". The rake's sexual desires can be seen as a call for freedom and a break from social order. He balks at the idea of marriage and family in pursuit of personal gratification. While a common characteristic of the rake is his pursuit of personal gratification there are a number of different types of rakes: the Hobbesian libertine, best explained by Horner in *The Country Wife*; the philosophical libertine, seen through the writings of Sir William Temple; the polite-rake; the debauchee; the extravagant rake, and finally the penitent or reformed rake. The rake figure played an important role in the Restoration Comedies which were popular from 1668 to 1710.

The Restoration Stage was closely related to the Court of this time period. In 1660 when Charles II ascended the throne in England, the emphasis of his court was on fashion, art, and love. King Charles led a rakish lifestyle; he was well known as a skilled pursuer of women. Many members of Charles' court became playwrights for the Restoration stage. The themes of the comedies often reflected themes at court. These themes included: the pursuit of love and pleasure; the deception and mistreatment of others; and changing attitudes towards marriage and sexuality.

The Restoration Stage became the forum to discuss changing views towards sexuality. As Weber explains "the rake's career on the Restoration stage initiates the modern discourse on sexuality, for the rake represents the initial attempts of English culture to transfer control of sexuality from the divine to the secular world". The Restoration period saw a change in the views of sexuality. The character of Horner in *The Country Wife* best exemplifies the changing attitude towards sexuality. He feigns impotence in order to gain the affections of married women. Weber explains "Horner takes an exquisite pleasure in both his sexual and social manipulations". Horner's pursuit of sexuality and duping of other characters becomes the clear definition of the rake's pursuit of gratification. It is also during the Restoration period that women are first allowed on stage. The Restoration stage introduced a more liberal view towards a woman's sexual needs and desires. The acknowledgement of sexuality on the Restoration stage did not guarantee that it was immune from criticism off the stage.

William Hogarth used his art as a form of criticism. Hogarth's works often depict the debauched lifestyle of a character which eventually leads to the demise of that character. In 1735 William Hogarth introduced eight panels entitled *A Rake's Progress*. These eight scenes depict events in the life of Tom Rakewell, a middle class youth. Although not quite as popular as the Harlot series, the Rake proved to have a longer lasting impact.

He is a walking, talking, living example of what Hogarth regarded as the great folly of the age – affectation. No person, or class, no institution, he was convinced, was immune; all were possessed by a crazed hankering to be other than they were. In more traditional language, they were whoring after false gods. Needless to say, this is exactly what we would expect in a traditional class society being challenged by commercial interests and considerations. (William Hogarth: A Rake's Progress)

Although the Rake series was not initially as popular as some of Hogarth's other works, it did prove to have a greater longevity. Hogarth's Rake series inspired many artists and served as a model for many rake figures.

Directly connected to Charlotte 's *Jane Eyre* are the first, third, fifth, and eighth plates. Each plate depicts a scene that relates to Edward Rochester's actions and attitudes. The first scene occurs after Tom has inherited his father's wealth. He is being measured for new clothing that will disguise him as an aristocrat. It is also the first plate that Tom attempts to pay off his pregnant fiancée, Sarah Young. This plate establishes two important traits about the rake: the desire to disguise himself in order to become something he is not, and a disregard for responsibility in the pursuit of pleasure. The third plate in *A Rake's Progress* depicts Tom's descent into a life of debauchery. The scene features couples in various embraces. The expression of wanton sexuality is key to understanding the driving force behind the rake. The fifth scene shows Tom Rakewell marrying an ugly, wealthy old woman in order to maintain his aristocratic lifestyle after squandering his wealth. The eighth and final scene shows Tom Rakewell in a madhouse, the victim of his excessive lifestyle. Hogarth's *A Rake's Progress* depicts one possible conclusion for the rake's debauched lifestyle.

John Wilmot, the second Earl of Rochester, depicts another conclusion for the rake's debauched lifestyle. John Wilmot was born in Oxford shire on April 1, 1647. Wilmot's mother was "the former Anne St. John, daughter of a Wiltshire knight". His father was a Royalist and awarded the title Earl of Rochester for serving Charles II. Wilmot was educated at Wadham College, Oxford; he traveled through France and Italy and returned to the English court in December of 1664.. Wilmot played an important role in the Restoration court. John

Wilmot has been described as "the youngest, handsomest and most talented of the writers and rakehells known as the Court Wits in the reign of Charles II". Wilmot was well known for his literary works, which included drama, lyric poems, satires and epistles. In July of 1680, at the age of 33, Wilmot died from syphilis.

John Wilmot became one of the most notorious figures at court. He was well known for his drunkenness, vivacious conversation, and womanizing. Samuel Johnson's *Lives of the English Poets* describes Wilmot as having "very early an inclination to intemperance [...] he addicted himself to dissolute [...] company, by which his principles and manners were depraved. He lost all sense of religious restraint, and, finding it not convenient to admit the authority of laws which he was resolved not to obey, sheltered his wickedness behind infidelity." Wilmot's actions were so scandalous that he was banished a number of times from court. Before his death Wilmot repented for his immoral lifestyle. He became the focus for a number of religious tracts which published his deathbed conversion.

John Wilmot's deathbed conversion sparked a new era for the rake, the reformed rake. This post Restoration literary character was often presented as a villain who paid the ultimate price of his debauched lifestyle, death. Samuel Richardson, in his novel *Clarissa,* creates such a figure, Mr.. Lovelace. In his essay "Clarissa and the Individuation of Character," Steven M. Cohan explains about Lovelace that "his sexual aggression and desire for revenge are similarly an exertion of power over others; and his love of plots and disguises makes him a perverse kind of artist figure". Lovelace relates to the historical rakes in his sexual aggression, his power over other characters and using disguises to deceive others. However, the rake figure moves away from a purely sexual figure. In regards to Lovelace's rape of Clarissa Cohan explains the new role of the rake.

In creating this situation where he and Clarissa are to respond according to the libertine code of behaviour [...] Lovelace thinks he can have some expectation of what is to occur. But when their two strong, willful, passionate personalities are locked together, the resulting explosion blasts the situation beyond the secure libertine arena, for neither he nor Clarissa respond according to the typical code. When she rejects him after the rape Clarissa forces Lovelace to acknowledge the many inconsistencies in his character which the rake type cannot include: for he loves and needs her deeply even after sexual conquest. Unlike the Restoration rakes who pursue women for pure sexual gratification, Lovelace begins the trend that a relationship with the woman, not sexual conquest, is the ultimate goal. Unlike the Restoration Comedies, *Clarissa* becomes a tragedy. Not only does Clarissa die, Lovelace is killed in a duel with Clarissa's brother. The restoration rake and his story has been altered. The rake's desire goes far beyond mere sexual conquests, his desire is to completely own and control the woman.

The rake became a popular definition of masculinity in the Restoration period. He was commonly defined by his pursuit of sexual gratification. However, society's fascination with the rake did not end with the Restoration period. The rake figure continued on in such literary works as Richardson's *Clarissa*. The allure of the rake was so strong that he continues to influence the perception of masculinity well in the twentieth century. Charlotte was attracted to rake model of masculinity and modeled Edward Rochester after this Restoration figure.

Establishing Rochester as the Rake

Q. Does Rochester fits perfectly in the character of a rake?

The rake became one of the most recognized figures of the Restoration Comedies. The rake character was seen as unmarried, cynical, coarse but with the manners of a gentleman, manipulative and self serving. By the twentieth century the rake had given away to the Regency dandy and the dark Byronic hero of Victorian literature. However, the rake does not completely disappear from twentieth century novels. Charlotte resurrects the Restoration hero in the creation of Edward Rochester in *Jane Eyre*. Edward Rochester exhibits many of the qualities associated with the Restoration rake; he manipulates the woman around him and his actions are self serving. 's rake varies just enough that she can present her character as both hero and villain which eventually allows for his reformation.

Readers are often deceived into believing that the rake should be viewed as a villain, hence their resistance in accepting Edward Rochester as a rake. However, as Harold Weber suggests that readers should not be concerned "with whether or not the rake emerges as a hero or a villain – he must [...] be both". The rake's mistreatment of women categorizes him as villain. Rochester's mistreatment of Jane and the other women in the story is detestable. He confesses that he used Blanche Ingram to make Jane jealous. Rochester admits that he "feigned courtship with Miss Ingram". Rochester deceives Blanche into believing his intent was marriage; yet she was merely a pawn in his romantic conquest of Jane. The whole time Rochester pursues Jane he is already married to Bertha. Rochester hides his marriage in an attempt to find his definition of a more suitable wife. He tells Jane that his "fixed desire was to seek and find a good and intelligent woman, whom [he] could love".

His marriage in no way hinders his search for a more acceptable wife. However, the actions which should classify Rochester as a villain often have the opposite effect. It is Blanche, not Rochester, who is depicted as the villain. Rochester relates the story of how Blanche's desire to marry him revolved around his fortune and that she "deserted [him]". By relating this tale, Rochester removes the blame from himself and redirects the reader's attention to Blanche's downfalls instead of his own. Rochester's treatment of the French prostitute Varens invokes sympathy from the reader. The reader blames for deceiving Rochester. However, 's betrayal of Rochester is no less than his betrayal of Bertha. Rochester manipulates his villainous past to create sympathy not only from Jane, but from the reader as well.

Rochester further invokes sympathy from readers when relating his marriage to Bertha. Historically the Restoration rake was seen as an unmarried figure, yet 's rake is not only married, but attempts to marry a second time. In Hogarth's *A Rake's Progress* the fifth plate shows the rake marrying a wealthy woman in order to gain a secure financial base. These are the same reasons Rochester agrees to marry Bertha. In his explanation of his marriage to Bertha, Rochester explains that he "must be provided for by a wealthy marriage" Rochester's marriage to Bertha became one of necessity because of financial reasons. After his epiphany on his marriage to Bertha, Rochester realises that the "woman who has so abused [his] long-suffering – so sullied [his] name; so outraged [his] honour; so blighted [his] youth – is not [his] wife; nor [he] her husband". Rochester no longer believes Bertha to be his wife and this fact justifies, in his mind, locking her in the attic. Presenting Bertha as the mad woman in the attic allows the reader to sympathize with Rochester and blame Bertha, instead of Rochester, for hiding his marriage.

Locking Bertha in the attic allows Rochester to pursue other women. Rochester's recounting his past relationships shows that a rake has no past history that does not entail recounting his mistress and past sexual escapades. Days after their initial meeting, Rochester explains to Jane his past relationship with Varens. It is odd that Rochester would be relating such a tale to a young, virginal Jane. However, nowhere in the novel is Rochester's past separate from his sexual encounters. After the discovery of his marriage, Rochester boasts of his sexual conquests to Jane. He confesses that he "could not live alone; so [he] tried the companionship of mistresses [...] first [he] chose Varen [...] she had two successors: an Italian, Giacinta, and a German, Clara". Rochester then wonders if Jane will think him "an unfeeling, loose-principled rake". Rochester's self declaration as the rake begins his journey away from the Hobbesian rake, whose sole concern was self gratification, towards the reformed rake who regrets his debauched lifestyle.

After the discovery of Bertha, Rochester begins his reformation from the rakish lifestyle. Rochester confesses that he "tried dissipation – never debauchery: that I hated, and hate". Rochester comprehends the evil of his past life.

I did not like it. It was a groveling fashion of existence. I should never like to return it. Hiring a mistress is the next worse thing to buying a slave: both are often by nature, and always by position, inferior: and to live familiarly with inferiors is degrading. I now hate the recollection of the time I passed with, Giacinta, and Clara. Until this point Rochester has shown no remorse for his lifestyle. This declaration moves Rochester away from his rakish lifestyle and creates him as the reformed rake. The disassociation with the rake leads into the powerful message Charlotte expresses with the character of Edward Rochester. Unlike the reformed rakes of the past who repent for their debauched life on their deathbed, 's reformed rake pays a small price for his reformation.

In the creation of her hero, Edward Rochester, Charlotte resurrected the Restoration rake. Rochester posses many characteristics associated with the rake. His past life is nonexistent without discussing some former lover. He deceives Jane into believing he is unmarried. Like many rakes, Rochester can be viewed as both villain and hero. While his actions towards the other characters in the novel are villainous, presents them in such a manner that the reader's sympathies lie with Rochester. Rochester repents for his debauched lifestyle and is rewarded by the death of Bertha and his marriage to Jane.

The Real Rochester

Q. What are the special characteristics of being a Rochester?
Or
Q. Is Edward a perfect example of Rochester?

John Wilmot, the second Earl of Rochester was one of the most infamous rakes from the Restoration period. While Wilmot's debauched lifestyle was well recorded, his deathbed conversion became even more popular. Through these early biographies and the poetry written by Wilmot, Charlotte became familiar with this historical figure. modeled her character of Edward Rochester on Wilmot. There are many instances in the novel *Jane Eyre* that link the two figures. In his essay "John Wilmot and Mr.. Rochester" Murray Pittock establishes the link between Rochester and Wilmot. Pittock does such a thorough job of supporting the claim that Rochester and Wilmot are related. However Pittock fails to explain why Charlotte chose to compare her Rochester to the historical Rochester. The key to understanding 's motivation in selecting John Wilmot as the model for Rochester lies in Wilmot's deathbed confessional.

By the end of his short life Wilmot repented his immoral lifestyle. After his death, Wilmot became the focus of a number of religious tracts publishing his deathbed conversion. It is this aspect of Wilmot's career as the rake that intrigued. In *Jane Eyre* Charlotte not only establishes a connection between John Wilmot, the second Earl of Rochester, but she also links Rochester's reform to the reform of Wilmot. However, unlike Wilmot's reform which occurs on his deathbed, allows her character to reform and continue his life.

The similarities between John Wilmot and Edward Rochester go far beyond the traits associated with the rake. Charlotte uses names for her characters that link the two characters. Wilmot's title as the Earl of Rochester directly relates to the name of Edward Rochester. John Wilmot's grandfather had the name Sir John St. John (Pittock 464). Edward Rochester's main rival for Jane's affection is St. John Rivers. Again the use of a name closely related to John Wilmot is remarkable. The repeated usage of names links the character of Edward Rochester with John Wilmot, the second Earl of Rochester.

That Charlotte would have been familiar with the second Earl of Rochester is undeniable. In his *Lives of the Poets,* Samuel Johnson included a biography on Wilmot. That would have been familiar with Johnson's work can be established in the references she makes to Johnson's novel *Rasselas*. Gilbert Burnet, a Scottish Bishop and famed historian, wrote *Life and Death of John Rochester* based on interviews he had with Wilmot on his deathbed. By 1848 this biography had gone through ten editions. This book was so famed that both Horace Walpole, writer of the first Gothic novel, and Samuel Johnson wrote critiques which ere incorporated into the 1820 edition.

Receiving critiques by both Walpole and Johnson serves as an indicator of the importance of this biography. In 1814 *The Conversion of the Earl of Rochester* was published. Finally, as Pittock explains, "such widely disseminated tales of reformed rakes and deathbed conversions were an important part of the literary culture of 's youth". Pittock recognizes that these deathbed conversions were an important part of 's reading; yet, he never establishes the influence these writings would have on 's work. As stated before, the link between Rochester and Wilmot can be seen through their reformation.

Rochester's conversations with Bishop Burnet sparked the deathbed conversion, *Life and Death of John Rochester*. The novel greatly influenced religious tracts which discussed the evils of a debauched lifestyle and salvation through repentance. Samuel Johnson in his *Lives of the Poets* discusses not only the importance Burnet played in Rochester's reformation but the influence his deathbed conversion had on society:

At this time he was led to an acquaintance with Dr. Burnet, to whom he laid open with great freedom the tenour of his opinions, and the course of his life, and from whom he received such conviction of the reasonableness of moral duty, and the truth of Christianity, as produced a total change both of his manners and opinions. The account of those salutary conferences is given by Burnet, in a book intituled, *Some Passages of the Life and Death of John earl of Rochester*, which the critick ought to read for its elegance, the philosopher for its arguments, and the saint for its piety. It were an injury to the reader to offer him an abridgement.

Wilmot confesses to Bishop Burnet the evils of his past life. Bishop Burnet in turn helps Wilmot forsake his former life and accept religion. uses this model of Wilmot's deathbed confessional and conversion in the dealings of Rochester and Jane.

When Rochester and Jane are reunited after the fire at Thornfield, their conversation resembles that of a confessional and rebirth. When Jane encounter Rochester at Ferndean his life has become meaningless. Jane decides that "it is time some one undertook to rehumanize" Rochester). It is Jane that will save Rochester from his meaningless existence and bring him back to humanity. Finally, much as Wilmot discovered Christianity at the end of his life, Rochester praises the God that has brought his Jane Eyre back:

But my heart swells with gratitude to the beneficent God of this earth just now. He sees not as man sees, but far clearer: judges not as man judges, but far more wisely. I did wrong: I would have sullied my innocent flower – breathed guild on its purity: the Omnipotent snatched it from me. I, in my stiff-necked rebellion, almost cursed the dispensation: instead of bending to the decree, I defied it. Divine justice pursued its course; disasters came thick on me: I was forced to pass through the valley of the shadow of death. *His* chastisements are mighty; and one smote me which has humbled me for ever. [...]. Of late, Jane – only – only of late – I began to see and acknowledge the hand of God in my doom. I began to experience remorse, repentance; the wish for reconcilement to my Maker. I began sometimes to pray: very brief prayers they were, but very sincere. Rochester has repented for the misdeeds of his previous life. 's hero, unlike John Wilmot, repented before his deathbed and was rewarded with his marriage to Jane. allows her reformed rake to celebrate in his reformation and continue on with his life.

Charlotte followed the literary tradition of the epistolary novel in the story of Edward Rochester as the rake. She looked to the historical figure of John Wilmot as a model for her character. Wilmot's fame as one of the most infamous rake's at the Restoration Court was well recorded. His deathbed conversion and repentance for his debauched lifestyle sparked the well known novel *The Life and Death of John Rochester*. Instead of having her hero repent on his deathbed, allows her character to repent on his metaphoric death (the loss of his eyesight and hand). balks at the idea that salvation comes at the price of death, instead she allows Rochester to repent and rewards him by allowing his marriage to Jane.

"I Never Met your Likeness": The Sexually Distinctive Jane Eyre

Q. Describe the development of Jane Eyre throughout the novel in special reference to love and sex.

In ways that are not always flattering, Jane Eyre is desexed. The narrator, main character, and namesake of Charlotte Brontë's *Jane Eyre* is a young woman through most of the novel—excepting approximately the first quarter of it, when she is a young girl—but she is rarely described with the degrees of femininity accorded to her fellows. Rather, plain Jane is sometimes referred to using terms more fitting when speaking of children, even addressed with that more impersonal pronoun, "it," which is usually reserved for beings that are either inhuman or unfamiliar to human society. What is the root of this innate otherworldliness in Jane that effects such language? Simply put, Jane does not belong with Victorians who vie for sexual prominence, though most of her contemporaries do.

This claim may seem reductively bawdy, but Maynard points out that "the Victorian angel in the house was not so much less sensible about sex than the Victorian woman in the street as has been supposed" (2). We also know that writers like Brontë did their best to "attempt... to pose and discuss the problems of sexual experience as they found them," so a discourse on the attitudes toward sexuality shown by characters in the novel is definitely called for.

The novel follows Jane from her pre-pubescent formative years to her marriage as a young adult; it is apparent throughout that she is markedly different from other females in her company. She is above them in a way that is hard to pin down, and she asserts as much. She is an exercise in moderation, an idealized balance of the modest but not prudish, and the liberal but not libertine. As Brontë biographer Moglen explains, "Paradoxically, in freeing Jane Eyre from the conventional trappings of femininity and granting her liberty to feel and express her feelings, to think and express her thoughts, in asserting her 'humanness,' Charlotte Brontë created the first 'anti-': one who defied the conventions of both fiction and society". This qualification is thrown into its greatest relief when Jane is juxtaposed with the other sexual creatures in the novel, her foils.

Jane admits as she dresses one day, preparing for her first adult role outside of Lowood, "I sometimes regretted that I was not handsomer; I sometimes wished to have rosy cheeks, a straight nose, and small cherry mouth; I desired to be tall, stately, and finely developed in figure; I felt it a misfortune that I was so little, so pale, and had features so irregular and so marked". Though her occupation of governess is decidedly gendered, her physiognomy is not. While contemplating the life ahead of her, she makes self-deprecating remarks, the kind mirrors notoriously generate. However, Jane's candidness regarding her appearance should not be dismissed as mere humility: she really is imperfect as a woman. Even the most feminine of clothes—a veil and other bridal attire—do not add anything significant to invoke the image of a woman in Jane. After dressing for her first marriage ceremony, she looks in the mirror and relates, "I saw a robed and veiled figure, so unlike my usual self that it seemed almost the image of a stranger". None of the descriptive language she uses is unique to a woman.

Blanche Ingram

On the other hand, when compared to Blanche Ingram's blatant display of femininity as desperate sexuality, Jane's plainness is ironically more desirable. Blanche Ingram's first name is the colour of private Victorian skin, that which sunlight has not touched or that clothing has not revealed; yet, it is the moniker she uses in public. Mrs. Fairfax describes Blanche's uniquely feminine exhibitionist tendencies when attending social gatherings: "She was dressed in pure white; an amber-ed scarf was passed over her shoulder and across her breast, tied at the side, and descending in long, fringed ends below her knee. She wore an amber-ed flower, too, in her hair: it contrasted well with the jetty mass of her curls". Seedily desirous of amorous attention, she wears her physical beauty on her sleeve and in her hair.

She matches the colour of the swarthy cloth—draped around her body and "across her breast" like an arm—with that of the virgin symbol atop her head. The symbolic flower "contrast[s] well" with the "mass" of curly hair that is decidedly pubic. Jane is never allowed such a depiction because she never wants one; her sexual prowess and identity are not matters of public opinion. Even to her future husband, as they are not yet married, she denies this kind of flattery. He begins:

"I will make the world acknowledge you a beauty, too.... I will attire my Jane in satin and lace, and she shall have roses in her hair; and I will cover the head I love best with a priceless veil."

"And then you won't know me, sir; and I shall not be your Jane Eyre any longer, but an ape in a harlequin's jacket—a jay in borrowed plumes. I would as soon see you, Mr.. Rochester, tricked out in stage-trappings, as myself clad in a court-lady's robe..." Jane's response is quite fitting in that it differentiates her from the too-feminine Blanche. Blanche had earlier admitted to Rochester that she prefers, rather than Rochester's actual self, a Rochester in the false stage-trappings to which Jane has just alluded—that is, Blanche desires her idealized conception of Rochester and the status that a marriage to him might bring to the public opinion of her and her family. Jane, however, rejects the showy display Blanche embraces; and though Blanche looks better the part of a respectable lady, only Jane plays it.

"And this beautiful and accomplished lady, she is not yet married?" Jane asks of Mrs. Fairfax regarding Blanche. Surely a woman like Blanche—admired "not only for her beauty, but for her accomplishments" in the realm of musical performance—should have a suitor. As it turns out, though, she is lacking something integral to the upper class portrait of femininity: a sizable dowry. The Victorian patriarchy card has already been played in her family: her brother has taken over the affairs of the Ingram estate without leaving her mu She is similar to Jane in this respect: she enters Rochester's life without being able to offer a monetary contribution to the marriage. The difference is that this lack of dowry is the only reason some equally eligible and equally shallow Victorian bachelor has not already snapped up Blanche.

Blanche is not a bachelorette for lack of trying. Her physiognomy communicates that she is confident, eager, and impetuous. On seeing her for the first time, Jane observes that "her face was like her mother's; a youthful unfurrowed likeness: the same low brow, the same high features, the same pride". In the quest for a rich husband, she is relentless: "Blanche was moulded like a Dian," physically resembling the goddess of the animal hunt. Blanche's mother shares with her "a fierce and a hard eye: it reminded [Jane] of Mrs. Reed's."

Rather than taking after any of these upper-class matriarchal figures, Jane is not jealous, does not flirt in public, and refuses to play her attractive qualities like trump cards. Her appeal, to use the cliché, is not skin deep, as she argues to Rochester: "Do you think, because I am poor, obscure, plain, and little, I am soulless and heartless?... My spirit... addresses your spirit; just as if both had passed through the grave, and we stood at God's feet, equal,—as we are!" (). Despite the fact that she has just equated herself with a man, Jane explains that what she has to offer is something above the physical and sexual realm, something a Blanche could never provide, dowry or none. In fact, when Rochester attempts to make Jane's "fairy-like" appearance more feminine, he claims, "I will clasp the bracelets on these fine wrists, and load these fairy-like fingers with rings," and she denies him, "No, no, sir! think of other subjects, and speak of other things, and in another strain. Don't address me as if I were a beauty; I am your plain, Quakerish governess". She prefers plain, asexual attire to the gaudy; she prefers simple, honest marriage offers to desperate, rich-fiancé hunts.

Rosamund Oliver

One comment goes a long way when it is about Rosamund Oliver, another logical foil of Jane. After getting to know her for quite some time, having "learnt her whole character," Jane describes Rosamund with less-than-flattering adjectives: "coquettish," like Blanche; "exacting"; "hasty"; "vain"; only "sufficiently intelligent"; "very charming"; but "not profoundly interesting"). None of these actually contradict her "perfect beauty"), as she "is ever surrounded by suitors and flatterers"). However, one of Rosamund's more telling qualities is explained by something she makes known to Jane: "she was sure my previous history, if known, would make a delightful romance". Immediately, a perceptive reader will see the connection between what Rosamund suggests and what the narrator is doing; and the pun is that, while the narrator adds this self-congratulatory comment deliberately, so does the author. An especially perceptive reader will note that Jane and her cousins—ironically in the case of Jane—are not in the habit of reading novels, while Rosamund is, as it is a pastime accepted as belonging to typical Victorian women.

Jane, Mary, and Diana prefer to translate, a task slightly more practical and arduous than novel-reading, and therefore more meritorious. Jane admits about Rosamund, "A very different sort of mind was hers from that, for instance, of the sisters of St. John". This difference is apparent in the literature with which they respectively "delight" themselves. The Riverses—who, really for lack of dowries, never marry—translate, as does Jane, while Rosamund reads novels and marries first.

Phonetically, Brontë has constructed quite a convoluted line separating Rosamund Oliver and St. John Rivers. As St. John's name implies, he is a dedicated "follower of the sect of Jesus". Rosamund Oliver, however, could be "Rose-à-Monde Lover", a lover of worldly things. Jane even qualifies her immaculate beauty as decidedly "earthly". St. John's marriage to her, then, would have run contrary to a Bible text he would have been familiar with, as he shares a name with its writer: "Do not be loving either the world or the things in the world. If anyone loves the world, the love of the Father is not in him; because everything in the world—the desire of the flesh and the desire of the eyes and the showy display of one's means of life—does not originate with the Father, but originates with the world". St. John has already dedicated his life to a cause that prohibits his love of the likes of worldly Rosamund. She should know this about St. John, but her naïveté is not the noble and pitiable kind that comes from mere inexperience. Jane, in the catalogue of Rosamund's undesirable attributes, recognizes the simple ignorance that keeps Rosamond cruelly vying for St. John's attention: Rosamund is "gay, lively, and unthinking". While Blanche Ingram represents the camp of women who "have neither souls nor hearts", at least she has a head on her shoulders in that she knows to quit when things cease to seem profitable for her.

While Rosamund is worldly to the core, Jane is the polar opposite, so, not of this world. This manifests itself in the portrayals of their sexuality. Rosamund's picture-perfect beauty is described in such detail that it would be redundant to repeat; luckily, the narrator sums it up: "all advantages, in short, which, combined, realise the ideal of beauty, were fully hers". St. John, who prides himself on his ability to control, confesses to being helplessly affected by Rosamund's beauty: "I love Rosamond Oliver... wildly—with all the intensity, indeed, of a first passion, the object of which is exquisitely beautiful, graceful, fascinating...".

He is attracted to her instinctually, like any animalistic creation. She is what Blanche paints herself to be, the very portrait of femininity that attracts men of all types. St. John, however, recognizes that Rosamund's external beauty is not for him or the ministry he has undertaken: "she could sympathise in nothing I aspired to—co-operate in nothing I undertook. Rosamond a sufferer, a labourer, a female apostle? Rosamond a missionary's wife? No!". He has a prior engagement, so to speak, in that he is dedicated to self-denial, the rejection of anything viscerally feminine that would please the prurient part of himself he so desperately wants to kill.

That said, he desires Jane for a wife, her beauty so removed that he is convinced he will never be sexually attracted to her. Her lack of femininity has been dictated by forces higher than her own: "God and nature intended you for a missionary's wife. It is not personal, but mental endowments they have given you: you are formed for labour, not for love. A missionary's wife you must—shall be.... I claim you—not for my pleasure, but for my Sovereign's service"

Bertha Mason Rochester

Jane contrasts, not only to unmarried women, but also to married women. Bertha Mason Rochester is the most physically powerful female in the novel, nearly getting the better of her husband: "the lunatic sprang and grappled his [Rochester's] throat viciously, and laid her teeth to his cheek: they struggled. She was a big woman, in stature almost equalling her husband, and corpulent besides...". On the other hand, the small wife Rochester desires, Jane, is hardly a force to be reckoned with: the most direct physical harm she does to Rochester is "[crush] his hand... and thrust it back to him" without even drawing blood.

Bertha's power is also sexual; she shows "virile" force. If Jane is hot compared to St. John, Bertha is simply on fire; it is her fire that burns down Thornfield. Whereas Jane's explicit sexuality is relegated to a position of secondary importance when she is referred to in mythical terms or using the pronoun "it," Bertha's sexual power is given more importance with similarly metaphorical language: "a figure ran backwards and forwards. What it was, whether beast or human being, one could not, at first sight, tell: it grovelled, seemingly, on all fours; it snatched and growled like some strange wild animal..." Whereas Jane has an ethereal, fairy-like power for those she influences, Bertha has a physical, beastly power over those she affects. Because of her madness, she is a slave to uncontrollably animalistic tendencies that are not governed by the mores of polite society.

The negative effects of her madness are magnified with the unyielding position into which she is forced by her family and by Rochester's. Her fiery femininity belongs in a less-structured society or in a society where women are not dominated by the cold and calculating systems of patriarchy. John Maynard, in his book on sexuality in Brontë's writing, explains that "the 'hot' world of [Brontë's] early tales and novelettes is here relegated to the offstage accounts of Rochester's early life with his unstable wife Bertha in the appropriately warm West Indies".

Finally, whereas Rochester does not examine Bertha mentally before entering into marriage bonds, he is given no other choice with Jane. After accepting his proposal, Jane coolly informs him that she will not give in to burning desires for physical gratification. "I shall keep out of your way all day, as I have been accustomed to do: you may send for me in the evening, when you feel disposed to see me, and I'll come then; but at no other time".

Edward Fairfax Rochester

In this way, Rochester illustrates that women are not the only sexual foils for Jane in the novel. While comparing Jane's journey to a conflict between Dionysiac and Apollonian forces, R. E. Hughes explains that Rochester undoubtedly signifies the former, the "frenzied, demonic, and unrestrained" sexual ethos in Jane's life:

There is probably no other hero of early Victorian fiction so embroiled in sensualtiy as Rochester. His several allusions to his mistresses of the past; the frankly erotic reasons which first attracted him to Bertha Mason; above all, the symbolic presence of Adèle, who may not even be his natural child but whom he keeps by him as a reminder of his descent into passion, is a constant reminder of the sensuality of this man. Rochester is sexual enough for both himself and Jane, indeed, desirous enough to be punished for it. Referring to Rochester's crippling from Thornfield's burning, a former butler of the estate comments, "Some say it was a just judgment on him for keeping his first marriage secret, and wanting to take another wife while he had one living". What St. John lacks, Rochester has too much of at first, so the balanced Jane can choose neither. St. John wants commitment without passion for Jane, while Rochester has passion for Jane, but is not in a position to offer fair commitment Both are unbalanced sexually.

For a man so invested with sexuality, Rochester also describes Jane in other strangely sexless terms. He emphasizes their similarities as individuals: a strongly sexual description would contain their complementary differences, as the etymology of sex (related to divisions or disparities) implies. When he proposes marriage to Jane, he removes sexual inequality from the equation: "My bride is here... because my equal is here, and my likeness". He qualifies Jane above women; she is so different from the feminine spectrum he has known in the past that she must be completely removed from their presence in thought and gender. Note how the conversation moves from "women" to a sexually unimportant "character":

"To women who please me only by their faces, I am the very devil when I find out they have neither souls nor hearts... but to the clear eye and eloquent tongue, to the soul made of fire, and the character that bends but does not break... I am ever tender and true."

"Had you ever experience of such a character, sir? Did you ever love such an one?"

"I love it now... I never met your likeness." Women's faces (Bertha's, 's, perhaps Blanche's) have all proved deceitful regarding what they hide. With Jane, Rochester does not have to see through a painted, feminine face to see her soul, so her sexuality has no bearing, and escapes his attention.

Unwittingly, Rochester makes the case that Jane is not a sexual creature at all, regardless of his lascivious intentions. In his fantasy world, Jane is not a Queen, earthy vixen, nymph, dryad, or other gender-specific creature. She is an elf, a fairy, and a sprite: "If I dared, I'd touch you, to see if you are substance or shadow, you elf!... Tell me now, fairy as you are—can't you give me a charm... to make me a handsome man?" Flirtatiously teasing his paramour, Rochester addresses Jane fantastically: "If that will be *your* married look, I, as a Christian, will soon give up the notion of consorting with a mere sprite or salamander. But what had you to ask, thing?" Explaining to Adèle—a symbol of his egregious former lifestyle— his love for Jane, Rochester paints a picture of Jane's peerless personality, transferring their life together to an extra-terrestrial setting, fit for the unique sexuality of his alien bride. "It was a fairy, and come from Elf-land, it said... I must go with it *out of the common world* to a lonely place—such as the moon, for instance—and it nodded its head towards her the moon's horn, rising over Hay-hill".

When juxtaposed with the idea of marriage to Rochester, Jane still is not entirely gendered: "You—you strange, you almost unearthly thing!—I love as my own flesh. You—poor and obscure, and small and plain as you are—I entreat to accept me as a husband". Her actual "unearthly" magical powers are figurative, as Maynard explains, with a view to demonstrating the influence she has over her company, an influence that cannot be exclusively sexual. "The few examples of what can be taken as devices more stylistic than mythical—primarily versions of that barely undergraduate device they call foreshadowing—are essentially all there is of primary myth.... On the whole [Brontë] subordinates the dogmatic or mythic content of Jane's tale to the aims of psychological understanding" Jane Eyre

Jane's youthfulness, her physically underdeveloped state (due in part to malnourishment at Lowood), and her decidedly otherworldly nature combine to draw the fine line between the childish and the childlike: Jane is never the former, and mainly the latter. When she is depicted with particularly young features or during the parts of the narrative when she is in fact a child, she displays a piercing understanding of human relations as well as a very acute and mature sense of justice. More importantly, she is cynical and brutally truthful; if she has not been this way since birth, she begins to be this way as she begins her narrative journey. In her scathing denunciation of Mrs. Reed, Jane leaves nothing to the imagination."I am not deceitful: if I were, I should say I *loved* you; but I declare I do not love you: I dislike you the worst of anybody in the world except John Reed; and this book about the liar, you may give to your girl, Georgiana, for it is she who tells lies, and not I". Dialogue as brusque and adult as this cannot escape attention; Jane knows her mind on the topic at hand, and speaks it. Her confidence is hardly childish, but its frank nature is childlike in that it is devoid of the guile that belongs to clever and scheming adults. She is unlike the two-faced adult Mr.. Brocklehurst, who offers either a nut or a Psalm to a boy, then rewards the false piety for the Psalm with two nuts.

Mrs. Reed recognizes Jane's bluntness and maturity without thinking twice about it: "'What more have you to say?' she asked, rather in the tone in which a person might address an opponent of adult age than such as is ordinarily used to a child". Indeed, Jane is mature enough as a youth to pose a serious threat to the authority wielded by her guardian, a threat posed by neither of her guardian's daughters. Maynard observes that relationship with Jane quickly emerges as highly competitive; and the competition is ultimately shown to have its main motive in sexual jealousy". If we choose to read Jane Eyre as an extension of Charlotte Brontë, we do well to note that Brontë's choice of the pseudonym, Currer Bell, is also devoid of sex as a label.

Brontë eschews gender in this; she omits it as a measurement of the quality of her work. Similarly, through the voice of a narrating, older Jane, we find that a Jane unencumbered by the strictures of Victorian femininity and sexuality enjoys an enviable place among her peers. She passes unthreateningly by those whom she does not intend to affect, and thereby escapes the expectations of femininity placed upon the likes of Blanche Ingram or Bertha Mason.

Jane shows unparalleled control of her faculties, not because she is actually loveless or sexless, but because she does not let her sexual desire dictate her actions. Blanche, Bertha, Rosamund, Rochester, and St. John all bow before their sexualities (St. John away from, the others towards), slaves to what Jane rules rationally. Gordon fleshes out these extremes, "The subtitle, *An Autobiography*, is true... in its polarities: the tensions... of chill and fire, the iron grip of rational control and the anarchic abandon that Charlotte had known..." If Jane is a child instead of a woman, she is a child in that she is guileless, honest, and innocent instead of silly or indiscreet. If she is an elf, a fairy, and a sprite, it is because her deliberate femininity removes her so far from the world of the recognizable, deviant, and uncontrollable women that she must be described in alien terms.

Thornfield: Jane's Crown

Q. What role does Thornfield play in the life of Jane Eyre?
Or
Q. Is her meeting and marriage justified in this novel?

Each setting in *Jane Eyre*, as was stated previously, affords a new perspective on the single masculine figure surrounded by figures that are qualified, or feminized, according to their relative distance from the center. What I had labeled a microcosm becomes more like a universal model during the Thornfield episode, with Rochester as the sun, and numerous planets in either relatively near, or relatively remote, orbit around him. His purchase power, his money, and the physical manifestations of his money, such as his tenants, his estates, his travels abroad, his servants, his guests, his horse and dog, his ward's mother, and finally his ward's governess, define Rochester. Rochester has inherited his family's property, not through primogeniture, but because everyone else is dead. This includes his cousin Mr.. Fairfax, whose widow works as housekeeper for Rochester, and who offers Jane the position of governess at Thornfield.

Mrs..Fairfax assumes all of the responsibilities that would normally fall to Rochester's wife. She is his relation by marriage, but widowed, and his employee, as her husband did not leave her sufficient means at the time of his demise, but she is not his wife. After reading Jane's advertisement of her qualifications, she invites Jane to Thornfield to provide an education for Adéle, whose mother is also not Rochester's wife. Adéle is a little girl who may or may not be Rochester's daughter, but whom he has nonetheless accepted as his ward. It becomes apparent then that at Thornfield the female lives are completely dependant on the surviving son, whose gravitational pull will nearly draw Jane into orbit with the others, but that the event of the red-room pulses like a subconscious danger signal from the beginning of her story.

Jane steps into this new setting from a coach that stops at Millcote, a community located on the outskirts of Rochester's familial lands, where she, in fact, languishes at the George Inn (one imagines she could as easily languish in the Rochester Arms), reviewing the ambitions leading her forward while waiting for her future to receive her. Jane is, as Rich points out, "young, inexperienced, and hungry for experience, [she] has to confront the central temptation of the female condition – the temptation of romantic love and surrender," and Thornfield is her first journey outside the vicinity of Lowood in ten years. Despite having been qualified for such a position at Lowood, Jane finds she is not entirely satisfied with her experience at Thornfield, and is therefore, in a measure adequate to the task, capable of resisting her "central temptation." Her position as governess is a painful disappointment to her from the beginning:

"And why had I these aspirations and these regrets? It would be difficult to say: I could not then distinctly say it to myself; yet I had a reason, and a logical, natural reason too," because her "new servitude" is become a new awareness, that her work is an occupation until she starts her only legitimate career as a wife. Again, the autobiographical voice of Jane describes this scene from ten years after her marriage when she is able to pinpoint exactly what she could not even approximate at the time. In the chapter following this admission, Jane gives her often-cited feminist manifesto from the parapets of patriarchal repression, though she is no more able to delineate her frustrations at that moment than she is in this earlier passage.

It is emblematic of the novel that "[Jane] rebels against exclusion yet ultimately does not seek to overturn the existing social order," or as Rochester informs Jane, "When I look in your face, one trait contradict[s] another," Admirable as Jane's heroism is, the narrative carries a number of tragic overtones rooted in the text's ambivalence about patriarchy. While Helen Burns's story is affecting in Thomas Gray's vein of "the short and simple annals of the poor," the tragedy of Bertha is the most illustrative example of this ambivalence. Grace Poole, like Mrs. Fairfax, is a husbandless, paid replacement whose nursing duties ironically serve the wife who would typically see to the dispensation of such care at her own home rather than being its recipient.

Instead, while Mrs. Fairfax is a surrogate for performing the household responsibilities of Rochester's wife, Nurse Poole perpetually monitors Rochester's violently insane wife, Bertha, in the attic of the Thornfield house, where they are both shut away from the sun. Bertha Mason is married off by the men in her family, through the inducement of a large cash dowry, as Rochester lets slip while relating her family history to Jane, "My father, and my brother Rowland, knew all this; but they thought only of the thirty thousand pounds, and joined in the plot against me".

This outside money is purchased as security for the second son, the price is a young girl of dubious lineage from Jamaica, who is thence married, in a manner as belittling for her as it was for Rochester, whose father and older brother forced his capitulation, in a manner similar to Mrs. Reed's attempt to force Jane's capitulation. This transaction is merely one example, concerning a character that only speaks for herself with violence, of how unfairly she may have suffered all her life. Rochester tells the story of her mother's similar fate, and Jane recounts the viciousness of the attack on her brother from hearsay rather than after bearing witness. In fact, in the only moment Jane and Bertha are alone; Bertha never harms Jane, and only tears the bridal veil in two. Perhaps she does this as a warning to Jane, or out of contempt for Rochester, as the veil is the only garment remaining of his selections and indicative of his style, or else as an act of self-criticism, or perhaps as a symbolic destruction of her marriage, or of marriage itself.

When considering Bertha, Rey Chow reminds us, "In a text that is considered one of the first major examples of a woman overcoming the patriarchal domination in modern times, we have an uncanny reminder and remainder of the non-Western other," an other without a voice of her own, and for whom the supposed homogeneity of the Christian union has become a living hell. What is purchased therefore is never the genuine article in *Jane Eyre*, only what is freely given constitutes something worth having. Money is another tool of the patriarchy that corrupts through careless use, and with which Rochester can only buy functionaries to replace his wife.

Bertha's non-existence is the foremost example of the charades Rochester plays at Thornfield, but the charades played by Rochester and Blanche stand out for their utility in condensing the subjective layers of meaning Jane must interpret on the matter of her "central temptation." In the space of a few introductory paragraphs, Brontë introduces the carefully interlinked connotations of "merry days," "patriarchal days," and "the pantomime of a marriage".

During the performance enacted between Rochester and Blanche, both dressed in eastern garb (where the western imagination suggests such transactions are culturally acceptable), he lays his treasure at her feet, for Blanche too is available for purchase, and "fasten[s] the bracelets on her arms, and the rings in her ears," alluding to connotations of marriage everywhere in the narrative Miss Temple's wedding, for instance, which resulted in the loss of the Temple name, and her name was her meaning, and coincidentally the loss of her position at the school, or a foreshadowing of the significance of St. John Rivers, as a symbol of holy water, a proposer of marriage, and seemingly a good husband, the bride's well.

It is the awful pantomime of a marriage that costs a woman her identity, and imperils Jane at Thornfield. Just such a pantomime is enacted daily at Thornfield, one which is alarmingly similar to the Bridewell Prison that is the subject of the charades, only it is to the certain knowledge of no one but Rochester, the occasionally lucid Bertha (a bride unwell), and Grace Poole (another holy water reference), who keeps Rochester's bride under lock and key.

Finally, Jane avoids such a marriage to Rochester by virtue of its having come to light that Rochester is already married. Yet, despite her deep and abiding "romantic love" for Rochester, Jane brings about the dissolution of this marriage herself. As a maturing young woman who has outgrown the mania of her neglected girlhood, she meets her resistance to becoming the master's property with a level head. When she considers living with Rochester she recalls, "I thought of Helen Burns...her doctrine of the equality of disembodied souls," and when she later resolves to abandon him to his own devices she admits, "I wanted to be weak that I might avoid the awful passage of further suffering". She writes to her uncle in Madeira, whom she has never met, on the chance that he might want her to come there and care for him. Mason has stopped in Madeira on his way home, but he returns to London upon hearing of this letter from Jane's uncle, and once there he joins the uncle's attorney in traveling with haste to Thornfield, where they arrive just in time to spare Jane from the fate of the red-room, "the pantomime of a marriage." While preparing for their wedding day Rochester again informs Jane as to her own character, and ironically identifies the source that undoes all his careful planning.

"You seem to submit, ...and I like the sense of pliancy you impart," for Jane is not at all pliant, a fact she will readily confess to St. John Rivers, *Jane Eyre* and Governess Relationships. The Victorian governess suffered socially because of her position. The relationship between her and others that were in her class was strained because of her financial situation. She often suffered from "status incongruity." The relationship between a governess and a gentleman was difficult because she was not his financial equal. While the relationship was strained in her novel *Jane Eyre,* leads us to believe that it is not altogether impossible.

When speaking of the governess and relationships we must first deal with "status incongruity" in the novel. There are several instances in *Jane Eyre* where the social strain is clearly displayed. The scene that takes place just before the charades give us a clear depiction of "status incongruity":

Will you play? he [Rochester] asked. I shook my head. He did not insist, which I rather feared he would have done: he allowed me to return quietly to my usual seat. He and his aids now withdrew behind the curtain: the other party which was headed by Colonel Dent, sat down on the crescent of chairs. One of the gentlemen, Mr.. Eshton, observing me, seemed to propose that I should be asked to join them; but Lady Ingram instantly negatived the notion. "NO" I heard her say: "she looks too stupid for any game of the sort." "Status incongruity" is well displayed here. Rochester (not willing to exclude her) invites Jane to play charades, but offers no protests when she rejects his offer. Jane does not want to participate because she feels uncomfortable. Avoiding the game of charades was Jane's way of escaping a situation which might have made both parties uncomfortable. She does not want to be placed in a situation where she is not entirely welcome. Another gentleman Mr.. Eshton, perhaps uncomfortable with the fact that she is excluded from the group, inquires if his counterparts think they should invite Jane to play. Lady Ingram is the one quick to reject the notion, reminding everyone in a subtle way that Jane is in fact beneath them. The whole Ingram family has a negative attitude toward the governess. Blanche claims: I have just one word to say of the whole tribe; they are a nuisance Lady Ingram's response to inviting Jane to play shows the attitude Victorian women had toward the governess.

Not only does Jane's station as a governess bring a social strain, but it also offers a potential threat. Victorian ladies viewed the governess as a threat to their happiness, and feared losing their husbands to the governess. Earlier in the novel when asked on the governess Lady Ingram admits "the word [governess] makes me nervous" Because the governess was a woman who worked for her living, she was associated with the working-class woman. The working-class woman was possessed sexual aggressiveness which was seen inseparable from her economic independence. The governess took her position in the very heart of the home, which brought about an explosive threat of unregulated sexuality Perhaps the threat the governess posed is best displayed when Blanche tells the story of her governess and her brother's tutor:

I helped you in prosecuting (or persecuting) your tutor, whey faced Mr.. Vining–the parson in the pip, as we used to call him. He and Miss Wilson [Blanche's governess] took the liberty of falling in love with each other–at least Tedo and I thought so; we surprised sundry tender glances and sighs which we interpreted as tokens of 'la belle passion,' and I promise you the public soon had the benefit of our discovery: we employed it as a sort of lever to hoist our dead-weights from the house. The Ingrams held no romantic interest in either the governess or the tutor, but their falling in love meant that they would have to find a replacement. Besides for finding a replacement tutor and governess the Ingrams felt that they were a "danger of bad example to innocence of childhood."

While Lady Ingram holds no romantic interest for Rochester, Jane presents a threat to her. Jane is not only a threat to Lady Ingram, because she is in direct competition for Rochester with her daughter, but if Jane is chosen over Blanche the financial stability she seeks for her daughter is lost. The Ingrams want of financial stability is discovered by Rochester later on in the novel. Rochester poses as a gypsy, when Jane asks the gypsy if Rochester will marry Blanche the response is as follows:

Appearances would warrant that conclusion; and, no doubt (though, with an audacity that wants chastising out of you, you seem to question it), they will be superlatively happy pair. He must love such a handsome, noble, witty, accomplished lady; and probably she loves him: or if not his person, at least his purse. I know she considers the Rochester estate eligible to the last degree; though (God pardon me!) I told her something on that point an hour ago, which made her look wondrous grave: the corners for her mouth fell half an in I would advise her blackmailed suitor to look out: if another comes, with a longer or clearer rent-roll,–he's dished.

The Victorian governess was not meant to capture the heart or attention of a gentleman, especially her master. This belief led to strained relationships between the governess and her master. However, the governess was bound to find herself the "daily object of scrutiny" by men of similar age or in Jane's case a man who is considerably older.

Throughout the novel we are given instances where their relationship is strained because of the differences in their classes. Upon their initial meeting Rochester is rude and blames Jane for his fall). Rochester also does not expose his love for Jane until he has first convinced her that he is going to marry Blanche Ingram The uneasy attraction in the novel leads to the discovery of Rochester's first wife, Bertha. The marriage of Rochester and Jane is accomplished at the end of the novel only because of two events; the death of Bertha and Jane coming into independency. It is only when Jane has money of her own and is re-established in the social class to which she belonged that her marriage is able to take place without objections, or further complications.

Takes the impossible relationship, and makes it a reality. She does this, however, without losing the realism of the relationship. *Jane Eyre* is not a story of Cinderella and Prince Charming, Jane does not get rescued. In fact Jane works her way up the social ladder, accomplishing marriage without the social strain it would have hd if she were still a governess.

The Essential Role of Victorian Servants, Especially the Housekeeper and Nursemaid

Q. Discuss the essential roles played by the servants and housemaids in the lives of their owners.

I desired liberty; for liberty I gasped; for liberty I uttered a prayer; it seemed scattered on the wind then faintly blowing. I abandoned it and framed a humbler supplication; for change, stimulus: that petition too seemed swept off into vague space; "Then" I cried, half desperate, "Grant me at least a new servitude."

Jane was not approaching any new territory when she wanted a new servitude. In fact 12.8 percent of the female population in England and Wales were engaged in domestic service in the nineteenth century. In nineteenth-century England, for any household with social pretensions at least one domestic servant was essential. The guide to the social status of a well-off Victorian family was the status of the domestics employed in the well-to-do families employed as large a staff as they could afford, while middle-class families held to the minimum of one.

There were many types of servants, among them the housekeeper, and the nurse. On the female side of the domestics, there were numerous servants. Since this essay is not concerned with male domestics, only a list of female domestics is provided. Female domestics would include the housekeeper, the cook, lady's maid, nurse, housemaids, kitchen maids, scullery-maids and laundry staff The housekeeper was responsible for hiring and dismissing the female staff. The housekeeper was expected to be a "steady middle-aged woman... morally exemplary and assiduous to the harmony, comfort, and economy of the family" Most often a housekeeper would stay with the same family for several years, forming a close bond with the family.

If the family came into financial trouble, a loyal housekeeper might stay behind as a general servant, while the rest of the staff would be dismissed. Housekeepers that worked for kin were either unmarried daughters of any age or widows Middle and upper class families with children also kept a nurse maid. She would be a young girl under the age of twenty. The nursemaid was responsible for dressing and undressing the children, playing with them, and taking them out of a walk. The nursemaid was often spent more time with the children then their own mother. She acted as a mother figure, performing most if not all of the duties that belong to the mother. The nursemaid's continual involvement with the children spawned a type of mother-child relationship.

The head nurse of larger households would run a separate department. She was not under the rule of the housekeeper. The nurse directly served the children. They had separate meals in the nursery away from the rest of the household. In most households the nurse was depended upon to administer punishment and enforce discipline on the children. Some nurses used their authority to make their charges miserable Servants were an essential for households with social pretensions. They defined the social status of those they worked for. Servants played a substantial role not only in the homes of their masters, but in the lives of the children and other servants.

Q. "Being an orphan Jane is succeeded in every step of life" Explain.

Or

Q. "Jane acquires all her dreams in reality" Discuss.

Or

Q. Is Jane unfortunate enough to be deceased like anything useless?

Or

Q. How does Jane faces success in blowing out male oriented society?

In Victorian literature, the orphan can be read as an unfamiliar and strange figure outside the dominant narrative of domesticity. They were often portrayed as poor children without a means of creating a successful life for themselves. Charlotte's *Jane Eyre,* however, is a portrayal of a female orphan who triumphs over almost every environment she enters. Therefore, Jane's ability to overcome the hardships that she encounters is a fictional success story. By discussing Jane's early life as an orphan at Gateshead and Lowood, and also her relationships with Helen Burns and Adele Varens, one can see how 's novel is an escape from the familiar predestined fate of at least one orphan in the novel—Jane.

Jane becomes an orphan after her father, a poor clergyman, is infected with typhus fever while visiting among the poor of a large manufacturing town. Jane's mother becomes infected from him, and both die within a month of each other. Because Jane is still a young child when this occurs, she knows no other life but of that as an orphan. Mr.. Reed, her uncle who informally adopts her, wants Jane to be brought up in a positive familial environment. After his death, however, Mrs. Reed makes certain that this is not possible. Through her character, draws on the archetypical literary figure of the wicked stepmother. Although Jane now lives with the Reeds, a financially well-off family, she is still treated like a poor, working-class orphan.

While at Gateshead, Jane is constantly reminded of her lower class, orphaned status. Jane's position in the Reed household is inferior and intolerable. Even the Reeds' servant, Miss Abbot, tells her, "you ought not to think yourself on an equality with the Misses Reed and Master Reed, because Missis kindly allows you to be brought up with them". Jane is at the mercy of the Reed family's demands and is severely punished for anything they deem improper. Although she does possess a passionate disposition that the Reeds often use as a justification for punishment, Jane is forced into a "habitual obedience." Therefore, she obediently listens to John as he reminds her of her insignificant, poor status: you are a dependant, mama says; you have no money; your father left you none; you ought to beg, and not to live here with gentlemen's children like us, and eat the same meals we do, and wear clothes at our mama's expense. The constant verbal and physical abuse from the Reeds makes Jane's time at Gateshead, for the most part, intolerable. She is a social outcast in the Reeds' home. The only peace that she finds at Gateshead is during times of voluntary solitude and while reading. Like orphans throughout English literature, she must develop an identity through the challenge of social mobility, a challenge that keeps her inferior while at Gateshead.

Because of her young, orphaned status, Jane is unable to escape from the torment at Gateshead until Mrs. Reed decides to send her away. But her experience at Gateshead becomes the ground on which she is able to build her future character. Jane is alone without any parental love to guide her except for Bessie's occasional show of affection. She must make a life for herself by herself. With the lack of parental attachment, Jane welcomes the liberation from the Reeds and is able to embrace the parting even with the insecurity that pervades her.

Although Lowood, which is a charity school, provides Jane with a means to escape the abuse of the Reeds, the living conditions are extremely poor. The winter snows keep the girls confined within the walls of the garden, clothing is insufficient, often resulting in frostbitten toes and fingers, and the supply of food is inadequate. For the first time, however, Jane is able to live with and interact with other orphans. It is here where she is able to truly begin her transformation from a miserable, lower class, orphaned child into an ambitious, independent woman.

Unfortunately, Jane's oppressive misfortunes do not immediately cease simply because her living environment changes. Soon after her arrival at Lowood, she is demeaned by Mr.. Brocklehurst and once again reminded of her inferior status as an orphan. After he refers to her as "a liar", he adds the following:

This I learned from her benefactress; from the pious and charitable lady who adopted her in her orphan state, reared her as her own daughter, and whose kindness, whose generosity the unhappy girl repaid by an ingratitude so bad, so dreadful, that at last her excellent patroness was obliged to separate her from her own young ones, fearful lest her vicious example should contaminate their purity. Mr.. Brocklehurst nullifies Jane's credibility by using her orphaned status against her. He insinuates that Jane is evil and incapable of interacting with a normal family unit and, therefore, that she should not be trusted by anyone at Lowood. This accusation of Jane's malevolence is one of the many examples throughout the novel that displays her passionate disposition and is consistent with the manner in which orphans were depicted by many Victorian novelists. Even as she struggles for independence as a woman, Jane is often reminded of her wicked qualities. Jane's story is even more profound because she gradually overcomes this wicked disposition, mostly while at Lowood.

Although Helen Burns is technically not an orphan (her father is still alive), she attends Lowood in order to get an education. As does Jane, Helen also fits into the "angel-demon" mold. On one hand, Helen is often punished by Miss Scatcherd and referred to as a "dirty, disagreeable girl!". She is a feeble child, and like the nineteenth century literary portrayal of orphans, she is a social outcast. Unlike, Jane, however, Helen never breaks free from this stereotype. But Helen also possesses qualities that are almost angelic. After Helen is unjustly punished (at least Jane feels that she is), Jane states, "The punishment seemed to me in a high degree ignominious, especially for so great a girl [...]". Because this incident occurs before Jane and Helen become close friends, Jane still does not quite know what to make of Helen Burns. She asks herself, "I wonder what sort of girl she is—whether good or naughty". Jane soon learns that Helen is good, and Helen's counseling undoubtedly helps Jane come to terms with her past and move on with a clear sense of true goodness.

In comparison to her life at Gateshead, Lowood offers Jane the opportunity to grow out of her "childlike disposition" and strive for a meaningful life on her own. As she matures, Jane realises that her orphaned status does not limit her to living a meaningless, oppressed existence, and she ultimately grows tired of the mundane lifestyle that Lowood offers. She begins to loathe the confinements of Lowood: "school-rules, school-duties, school-habits and notions, and voices, and faces, and phrases, and costumes and preferences and antipathies: such was what I knew of existence. And now I felt that it was not enough". When Bessie visits Jane after not seeing her for eight years, she states, "Oh, you are quite a lady, Miss Jane! I knew you would be: you will get on whether your relations notice you or not". Bessie, knowing Jane's orphaned status, concludes that Jane has become a well-rounded, skillful individual and will undoubtedly be able to lead a successful life on her own.

Jane's desire for a new servitude is fulfilled, and she leaves Lowood to become the governess of another orphan, Adele Varens. Although it can be argued that Rochester is the father of Adele, her status at Thornfield is still that of an orphan. Adele's living environment is much better than Jane's while at Gateshead, possibly because there are no other children around to demean her; however, like Jane, she lacks the ability to garner any form of familial love. Although Rochester supplies Adele with a home, a servant, and even a governess (Jane), he seems to view her as more or less a living object. Rochester insults Adele's existence as he informs Jane of her pitiful history before he brought her to Thornfield:

I even took the poor thing out of the slime and mud of Paris, and transplanted it here, to grow up clean in the wholesome soil of an English country garden. Mrs. Fairfax found you to train it; but now you know that it is the illegitimate offspring of a French opera-girl, you will perhaps think differently of your post and protégée. Through her past experience as an orphan, Jane realises the importance of nurturing Adele. Jane's compassion for Adele is evident, for she tells Rochester that "Adele is not answerable for either her mother's faults or yours: I have a regard for her, and now that I know she is, in a sense, parentless—forsaken by her mother and disowned by you, sir,—I shall cling closer to her than before". She realises that Adele is not to blame for her fate, and to view Adele in a negative manner would not only be hypocritical, it would also be wrong.

Jane's lowly status as an orphaned child is a major factor in shaping her character as she develops into adulthood. She learns from her hardships at Gateshead and her early days at Lowood, and these experiences serve as the foundation on which her later independence develops. Along with these experiences, she is involved in relationships with other children of orphaned status. Both Helen Burns and Adele Varens play a significant role in helping Jane become a successful governess and the eventual wife of her true love. Because of these experiences and relationships, Jane's past as a passionate, oppressed, insignificant, orphaned child is buried by her ability to overcome it. Her ability to overcome this sentence for failure is, indeed, like a fairy-tale.

Q. Explain Bertha Rochester as the Vampire in the Attic.

While the character of Bertha Rochester has provoked countless essays and discussions on the treatment of the mentally insane in the Victorian era, her madness has an underlying theme of power and sexuality. She is exotic and majestic, dark and fine: Bertha Rochester, in short, is a dream woman before her madness comes into fruition. Her actions, however, are hardly ideal, and her madness drives her husband to extreme measures.

In a sort of fairytale fashion, Bertha is carried away to the top floor of Thornfield Hall and locked in the attic, guarded by her drunken keeper, Grace Poole. She comes out on full moon nights, stalking the halls of Thornfield whenever her gatekeeper falls into a drunken slumber. Bertha's animal nature makes her a threat to all who come in contact with her, and she can drive grown men to tears and frustration. She appears more masculine than feminine, being described as "a big woman, in stature almost equalling her husband, and corpulent besides: she showed virile force…" (Brontë 290; 26). Bertha Rochester is the epitome of the female vampire; therefore, she must be destroyed.

Bertha's appearance after her transition into the madwoman evokes a sense of fear to all who see her. While this image of the unchaste, immoral "madwoman" becomes the cultural icon for the Victorians, Bertha's resemblance to vampires is what causes the greatest concern and reproach. She is a dark figure dressed in white, with bloodshot eyes and a purple, swollen face, as if her very face has been overfilled with blood, or as if she has been gripped by death and turned into a corpse. While many believe that vampires must be pale, their visage takes on a new vitality once they have fed from their victims. They can "appear in all parts, as the nostril, cheeks, breast, mouth, etc. turgid and full of blood". Bertha exudes a more animal like stance than that of a human, seen on all fours and growling when first revealed to Jane after the wedding ceremony is disturbed. Madness has made her into a savage beast, a prowling predator; thus, she remains locked in her tower until she can escape, or until she dies.

Like a typical vampire, she cannot cross the threshold uninvited, or without her keeper allowing her to venture forth. When Jane learns of Thornfield being burnt to the ground, the messenger tells the story of how Grace gave into drink and passed out while guarding the door; thus, Bertha was able to escape and start the fire that would consume Thornfield and herself. Bertha attacks at night when the moon is high, since "the undead ramble at night and spend the daytime in their tombs...". The night she attacks her brother, Mason, the moon is full and red, alluding to the bloodshed that will follow that night. The only way she can die is if she is incinerated. Even though Bertha's last act is one of suicide since she jumped off the roof, the fire that takes Thornfield Hall drives Bertha to her ultimate demise.

The characteristic that makes Bertha most like a vampire is her bloodlust. While her first attack on Rochester did not draw blood, her intent was to murder him in his sleep and secure her freedom. When this fails, Bertha attacks the next powerful male who enters her chamber: her brother, Mason. He had a hand in marrying Bertha to Rochester, and in a sense of revenge, she assaults the surviving patriar As he lies in the bedchamber, blood pouring out of his stab wound, his flesh ripped by her teeth, Mason recalls Bertha's actions: "She sucked the blood: she said she'd drain my heart"). She uses her teeth once more when she attacks Rochester for the second time, clamping onto his cheek with her bite. These two men could have certainly died by Bertha's actions, and both had to struggle and fight against her in order to sustain their lives. Mason barely escaped, suffering from extreme blood loss. Had Rochester not been able to escape the final fire that brought down Thornfield, Bertha would have taken his life along with hers. She poses a serious threat to the two men who held power over her: a brother and a husband.

Bertha's defiance against her patriarchs could have certainly been a cause for her prisoner's sentence in the attic, since both madness and vampirism are revolutions that oppose male power. In protest, Bertha attempts to escape her lair and strikes out against those who have shut her up in the first place, making her even more of a threat and helping to develop her newfound vampire nature.

Her nightly ventures are the most obvious of Bertha's vampire qualities, especially considering they occur on full moon nights or when people are in a deep sleep. Her first attack on Mr.. Rochester jolted Jane awake after hearing a murmur in the hall, and her panic increased as a demonic laugh rang outside her chamber. Bertha's assault on Mason on the full moon night again awoke Jane when a cry was heard in the still night air along with a "deadly struggle".

The night when Bertha comes to Jane's own chamber, she rummages through the closet and scares Jane into unconsciousness. As the reader can tell, the common factor of all these attacks is the fact that Jane was either the first one to hear them, or they happened to her. Was Jane truly awake when these incidents took place? One key quality of vampires is their ability to send themselves into the dream world of their lover or their prey. Jane can be seen as competition for Bertha, and one way to rid oneself of an opponent is to scare her away. While Bertha was attacking her patriarchal oppressors, she was also trying to rid herself of the next powerful woman in the household. Unfortunately for Bertha, Jane was not willing to back down.

Bertha's sexuality does not hold precedence in Brontë's novel, but remnants of the woman Rochester's wife used to be are discussed in brief. In his account of their betrothal, Rochester refers to the Spanish Town inhabitant as a beautiful creature who "flattered me, and lavishly displayed for my pleasure her charms and accomplishments". He goes on to say that he was rather tricked into the marriage, for while Bertha had no great merit to her character, she over-stimulated his senses and excited him to the point of acceptance.

Rochester was tricked into marrying a woman he did not really love, and a woman who had a family history of overindulgence and madness. Bertha is seen as violently sexual, a psychosexual predator; this flaw takes away her humanity. In comparison to Jane, Bertha is the perfect antithesis to Victorian ideals: unchaste, bestial, and wild. Yet while Bertha may be more of a wild creature, a sexual symbol of women's nature, Jane still has much in common with this vampire vision. In the end, however, "consumed in the acceptable vampire manner, by a fiery leap", Bertha is destroyed in order for Jane to find happiness with a man long ago seduced by the perfect fantasy.

Q. Explain the conflicting terms of Vampire and Human in concern with Jane's character.

Or

Q. "As coin has two sides, the character can also have two sides" Discuss.

Jane Eyre tells Mr. Rochester in one of their moonlit meetings, "I am a free human being with an independent will," to which he replies, "And your will shall be your destiny". Jane is a strong woman who struggles to be independent in a patriarchal society, making her a threat to the Victorian framework, much like Bertha. Although she might not always be caged, like the young Jane had been in the famous red room at Gateshead, Jane longs to be free from the constraints of a society that appears to be ashamed of powerful women.

Her nearest counterpart, Bertha, also struggles with this need to be free, although she is fighting to leave the actual prison of Thornfield, as well as the patriarchal powers keeping her hidden. Bertha, in her caged state, represents the inner battle Jane must suffer to either be a typical Victorian woman, an ideal human female, or a self-righteous and liberated woman, a vampire in society. The major problem with rebellion, in the physical and sexual sense, is that it is a masculine subject.

Jane must be a silent revolutionary, as well as sexually repressed, in her battle if she wishes to remain a female figure, whereas Bertha is already seen as a masculine figure, and thus is a greater threat to her male repressors. Jane is given names of mythical creatures throughout the novel, often being called an imp or a fairy by Mr.. Rochester; although she is never referred to as a vampire, the similarities remain. Her bestiality, her power, and her sexuality, repressed as it may be, remain a theme throughout the novel, paralleling Bertha in many ways. In order to be victorious in finding her humanity, Jane must have Bertha destroyed. Though she might not have been the immediate cause of Bertha's vampiric demise, Jane does have an indirect impact on her death.

From the very beginning of *Jane Eyre,* Jane is given an animal like image. Unjustly as it may be delivered, she cannot escape these metaphors that are a constant, especially in Jane's younger years. John Reed calls her a rat, Bessie likens her to a cat, and the child Jane is locked up in the red-room like a caged animal. She is seen as less than human, much like Bertha, making her an outcast to society. Jane is seen as a different sort of human being, a foreigner in the lives of others, especially with the Reed children; thus, she is cast from her peers in a sort of xenophobia, giving her a "vampiric ambience of the [Victorian] period"). For this reason, Mrs.

Reed sends her away to the red room, and even to Lowood, in the hopes that Jane can assimilate herself with fellow human beings, especially her female peers. Her attacks on the men in her life can be seen as animal instinct as well. In her younger days, Jane would fight with her fists, as well as her words, against patriarchal figures; this scenario is best seen when she assaults John Reed in the breakfast room, where Jane "received him in frantic sort" after he refuses to stop the insults on her character and strikes out at her.

In her adult days, Jane, though less likely to have violent outbursts, still has moments where she must strike out in a powerful way in order to show her authority. With Mr.. Rochester, she performs a pseudo-castration in their carriage ride back from shopping: "I crushed his hand, which was ever hunting mine, vigourously, and thrust it back to him red with the passionate pressure". Although this scene can also be interpreted as repressed sexuality, Jane is also rebelling against a patriarchal figure who is trying to use her for his sexual desires. She does not necessarily act in modesty, but in a sense of self-control against the primary man in her life.

The theme of blood appears to follow Jane from childhood into adulthood. First occurring with John Reed, Jane recalls, "I felt a drop or two of blood from my head trickle down my neck...". Jane's neck will be referenced again later when Rochester speaks about Jane's station being in his heart and his foot "on the necks of those who would insult you, now and hereafter" (Jane's station in society, therefore, can be seen on the necks of her fellow citizens, including men. As is the custom of vampires, they pierce the necks of their victims, which can be seen in such tales as Le Fanu's *Carmilla,* when Laura talks about the mark left at her throat after seeing Carmilla in her room. Her next encounter with blood comes at Thornfield Hall, when Mr.. Mason is attacked by Bertha. Jane does not seem to mind the blood and chaos of the situation, being more afraid of Grace Poole than of the wounded man: "A pale and bloody spectacle under my eyes and hands...the rest I could bear; but I shuddered at the thought of Grace Poole bursting out upon me. During the entire night, Jane calmly dips her hands into bloody water and washes Mr.. Mason's wounds, no questions asked.

This submersion in blood can be likened to another scene in *Carmilla.* The vampire, Mircalla – an anagram of Carmilla – is found lying in a pool of blood seven inches deep within her coffin, since this blood is crucial to her vitality. Jane, herself, submerges her hands into the blood of Mason, another patriarchal figure, and monitors his state between life and death. Still later at Thornfield, after Bertha is revealed, Mr.. Rochester alludes to Jane's stubborn nature and lack of emotions when he says, "But I err: you have not wept at all! I see a white cheek and a faded eye, but no trace of tears. I suppose, then, your heart has been weeping blood?". Again, Jane's character and self-control are being called into question because of her inability to shed a tear, as though she were a dead creature. Jane wounds Mr.. Rochester, emotionally if not physically, and regains the power she needs to leave him behind.

Another vampiric quality possessed by Jane is immortality. While Mr.. Rochester wishes for Bertha to perish, being almost appalled at her resilience, he sees Jane as this immortal and mythical creature that haunts his every waking moment. Mr.. Rochester even ventures to tell Jane that "Death was not for such as [she]" This reference to immortality is not the first one within the novel. When Jane first meets Mr.. Brocklehurst at the Reeds', he inquires as to where "the wicked" go at death and how one might avoid such a place. Jane replies, "I must keep in good health, and not die". Good health merely means that one must sustain life to Jane, who does not even think about the faith aspect of Mr.. Brocklehurst's questioning. Even after Jane leaves Thornfield, her immortality can be seen. She must wander through the streets alone, without food or shelter, until she finds Marsh End. When Hannah refuses Jane entry, she practically begs for death; however, Jane does not die, despite her pleas.

Instead, Jane is taken in by and nursed back to health by the Riverses, especially Diana and Mary. When they first take in the sick Jane, the women see her as "white as clay or death" and remark that she must be famished due to her being "very thin, and how very bloodless!" Jane attaches herself to Diana and Mary, much like Carmilla attached herself to Laura, when Laura's father took in Carmilla during her sickness. St. John even remarks to Jane "my sisters had evidently become attached to you, and your society gave them unusual pleasure, making Jane's relationship to Diana and Mary seem odd in their closeness. St. John goes on to explain that he had to break up this comfort level so that his sisters could leave Marsh End, though one could say he broke up this comfort out of his need re-establish his power over Diana and Mary. Jane seems to play a stronger role in their lives than their brother, which causes a threat to yet another patriarchal figure.

Although Jane is not a sexual character in the novel, she has a sense of suppressed sexuality that makes her appealing to Mr.. Rochester. Jane is a dark and mysterious figure who appears at Thornfield Hall in a fairytale setting. She encounters her master in the moonlight when thinking about Bessie's story of the Gytrash. Her mystical appearance seems to throw off Mr.. Rochester; thus, whenever he recalls that night's events, he likens Jane to an elf or a sprite. Jane was not like her aunt and cousins, with their graceful appearance and fair features. She is a plain woman with dark hair and eyes. The most intriguing aspect of Jane's personality, however, is how she seems to seduce the men in her life without even trying. Even if St. John's proposal was not sexually driven and attraction was not necessarily a factor, he was intrigued by her sense of duty, her entire being. St. John declares to Jane, "I have watched you ever since we first met: I have made you my study for ten months". Her very presence in his life made St. John stand up and pay attention. The same can be said for Mr.. Rochester, though in a more violent manner.

He is absolutely taken by Jane in every way. She seems to seduce him, just as Bertha had once done to him back in Spanish Town. The difference between these women, however, is that Bertha knew she was being a seductress, whereas Jane was being herself. Vampires are known for being mysterious and alluring, whether in appearance or action. Carmilla was a beautiful young woman who won over Laura by her sheer beauty, as well as her magical words. Jane may not be a beauty like Bertha, or even Céline, but she is able to craft herself in a way to be appealing to Mr.. Rochester. The night he proposes to Jane, Mr.. Rochester expresses just what she has done to him:

I have never met your likeness, Jane: you please me, and you master me – you seem to submit, and I like the sense of pliancy you impart; while I am twining soft, silken skein round my finger, it sends a thrill up my arm to my heart. I am influenced – conquered; and the influence is sweeter than I can express; and the conquest I undergo has a witchery beyond any triumph *I* can win. Jane has conquered Mr.. Rochester in much the same way as Bertha, even though he may not admit it. Now that Jane has bewitched her lover, she can move in and master his heart even further. She can fight against a patriarchy that had suppressed her long ago, and her immortality will help ensure Jane has plenty of time to dine on her prey.

Bertha and Jane, the two women of Thornfield Hall, epitomize the antithesis of Victorian women. Their actions constantly cause revolutions. From Spanish Town to Thornfield, Bertha uses her vices to win Mr.. Rochester, and then destroys his life because of them. From Gateshead to Thornfield, Jane uses her determination and will to win Mr.. Rochester, and then takes over his life with them. While both women possess "female traits that can be accepted in fantasy but not in male-dominated society"), Jane represents a tamer Bertha. Victorian society can deal with this hybrid, half human and half vampire, better than they can deal with a mad woman with a bloodlust. Bertha must not die for Jane to win the battle for the patriarch, Mr.. Rochester, but because she cannot pretend to be part of the society. In the end, Jane played the role of domesticated wife, even sending Adèle to a boarding school because being a governess once more was "impracticable; my times and cares were now required by another – my husband needed them all".

Bertha could never have played this role with Mr.. Rochester; thus, she commits suicide in the flames caused by her own hand, and Jane emerges from her hiding a victorious woman. Still, Jane remains a powerful figure in the novel until the very end, even though she appears to take on "a 'position of powerlessness' as her source of authority and authenticity", which becomes a sort of silent rebellion. Although her authority may not threaten Mr.. Rochester, most Victorian men would not be so quick to accept such a woman who could test their authority in this manner. Of course, turning fantasy into reality squashes the dream, and the perfect female vampire can never be more than a passing fancy in a period where powerful women cannot be accepted.

Q. What is the significant role of Gypsies in the plot of Jane Eyre?

Despite the important role Gypsies played in the nineteenth century, they were not automatically accepted as equals in society. In fact, from the moment they set foot on European soil, the Gyspies were misunderstood and even feared. These feelings became manifest in prejudices, which led to discriminatory actions. At the same time, however, Victorian society found itself fascinated with these strange Gypsies. The gypsy motif in *Jane Eyre* reflects the ambiguous attitude of Victorian society toward Gypsies. The depiction of "the Gypsy" at Thornfield Hall and the characters' reactions to her are reflections of prejudices based on the Gypsies' skin colour, way of life, and traditions, and are also reflections of discriminatory treatment the Gypsies suffered. Simultaneously, many of the descriptions of the Gypsy are also the product of a romanticized view of Gypsies, which manifests itself works of fiction by many other authors throughout the Victorian Era.

The Victorians' initial impression of the Gypsies was not a favorable one. At first, the prejudices against Gypsies had obvious sources. Settled society has always had a fear of foreigners, so naturally, "the earliest response to the 'Egyptian' immigrants was rooted, generally, in a xenophobic fear and mistrust of aliens". Besides being mistrusted as foreigners, the Gypsies fell victim to racial prejudice because of the colour of their skin. Even long before the nineteenth century, "the conviction that blackness denotes inferiority was already well-rooted in the Western mind. The nearly black skins of many Gypsies marked them out to be victims of this prejudice"). Even if Charlotte never saw a Gypsy, she reflects these perceptions of them in her description of "the Gypsy" that visits Thornfield Hall. The Gypsy's most noticeable feature in Sam's mind as he describes her to the assembled guests is that she is "'almost as black as a crock'".

Later, when Jane goes for her interview with the Gypsy, she notes that her face "looked all brown and black". Since the Gypsy turns out to be Mr.. Rochester, and there is no indication that he actually blackened his face for his disguise, it may be that the Gypsy's black skin is an imagined product of the characters' preconceived notions about what Gypsies look like. Whatever the case, the fact that makes the Gypsy's skin colour prominent in the characters' description of her reflects the racial prejudice that existed toward Gypsies in Victorian England.

The Gypsies also faced prejudices about their way of life. The Gypsies' travelling lifestyle aroused suspicion because of the common belief that "itinerancy served merely as a cloak for a deviant range of predatory, parasitic, and criminal activities". People were distrustful of Gypsies simply because they moved around a lot. Accompanying this mistrust was "a belief in the superiority of the settled over the nomadic culture and the incompatibility between the two". Nineteenth-century England was the perfect breeding-ground for this notion. As society became more industrialized, the population moved out of the untamed countryside and into the cities.

While the rest of society settled down in permanent residences in the cities, the Gypsies continued their nomadic existence in what was now viewed as the wilderness. Thus, "In contrast to the new ways of civilised, industrial society [the Gypsies'] culture was seen as backward and primitive". As people became more settled, they began to feel that their way of life was normal. The presence of the wandering Gypsies challenged this, and caused many people to view them negatively because they were different. These prejudices are reflected in the guests' reactions to the Gypsy. Lady Ingram calls her "'a low imposter'". Sam observes that she is "'quite troublesome'" and that "'she looks such a rough one'" and "'such a tinkler'". Through the unfavorable reaction of her characters towards the Gypsies, articulates the prejudices of her society against the Gypsies.

The fortune-telling issue was also a source for suspicions about the Gypsies. Fortune-telling has always been associated with pagan ideas, so the presence of Gypsy fortune-tellers in a Victorian society dominated by the Church obviously caused a commotion. Added to the problem was the fact that the Gypsies "failed to practise with any conviction one or the other of the prevalent religions". Due to this apparent lack of religion, much of society in general thought Gypsies "to be inflicting their magical and devilish practices on an innocent, Christian society". Lady Ingram obviously feels this Gypsy will corrupt her innocent daughters as she "wrings her hands" and begs Blanche to "'pause—reflect!'". Some of the guests at Thornfield are certainly skeptical of the Gypsy's powers. The Misses Eshton are not sure, demanding, "'is she a real fortune-teller?'".

Blanche Ingram, after hearing an unfavorable fortune, is ready to dismiss the Gypsy as an imposter all together. She condescends to her fellow guests with her observation that their "'organs of wonder and credulity are easily excited'" at the prospect of "'a genuine witch'. She concludes that the Gypsy told her fortune "'in hackneyed fashion'" and told her "'what such people usually tell'" (. Here, actually pokes more fun at Blanche than she does at the Gypsy because, unbeknownst to Blanche, what the Gypsy has told her is an exaggerated version of the truth about Mr.. Rochester's fortune. But at the time, Blanche views the Gypsy as a complete fraud, thus supporting the prejudiced view of Gypsies.

The prejudices against Gypsies become manifest in scores of discriminatory legislation against Gypsies. The first anti-Gypsy Act in England was passed in 1530, just twenty-five years after the Gypsies' arrival there. The Act's intention was to rid the country of all Gypsies by banning further immigration and requiring the Gypsies already living in England to leave or suffer confiscation of their goods, imprisonment, and execution as felons. There are reports of deportations throughout the sixteenth century and of executions as late as the seventeenth century.

In 1783, all existing laws directed specifically at Gypsies were repealed, but the discriminatory treatment continued in the form of new laws. Throughout the nineteenth century the various Poor Law, Vagrancy, Hawkers, Highways, Health, Housing and Education Acts resulted in Gypsies, and other nomads, being prosecuted (or threatened with prosecution) for such offenses as setting fires, damaging grass by camping, possessing a dog without a license or collar, fortune-telling, taking sticks and ferns without permission, damaging crops, and begging.

Mr.. Eshton, a member of the party assembled at Thornfield, feels it within his duty as a magistrate to threaten the Gypsy with prosecution. He declares, "'Tell her she shall be put in the stocks if she does not take herself off'"). Stocks were common instruments of punishment in Victorian England. Mr.. Eshton's reaction reflects the discriminatory treatments that the Gypsies were receiving in real life at this time.

Victorian society was very hypocritical towards the Gypsies. As George K. Behlmer says, "precisely because the Gypsies stood apart from the mainstream of urban-industrial life, they held a special fascination for the critics of that life. What appeared to be a characteristic restlessness among Gypsies therefore evoked both romantic praise and systematic harassment during the last third of the nineteenth century". At the same time that the Gypsies were being discriminated against, they were also being romanticized. Behlmer cites as one reason for this the fact that Gypsies "could serve as representatives of the hardy competence associated with 'true' country folk" because they were "monuments to the Victorian ideal of mens sana in corpre sano (a sound mind in a sound body)". Some people in the crowded cities of the newly-industrialized society missed the simplicity of life in the country and were attracted to the free lifestyle of the Gypsies. Society's fascination with Gypsies manifested itself in the literature of the time. Beside the romanticized descriptions of the Gypsy by the characters of *Jane Eyre,* romantic images of the Gypsy also appeared in works of fiction by many other authors throughout the Victorian Era.

Romanticized notions of Gypsy life are first evident in the reactions of the ladies at Thornfield to the Gypsy. Prior to the Gypsy's appearance at Thornfield, they had "'talked of going to Hay Common to visit the gipsy camp'" They treat the Gypsies' homes as if they are museum exhibits, revealing their attitude of blind fascination towards a group of people that they obviously do not understand. One thing the young ladies may have been shocked to realise, however, is that they are acting like Gypsies themselves. The activities of the group of aristocrats, who travel around, spending a week or two at each friend's home, are really quite similar to the nomadic existence of the Gypsies. Charlotte uses this motif as a way to satirize the aristocrats.

Enticed by the magical and mysterious aspects of fortune telling, the young men proceed to romanticize the Gypsy even further. Frederick Lynn declares that the Gypsy is "'a real sorceress'," and his brother feels that "'it would be a thousand pities to throw away such a chance of fun'" The whole group considers the idea of having their fortunes told "'excellent sport'". When Sam leaves to summon the Gypsy, the "mystery, animation, expectation rose to full flow". These young people obviously share the romanticized notion their society has about Gypsies.

Jane's description of the Gypsy is also romanticized. The Gypsy wears "a red cloak" and " a broad-brimmed gipsy hat, tied down with a striped handkerchief under the chin". Real Gypsy women used this very image to promote the superstitious beliefs about their powers and to lure customers. The "impression [that Gypsy women had magical powers] was further enhanced if the Gypsy, dressed for the part by wearing colourful headscarves and droopy earrings, was old, ugly, and with the appearance of a 'wild-eyed hag'". Mr.. Rochester obviously picks the perfect disguise for making Jane think he is really a Gypsy.

Jane, despite her practical, no-nonsense nature, finds herself caught up in romantic ideas about the Gypsy as well. She describes how the Gypsy's "strange talk, voice, manner, had by this time wrapped me in a kind of dream. One unexpected sentence came from her lips after another, till I got involved in a web of mystification" *Jane Eyre* is not the only novel that mirrors this romanticized view of Gypsies. Inspired by the works of leading Gypsy scholar George Borrow, author of several fictional and semi-fictional works about Gypsy life, many prominent authors of the time began to include Gypsy characters in their works).

Borrow and other Gypsy scholars enjoyed warm relations with Thomas Carlyle, George Eliot, Bulwer Lytton, Algernon Charles Swinburne, and Theodore Watts-Dunton. As a result of this friendly relationship, "the [Gypsy scholars] and their literary friends generated 'a very craze for the Gypsy' that had no European equivalent".

This Gypsy craze was manifested in the formation of the Gyspy Lore Society in 1888. Society's fascination with Gypsies had its parallels in the literary community. As David Mayall notes, "the use of romantic notions of a separate, mysterious race of Gypsies was a device frequently adopted in poetry and fictions of all descriptions, from the 'highbrow' works of Sir Walter Scott...Charles Dickens and D.H. Lawrence to the anonymous 'penny dreadfuls' and railway literature".

Works by contemporaries of that involve Gypsy characters include George Eliot's poem "The Spanish Gypsy;" Matthew Arnold's poems "To a Gipsy Child by the Sea-Shore," "Resignation," "The Scholar-Gipsy," and "Thyrsis;" J.M. Barrie's "The Little Minister;" and, a later work, D.H. Lawrence's "The Virgin and the Gypsy." 's inclusion of this Gypsy character, even though a somewhat minor one, reflects on a small scale a society's reaction to a race that was both misunderstood and loved.

Q. How the novel depicts the prevalent racism in the Victorian society?

Or

Q. Does this class distinction also affects the education of children on whole?

Charlotte 's novel, *Jane Eyre,* conveys her main character's struggles at her Aunt Reed's house, through the horrible times at Lowood to the disrespect she received as a governess. Jane Eyre is mistreated by her aunt and her cousins, which eventually leads Jane to rebel against her family. She is sent to Lowood where she encounters the hardships of life at a charity school. Throughout the novel, describes the horrible conditions that children faced at school. In particular, she focuses on the problems with charity schools like Lowood.

Charlotte was quite familiar with the terrible conditions of these schools, having two older sisters who died as the result of the school's neglect. Charlotte brings a social awareness to the horrible conditions that school children suffered from. *Jane Eyre* is a critique of a society that would allow children to withstand such intolerable living conditions. These children suffered unbearable physical privation because they were from the lower class and treated as inferiors in society calls attention to the need for society to step in and take responsibility for children who are being mistreated, underfed, inadequately clothed, and lack proper hygiene, and who are dying as a result.

Schools like Lowood that were intended for charity children had a strong focus on preparing the girls for work, unlike private schooling for upper-class girls, which focused much more on acting like a lady (Pedersen, "Reform"). Charity children were taught based on their social status. They were given limited opportunities for work and strictly kept from moving up in society. There were very few employment options for the girls who would attend a charity school. Lowood, which was representative of charity schools, centered on an education that would allow the girls to become a governess or a school teacher.

Education there was not concerned at all with the abilities and talents of individual students. They were all taught strictly the same things to give them the kind of education that would prepare them for their limited future job options. In fact, often times, "The labouring classes...were frequently uninterested in education, because they could see no benefit in it: they had been conditioned to see themselves in a 'station' in life to which the available schooling seemed irrelevant" (Silver 75). At Lowood, the girls were taught very differently from those of the upper-class. Lowood students did not learn to act like a lady in upper-class settings. Instead they learned to be respectful of the upper-class and skills to teach when they became a teacher or governess since that is all that was expected of them.

As Helen explains to Jane why Lowood is different from other schools, she says, "Well, all the girls here have lost either one or both parents, and this is called an institution for educating orphans". Since the pupils at Lowood were poor and typically had no one to look into the living conditions there, the institution could get away with the horrible conditions that the students lived in. It was only after so many children had died of typhus fever that something was finally done, Jane tells us, about the inadequacies of the school:

When the typhus fever had fulfilled its mission of devastation at Lowood, it gradually disappeared from thence; but not till its virulence and the number of its victims had drawn public attention on the school. Inquiry was made into the origin of the scourge, and by degrees various facts came out which excited public

indignation in a high degree. The unhealthy nature of the site; the quantity and quality of the children's food; the brackish, fetid water used in its preparation; the pupils' wretched clothing and accommodations: all these things were discovered; and the discovery produced a result mortifying to Mr.. Brocklehurst, but beneficial to the institution. Previous to this outbreak of typhus fever, no one ever looked into the conditions of the school. The majority of the children there had no family to look into their well-being and, at that point, England did not have any mode of regulating schools and enforcing adequate living conditions for the students. Clearly, is making a statement that these schools should be under public scrutiny without it taking the deaths of countless children before anyone will take notice of the conditions at these schools. is using Lowood as an example of how terrible and unhealthy boarding schools could be and to demonstrate the need for change. Lowood is depicted as extremely bad in terms of sanitation, but, sanitation problems leading to disease was not uncommon during the Victorian period.

An outbreak like the typhus epidemic at Lowood was not an unusual situation at boarding schools during the Victorian period. There were many accounts of schools with improper care for the children, including a lack of sanitation and poor hygiene that led to outbreaks of disease. In fact, "Epidemics of either scarlet fever, diphtheria, whooping cough, or measles were regarded as part of the natural cycle of school life" (Charlotte was quite familiar with such situations, having experienced the death of two of her sisters after they became extremely ill at school. At the Cowan Bridge Clergy Daughters' School where Charlotte 's sisters, Maria and Elizabeth, attended, "Their illnesses were neglected by school officials until they were very severe.... [Charlotte 's] bitter impressions of the school and its Calvinist founder are recorded in *Jane Eyre* in her depiction of the Lowood school" Typhus fever killed many of the children at Lowood, which is what finally drew attention to the intolerable conditions there and instigated the changes that resulted.

The children who did survive the typhus outbreak benefited from the change that resulted in the much improved conditions at the school. As Jane tells us, "The school, thus improved, became in time a truly useful and noble institution". After the change in living conditions and excessive strictness enforced by Mr.. Brocklehurst, the students were then better able to benefit from the academics taught there. In Jane Eyre's case, she became a teacher for a while and then ventured on to advertise for a position as a governess. She desired more than what Lowood had to offer but, being a poor orphan, she had very limited options. Nonetheless, the novel demonstrates the function of a school as long as the conditions are healthy and the teachers and school officials are more compassionate towards the children's needs. Once Mr.. Brocklehurst's authority was reduced and the girls at Lowood benefited from healthier conditions, Jane becomes rather satisfied with the school.

Jane is finally able to leave Lowood when she secures a position as a governess, which is one of her very few job options being considered a lower class orphan. While there, she falls in love with Mr.. Rochester who does not treat her with the disrespect that is so common from people of his class. Not everyone, though, is so kind to Jane. When Mr.. Rochester has guests at the house, most of them are very rude to Jane. They treat her with disrespect and show no concern for her feelings. They act as though she is a stupid creature with no feelings, much like Jane's treatment at Gateshead from the Reeds. Jane is again put in a position that exemplifies the ill-treatment that people of the lower class experienced. However, stresses throughout the novel that Jane is actually superior to all the upper-class people who treat her so maliciously.

In particular, it is Blanche Ingram and Lady Ingram who treat Jane the worst. They talk about how awful they think governesses are in front of Jane. Even when Mrs. Dent whispers to Lady Ingram that there is a governess present while she is telling everyone how awful they are, Lady Ingram simply states, "Tant pis!, (Too bad!)... I hope it may do her good... I noticed her; I am a judge of physiognomy, and in hers I see all the faults of her class" conveys the poor treatment that people of the lower class endured from the upper-class.

Once Jane Eyre leaves Thornfield, she becomes a school mistress making low wages and is very unsatisfied with her position but, again, her options are extremely limited. Here, Jane is portrayed as being well-respected by her students and their parents. This is probably because the students she teaches are quite poor, so neither the girls nor their parents are of a higher social class that would likely create a situation where Jane was disrespected. Although Jane liked her students and was treated respectfully, she was not happy with the constraints that society put on her and she wished for more in life. When Jane reflects on her teaching position at Morton School, "[she] felt desolate to a degree. [She] felt—yes, idiot that [she is]—[she] felt degraded". Jane was lucky to be a teacher who did receive respect from her students and their parents, but she was still unhappy that she was so restricted in society because of her class that this was all she could do.

Although governesses and school teachers were expected to be polite to members of the upper-class, the upper-class felt no obligation to return the courtesy. During the nineteenth-century in England,

The polite fiction was that a lady who kept a school met her pupils' parents as an equal.... In fact, the private school-mistress was in a distinctly subordinate position, obliged to defer to parental demands in ordering her establishment. Parents often treated the teachers shabbily,...sometimes bullying them quite shamelessly.

Typically then, a school-mistress would not have encountered very pleasant interactions as a school teacher, but Jane was lucky in this case. However, Jane was well-respected because she was teaching children of a low social class so they would not look down upon her as those from the upper-class (such as the Ingrams) often did. Because her students were of low social status, though, they hadn't had much schooling and Jane was bored because she had far more talent than her position allowed her to utilize. Even though she was respected and well-liked by her students, Jane was very unhappy with the limits that society put on people of her status. She had very few employment options and she had exhausted all possibilities and was driven unhappily away from all of them.

Jane's misery began when she was ill-received by the Reed family. It continued with the inadequate living conditions at Lowood where no one took care of the lower class children. She took herself away from the problems of Thornfield and did what she had to at Moor House. It is not until Jane gets an inheritance that grants her independence that she is free from the societal restraints of her class and finally able to make herself happy. Jane no longer has to worry about people looking out for her when she can't help herself as was the situation at Lowood. Also, she doesn't have to work as a governess or schoolteacher, which are both positions that were looked down upon by the upper-class who felt they had the right to disrespect people in these positions.

Jane also does not have to feel indebted to Mr.. Rochester now that she has money. By the end of the novel, Jane is finally in a position where she does not have to suffer from the many drawbacks of being the poor orphaned child she started out as when she suffered through horribly unhealthy living conditions at Lowood. *Jane Eyre* illustrates many problems in Victorian England, many of which stemmed from class distinction. Jane Eyre was treated terribly because she was orphaned. It took an epidemic at her school for anyone to help the lower class children at Lowood. Later in her life, it took a huge inheritance for her to finally be able to break free from the expectations of a lower class person in England during the

Victorian period. 's novel is a social critique of the ills of society at the time. She focuses on the extremely terrible conditions at Lowood to exemplify the horrors that were being ignored in the schools that were killing children like her sisters at the Cowan Bridge Clergy Daughter's School.

Chapter 15

Further Study Questions

Chapter 1

- What purpose do the descriptive passages from Berwick's *History of British Birds* serve at this stage of the text?
- What are your impressions of John Reed? What do you make of the abuse that Jane suffers? Is it realistic?

Chapter 2

- On page 10, note Jane's thoughts of suicide.
- Jane Eyre was a watershed novel at the time it was written because it blended two styles of novels: the *romantic* novel and the *gothic* novel. According to Webster's *Encyclopedic Dictionary of the English Language*, romanticism emphasized content rather than form; encouraged "freedom of treatment," "introspection," and celebrated "nature, the common man, and freedom of the spirit." The same source defines the gothic novel as a type of fiction "characterized by picturesque settings; an atmosphere of mystery, gloom, and terror; supernatural or fantastic occurrences; and violent and macabre events." Where do you see both elements in the novel so far?
- Jane's fears of the ghost are consistent with her vivid imagination; yet the ghost never appears, and Jane is returned to cruel reality.

Chapter 3

- Most readers of today are familiar with the signs of child abuse, emotional abuse, and neglect. While these terms were arguably unknown to Brontë in the mid 19th century, how does her treatment of Jane reflect what we know about them?

Chapter 4

- On page 26, what is unexpected in Jane1s answer to how she plans to avoid going to Hell?
- How does the anecdote of the "little psalm angel" (26) heighten our contempt for Brocklehurst?
- Why does Bessie begin to treat Jane with kindness at this point in the text? What lesson does Jane learn on how to deal with people she fears? How is this unusual when compared with the depiction of the other children of this time period, such as the "little psalm angel" and the "girls of the school" (27-8)?

Chapter 5

- On page 40, notice "Jane's" first direct address of the "reader."
- How does Miss Temple fit in with your expectations of her from Brocklehurst's interview with Jane? In fact, how does her character compare to most of the other adult characters encountered in the text so far?

Chapter 6

- In this chapter, Jane receives another lesson in strength, this time from Helen Burns. What do you think of Burns' diction and speech? What do you think of her philosophy?

Chapter 7

- What do you think of Mr.. Brocklehurst's philosophy of education in this chapter?
- Discuss Brontë's feelings on the "nature of man" (60). Is she being serious or tongue-in-cheek?

Chapter 8

- Compare Jane Eyre to other mistreated s from children's stories (Cinderella, Rapunzel, Snow White). Knowing that Jane Eyre is the novel that broke many rules about how a mistreated should act, compare and contrast them to Jane.

Chapter 9

- Pay attention to the lush descriptions of Miss Temple

in chapter 8 and spring at Lowood in chapter 9. How would descriptions like these affect readers in the mid 19th century? How do they affect readers of today?

- Notice the parallels between life at Lowood in the spring and Jane's new lifestyle. How is this "pathetic fallacy" a form of foreshadowing?

Chapter 10

- Read the first paragraph of chapter 10. If Brontë means that she has only related events that are important, what are those important events and how are they important to Jane's development as a character?
- What do you think of Jane's prayers for a "new servitude"?
- What can you make of Bessie's character in her differing reactions to Jane's looks and her abilities? What is the effect that Brontë is trying to convey to the reader?
- Pay attention to the appearance of a mysterious Mr.. Eyre.

Chapter 11

- What do you make of the first two paragraphs in chapter 11? Analyse this passage with regard to literary theory and the nature of the narrator.
- What affect does Mrs. Fairfax's description of Rochester have on the reader? How does Brontë achieve this affect?

Chapter 12

- Read the passages on pages 100-101. What do you make of them? What is the link between the paragraphs? What opinions does Brontë show here, and how does she direct them through these paragraphs?

Chapter 13

- How has Thornfield changed with the arrival of Mr.. Rochester? What is the significance of this?
- On page 110, as well as other places in the text, Brontë makes liberal use of French in her dialogue. What does this say about her audience? How do you compare to that audience?

- Rochester studies Jane's paintings on pages 115-117. What do you make of the paintings? What does this incident add to the story?
- Comment on the character and appearance of Rochester. How does he measure up to other romantic heroes?

Chapter 14

- When Rochester says he is "paving hell with energy" and that he is "laying down good intentions," he is alluding to an old saying: "The road to Hell is paved with good intentions." This quote has been attributed to Karl Marx, but I think it has been around longer than that. However, this might make an interesting jumping-off point for someone to analyse *Jane Eyre* from a Marxist perspective.
- This chapter gives more insight on the nature of Rochester through his battle of wits with Jane. What is revealed about Rochester here? What is the outcome of their conversation?

Chapter 15

- Why does Jane become more affectionate and tolerant of Adèle, both literally and figuratively?
- We see that something odd is going on at Thornfield with Rochester's demand that he "like it if he can"(133), the strange laughter, and the attempt on his life.
- Note at the end of the chapter the change in the relationship between Jane and Rochester.

Chapter 16

- The discussion of Miss Blanche Ingram between Jane and Mrs. Fairfax should recall Rochester's opinions of love and jealousy in his romance with Adèle1s mother, Céline Varens.
- What do you make of Jane creating a harsh piece of artwork for herself and a lovely piece of artwork depicting Miss Ingram?

Chapter 17

- Beginning with the serving of coffee on page 162, Brontë shifts her narrative into the present tense. Why does she do this, and what is the effect on the reader?

- How does Brontë transmit the characters of the Ingram ladies successfully to the reader?

Chapter 18

- Sometimes Jane's naïveté offers Brontë a chance to satirize the attitudes and actions of aristocracy. In the first full paragraph on page 176, how does Brontë satirize love as seen by the upper class?
- Comment on the sudden appearance of both Mr.. Mason and the old gypsy woman.

Chapter 19

- This chapter shows another change in the relationship between Rochester and Jane. Analyse this new stage.
- Re-read the section beginning with "Here is to your health, ministrant spirit!" (192) until the end of the chapter. What do you make of this passage?

Chapter 20

- On page 198, Brontë again changes into the present tense. Why?
- At this point in the novel, it is very clear that Rochester is deeply involved with some mystery surrounding Grace Poole. At the end of the chapter, who does he initially hint may help him find happiness? When Jane can not respond to Rochester1s hinting, his tone and attitude change immediately. What does this say about Rochester as a character?

Chapter 21

- On pages 223-4, we are treated to an example of what the Reed sisters have become. How does Jane respond to their personalities. How does Jane compare and contrast to them?
- Describe the resolution of the relationship between Jane and Mrs. Reed. Is it different from what you expected? Would it have been different from what Brontë's audience would have expected?

Chapter 2

- Chapter 22 is short and ostensibly deals with Jane's return to Thornwood. What function might this chapter serve in terms of the entire text?

- Note again the switch in tense on page 231.

Chapter 23

- Pay attention to Brontë's description of Thornfield in summer at the beginning of the chapter. Notice how it contrasts the events of the rest of the chapter. Notice also the change of weather and the destruction of the chestnut tree. As a reader, what effect should these incidents of "pathetic fallacy" have on you?
- In Jane's impassioned speech beginning with "I tell you I must go!" (240) you should be able to find pieces of both Bessie and Helen Burns. How do the philosophies of these two influential characters colour Jane's words?

Chapter 24

- This chapter is pure Jane Eyre. How is Jane different than most brides of romance stories? What would Brontë's audience have thought of her behaviour?

Chapter 25

- When Jane regards her wedding gown on page 261, what mood does Brontë establish?
- Why does Brontë narrate with such a heavy hand when she writes "Stay till he comes, reader; and when I disclose my secret to him, you shall share the confidence." (262)?

Chapter 26

- What is the irony in Jane wearing "the plain square of blond" veil for her wedding (272)?
- What do you think of the fact that Jane's uncle and Mr.. Mason were business associates?
- Re-read Jane's recollections of the events leading up to the introduction of Bertha Mason (281). How are these events different from similar events in traditional romantic novels? Why does Brontë "play" the scene this way?

Chapter 27

- "Reader, I forgave him at the moment on the spot" (284). What is your reaction to this?
- When Rochester explains the circumstances of

marriage to Bertha Mason, how do you respond as a reader? Does Brontë succeed or fail to produce sympathy for this character? How?

- Compare the symbolism of "(a) wind fresh from Europe" (293) and the "fiery West Indian night" (292). What do these symbols represent? Are they ironic in any sense?
- On page 302, Jane explains her rationale for not complying with Rochester. Is this in character with the Jane we have come to know? How?

Chapter 28

- The suffering that Jane endures is compounded by her belief that she has "no claim to ask" for help (312). How is this philosophy in keeping with her character?
- As the author of the text, Brontë is the artist who chooses what events happen in the plot (much the same way a painter can choose the composition of a painting, or a sculptor can choose where and how to carve the elements of a sculpture). Why did she choose to create a section where her main character goes through so much pain? Is it appropriate?

Chapter 29

- Do a little resear Where do the names Mary, Diana, St. John, and Hannah come from, and what is the significance attached to those names? Compare the meanings of the names to their respective characters in the previous chapter and this one?

Chapter 30

- Compare the Rivers family to the Reed family. In what way are they similar? In what way are they foils? Do the names signify anything?

Chapter 31

- Jane's feelings toward her backwoods students and the "germs of native excellence, refinement, intelligence (and) kind-feeling" that "are as likely to exist in their hearts as in those of the best-born" (342) are likely to have caused a stir among non-romantics of the period. Why?

- Why does Jane begin this chapter in the present tense?
- Jane Eyre is running from an unattainable love. Who else is running as well, and what are the details?

Chapter 32

- A good minister is an example to his congregation; followers will learn "truth" by simply observing the daily actions of their pastor. Does St. James Rivers impart any "truths" to Jane?

Chapter 33

- In this chapter, the final pieces of the puzzle slip into place. Is this resolution too coincidental or is it satisfactory?

Chapter 34

- Characterize the similarities and differences between St. John's offer of marriage and Rochester's. Why does Jane refuse St. John when she is willing to accept a life with him in India? Couldn1t she grow to love him? How does her response fit in with what we know about Jane as a character?
- Hot climates seem to have a special symbolic meaning in the text (note Rochester's discussion of the West Indies). What do you make of it?

Chapter 35

- Jane's conversation with Diana (396-8), although acceptable and unexceptional to us, would have bordered on the scandalous in Brontë's day. What is it about Jane's viewpoint that would have drawn so much anger?
- Does Jane's near surrender to St. John Rivers, stopped only by "the voiceŠof Edward Fairfax Rochester" speaks to her "in pain and woe" (401) diminish her strength of character? Why would Brontë have slipped again into the realm of the supernatural if Jane had enough strength in her own convictions?

Chapter 36

- In this chapter we learn the fate of Rochester, Bertha Mason, and Thornfield Hall. How do these revelations sit with you, the reader? Did Brontë do a good job of tying up loose ends?

Chapter 37

- Notice that Brontë makes a direct jump from the inn at Millcote to Rochester's house at Ferndean. Why does she do this? What effect might she wish to achieve?
- On page 419, Jane has her own ideas of how to shake Rochester from his gloom. What are they?
- "To make a love story workŠyou gotta have heart. More important: The audience must believe it's real." This quote by Pat H. Broeske in his article "Save Yourself From *Trouble*" from the January 1995 issue of *Writer's Digest* was his thesis for why some Hollywood love stories work and some don't. Does Jane Eyre work as a love story? Do Jane and Rochester have "heart"? Are we glad to see them back together? What makes their relationship ring true for the reader?

Chapter 38

- Brontë ends the novel on a religious note. In fact, she has been building the religious closure since Rochester's admission of prayer in chapter 37. What effect does this have on you as a reader? What effect would it have had on Brontë's audience?
- If St. John Rivers was such a frigid (and in some ways unpleasant character), why would Brontë chose to end the novel with a reference to him?
- Note the parallel structure: The novel begins with the antics of John Reed and closes with the antics of St. John Rivers.

Chapter 16

Important Quotations Explained

I am Glad You are no Relation of Mine

Quotation

I will never call you aunt again as long as I live. I will never come to visit you when I am grown up; and if any one asks me how I liked you, and how you treated me, I will say the very thought of you makes me sick, and that you treated me with miserable cruelty... You think I have no feelings, and that I can do without one bit of love or kindness; but I cannot live so: and you have no pity. I shall remember how you thrust me back... into the red-room... And that punishment you made me suffer because your wicked boy struck me—knocked me down for nothing. I will tell anybody who asks me questions this exact tale. 'Ere I had finished this reply, my soul began to expand, to exult, with the strangest sense of freedom, of triumph, I ever felt. It seemed as if an invisible bond had burst, and that I had struggled out into unhoped-for liberty....

Explanation

This quotation, part of Jane's outburst to her aunt just prior to her departure from Gateshead for Lowood School, appears in Chapter 4. In the passage, Jane solidifies her own orphanhood, severing her ties to the little semblance of family that remained to her ("I will never call you aunt again as long as I live," she tells Mrs. Reed). Jane asserts her fiery spirit in her tirade, and she displays a keen sense of justice and a recognition of her need for love. Along with familial liberation, the passage marks Jane's emotional liberation. Jane's imprisonment in the red-room has its psychological counterpart in her emotional suppression, and it is not until she speaks these words to Mrs. Reed that she feels her "soul begin to expand." Lastly, the passage highlights the importance of storytelling as revenge and also as a means of empowerment. Jane declares that she will "tell anybody who asks me questions this exact tale"—via authorship, Jane asserts her authority over and against her tyrannical aunt.

Feeling... clamoured wildly. "Oh, comply!" it said. "... soothe him; save him; love him; tell him you love him and will be his. Who in the world cares for you? or who will be injured by what you do?" Still indomitable was the reply: "I care for myself. The more solitary, the more friendless, the more unsustained I am, the more I will respect myself. I will keep the law given by God; sanctioned by man. I will hold to the principles received by me when I was sane, and not mad—as I am now. Laws and principles are not for the times when there is no temptation... They have a worth—so I have always believed; and if I cannot believe it now, it is because I am insane—quite insane: with my veins running fire, and my heart beating faster than I can count its throbs."

Explanation for Quotation #2

In this quotation, near the end of Chapter 27, Jane asserts her strong sense of moral integrity over and against her intense immediate feelings. Rochester has been trying to convince her to stay with him despite the fact that he is still legally married to Bertha Mason. His argument almost persuades Jane: Rochester is the first person who has ever truly loved her. Yet she knows that staying with him would mean compromising herself, because she would be Rochester's mistress rather than his wife. Not only would she lose her self-respect, she would probably lose Rochester's, too, in the end. Thus Jane asserts her worth and her ability to love herself regardless of how others treat her.

The passage also sheds light upon Jane's understanding of religion. She sees God as the giver of the laws by which she must live. When she can no longer trust herself to exercise good judgment, she looks to these principles as an objective point of reference.

Jane's allusions to her "madness" and "insanity" bring out an interesting parallel between Jane and Bertha Mason. It is possible to see Bertha as a double for Jane, who embodies what Jane feels within—especially since the externalization of interior sentiment is a trait common to the Gothic novel.

The description of Jane's blood running like "fire" constitutes one of many points in the book in which Jane is associated with flames.

"Shall I?" I said briefly; and I looked at his features, beautiful in their harmony, but strangely formidable in their still severity; at his brow, commanding, but not open; at his eyes, bright and deep and searching, but never soft; at his tall imposing figure; and fancied myself in idea his wife. Oh! it would never do! As his curate, his coMr.ade, all would be right: I would cross oceans with him in that capacity; toil under Eastern suns, in Asian deserts with him in that office; admire and emulate his courage and devotion and vigour: accommodate quietly to his masterhood; smile undisturbed at his ineradicable ambition.... I should suffer often, no doubt, attached to him only in this capacity: my body would be under a rather stringent yoke, but my heart and mind would be free.

I should still have my unblighted self to turn to: my natural unenslaved feelings with which to communicate in moments of loneliness. There would be recesses in my mind which would be only mine, to which he never came; and sentiments growing there, fresh and sheltered, which his austerity could never blight, nor his measured warrior-march trample down: but as his wife—at his side always, and always restrained, and always checked—forced to keep the fire of my nature continually low, to compel it to burn inwardly and never utter a cry, though the imprisoned flame consumed vital after vital—this would be unendurable.

Explanation for Quotation #3

This passage occurs in Chapter 34. St. John Rivers has just asked Jane to join him as his wife on his missionary trip to

India. Jane dramatizes the interior conflict involved in making her decision. In many ways, the proposal tempts her. It is an opportunity to perform good works and to be more than a governess, schoolteacher, or housewife—the roles traditionally open to women. Jane's teaching jobs at Lowood, Thornfield, and Morton have all made her feel trapped, and she would not mind enduring hardships for a cause in which she truly believes. Yet, St. John's principles—"ambition," "austerity," and arrogance—are not those that Jane upholds.

Misguided religion threatens to oppress Jane throughout the book, and St. John merely embodies one form of it. He also embodies masculine dominance, another force that threatens Jane like a "stringent yoke" over the course of the novel. Thus she describes St. John's "warrior-march" and notes his assertion of his "masterhood." Jane must escape such control in order to remain true to herself, for she realises that her conventional manner of dealing with oppression—by retreating into herself, into the recesses of her imagination, into conversation with herself—cannot constitute a way of life. In her rejection of Rochester, Jane privileged principle over feeling; she is now aware of the negative effects such emotional repression can have. Feeling, too, must play a role in one's life: a balance must be struck.

I could not help it; the restlessness was in my nature; it agitated me to pain sometimes. Then my sole relief was to walk along the corridor of the third story, backwards and forwards, safe in the silence and solitude of the spot, and allow my mind's eye to dwell on whatever bright visions rose before it—and, certainly, they were many and glowing; to let my heart be heaved by the exultant movement... and, best of all, to open my inward ear to a tale that was never ended—a tale my imagination created, and narrated continuously; quickened with all of incident, life, fire, feeling, that I desired and had not in my actual existence. It is in vain to say human beings ought to be satisfied with tranquility: they must have action; and they will make it if they cannot find it. Millions are condemned to a stiller doom than mine, and millions are in silent revolt against their lot.

Nobody knows how many rebellions besides political rebellions ferment in the masses of life which people earth. Women are supposed to be very calm generally: but women feel just as men feel; they need exercise for their faculties, and a field for their efforts as much as their brothers do; they suffer from too rigid a restraint, too absolute a stagnation, precisely as men would suffer; and it is narrow-minded in their more privileged fellow-creatures to say that they ought to confine themselves to making puddings and knitting stockings, to playing on the piano and embroidering bags. It is thoughtless to condemn them, or laugh at them, if they seek to do more or learn more than custom has pronounced necessary for their sex.

Explanation for Quotation #4

This passage appears in Chapter 12, in the midst of Jane's description of her first few weeks at Thornfield. The diction highlights Jane's feelings of imprisonment (she paces the corridors like a creature caged), and her longings for freedom and equality. Jane's words are also relevant to Brontë's own experience as a writer, and to the general condition of Victorian women.

The images of restlessness and pacing, of feeling "stagnation" and "too rigid a restraint," are examples of the book's central theme of imprisonment. In addition to instances of physical imprisonment, Jane must also escape the fetters of misguided religion (represented by Brocklehurst), of passion without principle (represented at first by Rochester), and of principle without passion (represented by St. John Rivers)—not to mention those of society.

Brocklehurst, Rochester, and St. John may also threaten Jane with the fetters of patriarchy, which is the specific force Jane resists in this passage. Jane extends her feeling of entrapment to her fellow women, and these sentences constitute Brontë's feminist manifesto. As she describes the "doom" to which "millions in silent revolt against their lot" "are condemned," Brontë criticizes what she believed to be stifling Victorian conceptions of proper gender roles. The passage explicitly states that the Victorian wife suffers from being metaphorically "locked up." Bertha Mason, who is eventually rendered nearly inhuman when her neglected, suppressed feelings turn to madness and fury, may be viewed as a symbol of the imprisoned female's condition.

The passage suggests that Brontë's writing may have been her means of coping with such rage. Jane describes her retreat into her own mind, to find freedom in her imagination. While Brontë's greatest triumphs were the result of such self-retreat, her 's achievement is the balance she strikes between her need for autonomy and her desire to be an active member of society.

I have now been married ten years. I know what it is to live entirely for and with what I love best on earth. I hold myself supremely blest—blest beyond what language can express; because I am my husband's life as fully as he is mine. No woman was ever nearer to her mate than I am: ever more absolutely bone of his bone, and flesh of his flesh. I know no weariness of my Edward's society: he knows none of mine, any more than we each do of the pulsation of the heart that beats in our separate bosoms; consequently, we are ever together. To be together is for us to be at once as free as in solitude, as gay as in company. We talk, I believe, all day long: to talk to each other is but a more animated and an audible thinking. All my confidence is bestowed on him, all his confidence is devoted to me; we are precisely suited in character—perfect concord is the result.

Explanation for Quotation #5

This, one of the final passages of *Jane Eyre*, summarizes the novel's "happy ending." Its implications have generated much debate over the way Brontë chose to conclude her book. Some critics view Jane as having sacrificed her autonomy—no longer her own person, she and Rochester have merged, sharing one heart, each possessing the "bone" and "flesh" of the other.

One might also argue that Jane relinquishes her powers of thought and expression—two characteristics that have defined her for most of the novel. Suddenly, the otherwise imaginative Jane equates her "thinking" to her conversations with Rochester—she even finds the conversations "more animated." Similarly, although ten years have elapsed since the wedding, the otherwise eloquent Jane suddenly claims that she is unable to find any "language" to "express" her experiences during this period.

Other critics interpret this passage in a more positive manner. It can be read as Jane's affirmation of the equality between her and Rochester, as testimony that she has not "given up" anything. The passage is followed in the novel by a report on St. John Rivers. Jane writes: "his is the spirit of the warrior Greatheart... his is the ambition of the high master-spirit...." (Greatheart serves as guide to the pilgrims in Bunyan's *Pilgrim's Progress.*) Emphasizing St. John's desires for "mastery" and his "warrior" characteristics, Jane describes a controlling patriar While Rochester may have been such a figure at the beginning of the novel, his character has changed by its conclusion. He has lost his house, his hand, and his eyesight to a fire, and the revelation of his youthful debaucheries has shown him to be Jane's moral inferior.

Rochester can no longer presume to be Jane's "master" in any sense. Moreover, Jane has come to Rochester this second time in economic independence and by free choice; at Moor House she found a network of love and support, and she does not depend solely on Rochester for emotional nurturance. Optimistic critics point to Jane's description of St. John as her reminder that the marriage she rejected would have offered her a much more stifling life. By entering into marriage, Jane does enter into a sort of "bond"; yet in many ways this "bond" is the "escape" that she has sought all along. Perhaps Brontë meant Jane's closing words to celebrate her attainment of freedom; it is also possible that Brontë meant us to bemoan the tragic paradox of Jane's situation.

Bibliography

Barker, Juliet R. V. *The Brontës.* New York: St. Martin's Press, 1995.

Berg, Maggie. Jane Eyre: *Portrait of a Life.* Boston: Twayne Publishers, 1987.

Bloom, Harold, ed. *Charlotte Brontë's* Jane Eyre. New York: Chelsea House Publishers, 1987.

Brontë, Charlotte. Jane Eyre: *An Authoritative Text, Backgrounds, Criticism.* Richard J. Dunn, ed. New York: W.W. Norton & Co., 1971.

Fraser, Rebecca. *The Brontës: Charlotte Brontë and her Family.* New York: Crown Publishers, 1988.

Gates, Barbara Timm, ed. *Critical Essays on Charlotte Brontë.* Boston: G.K. Hall & Co., 1990.

Gilbert, Sandra M. and Susan Gubar, eds. *The Madwoman in the Attic: The Woman Writer and the Nineteenth-Century Imagination.* New Haven: Yale University Press, 1979.

Gregor, Ian, ed. *The Brontës.* Englewood Cliffs, New Jersey: Prentice Hall, 1970.

Rhys, Jean. *Wide Sargasso Sea.* New York: W.W. Norton & Co., 1999.

Vicinus, Martha, ed. *Suffer and Be Still: Women in the Victorian Age.* Bloomington: Indiana University Press, 1972.

Winnifrith, Tom. *The Brontës and their Background: Romance and Reality.* Houndmills, Basingstoke, Hampshire: Macmillan, 1988.

Bentley, Phyllis. *The Brontës*. London: Thames and Hudson Ltd., 1969.

Blom, Margaret Howard. *Charlotte Brontë*. Boston: C.K. Hall & Co., 1977.

Brontë, Charlotte. *Jane Eyre*. New York: E. M. Hale & Company, 2nd edition.

Cecil, David. *Early Victorian Novelists*. New York: The Bobbs-Merrill Company, 1935.

Evans, Barbara and Gareth Lloyd. *The Scribner Companion to The Brontës*. New York: Charles Scribner's Sons, 1982.

Fraser, Rebecca. *The Brontes: Charlotte Bronte and Her Family*. Crown Publishers, 1988.